SOLD SEPARATELY

SOLD
SEPARATELY

CHILDREN AND PARENTS
IN CONSUMER CULTURE

ELLEN SEITER

RUTGERS UNIVERSITY PRESS
NEW BRUNSWICK, NEW JERSEY

Library of Congress Cataloging-in-Publication Data

Seiter, Ellen, 1957–
    Sold separately : children and parents in consumer culture / Ellen
Seiter.
        p.   cm. — (Communications, media, and culture)
    Includes bibliographical references (p.   ) and index.
    ISBN 0-8135-1988-8
    1. Television advertising and children—United States.
    2. Children as consumers—United States. I. Title. II. Series.
    HQ784.T68S45   1993
    305.23—dc20   92-44227
                                        CIP

British Cataloging-in-Publication information available

In memory of Sheila Harrington Seiter
1919–1983

CONTENTS

LIST OF ILLUSTRATIONS

ACKNOWLEDGMENTS

T he Center for the Study of Women in Society and the Office of Research and Sponsored Programs, both at the University of Oregon, supported the research for this book.

Some material from Chapters Two and Four appeared in the article "Different Children, Different Dreams: Racial Representations in Children's Advertising," *Journal of Communication Inquiry* 14, no. 1 (1990): 31–47. A version of Chapter Seven appeared in *Cultural Studies* 6, no. 2 (1992): 232–247.

Thanks are due to many who granted interviews in connection with this research, including Bert Leiman, associate director of children's research at Leo Burnett; Sharon Wottrich, A Plus Agency; Jean Gramer, Stewart Talent Agency; and Linda Jack, Amelia Lawrence Agency. I also wish to thank Marsha Cassidy and Richard Katula, organizers of the Minority Images in Advertising Symposium (1989) sponsored by the Communication Department at De Paul University and funded by the Leo Burnett Foundation. Diane Foxhill Carruthers, communications librarian at the University of Illinois, Urbana, was very helpful. My research was guided by contact with the parents and children of the Lane County Relief Nursery and an encouraging show of interest among the members of my Birth-to-Three support group.

Roland Marchand provided me with many useful suggestions and kindly encouragement at the initial stage of this project. I benefited from the support and advice of Jacqueline Bobo, Susanne Bohmer, Charlotte Brunsdon, Gretchen Elsner-Sommer, Lisa Friedman, Jane Gaines, James Hay, Cheris Kramerae, Kristin Margolf, David Morley, David Dexter Nelson, David Thorburn, Kate Torrey, and Ellen Wartella.

Chuck Kleinhans, Julia Lesage, Barbara Corrado Pope, and Daniel Pope were helpful critics of early versions of the manuscript. Leslie Mitchner of Rutgers University Press and George Custen, series editor, read the manuscript with painstaking care. Their provocative questions and comments challenged me to write the best book I could. Thanks to Grace Buonocore for her skillful editing.

Rosemary Morrison gave me the original idea to write this book. Her insights into children's culture appear uncredited throughout its pages.

Kathleen Rowe made an immense contribution to my work through her careful research assistance, her first-rate editorial skills, her sage advice, and her kindly encouragement.

Roy Metcalf's faith in the book was undaunted over many years, and his countless, good-natured sacrifices made it possible. His enthusiasm for both parenting and popular culture is inspiring. Anne Metcalf showed me the way with her articulate judgments of toys and television. Henry Metcalf kept my spirits high.

Sheila Harrington Seiter taught me to appreciate how fascinating children are and to value the effort good writing requires—two things that sustained me in my work. While writing, I reflected anew on the enormous difficulties she faced as a widowed mother of five children in the 1960s and on her remarkable courage, grace, and wisdom. This book is dedicated to her memory.

Eugene, Oregon
January 1993

SOLD SEPARATELY

INTRODUCTION

The research for this book began during my first pregnancy, when I found, pushed through my mail slot every day, free magazines filled with cheerful advice and tempting offers for products that promised to cure illness, to provide good nutrition, to banish children's tears, and to turn my soon-to-be-born child into a person as clever as could be. Every time I watched television or picked up a magazine, I suddenly discovered that there were children everywhere: adorable babies in tender maternal embrace; laughing toddlers at play. Despite the fact that I am a professional media critic—a specialist in daytime television, in fact—I had never really noticed how many children and babies were selling not only diapers and baby food but soaps and detergents and shampoos and tires and automobiles. I had never listened to advertisers' messages so attentively before, because I had never felt spoken to so directly. In critical theory there is a term—interpellation—that refers to the moment in which ideology "hails" us, seems to say "hey, you!" When I had my first baby, I felt that advertising and advice literature buttonholed me in a way I never dreamed possible. When I had my second child, I learned that my ability to ward off this feeling through critical study had lessened only slightly. I was ready to listen. Struggling under the responsibilities of paid work, housework, and child care, I was really interested in advertising's promises of easier/better/quicker laundry, cleaning, and cooking. One of the most interesting and satisfying aspects of media depictions of children is that they portray emotional fulfillment through the experience of parenting. There is enormous promise held out in the language of advertisements—for joy, intimacy, fun, tenderness, gratitude. The message is no less than this: mothering is the most satisfying and fulfilling experience life has to offer—so long as one has the right equipment.

It was only on second take that I realized one reason I was so affected by media addressed to parents: I belonged to the target market. I was white and I had white babies, who resembled most of the models in the ads. I was married and lived in a house in a de facto racially segregated neighborhood. I had a car, a cat, a dog, a yard, and a middle-class job. My life looked a lot like the domestic scenarios usually depicted in ads and assumed as the status quo in advice literature. My family almost looked the part of advertising's idealized world—most important, we looked it enough to be able to ignore whatever discrepancies existed between that world and ours.

By the age of two, my children recognized themselves in the same way on the television screen and began channeling their desires toward the consumer goods offered there. In no time, our closets and usually our floors were cluttered with toys; our cupboards full of goodies; our television dominated by kids' programs and videos. This book is an attempt to understand how this happened in my household and to decipher the frequent arguments over toys and television I heard all around me.

When my daughter was one year old, a sabbatical from university teaching gave me the time to work once or twice a week in a therapeutic nursery for working-class children who had been classified by social workers as being "at risk" for abuse or neglect. Their parents were under enormous pressure—from poverty, unemployment, lack of education and housing, addictions to drugs and alcohol. In the nursery, these children were exposed to a "stimulating" environment, much like the one I had created at home, with a changing array of material goods (music on tape decks, paint on easels, puzzles, books, and the like). I repeatedly observed ways that toys and media experiences did indeed help children to talk and to learn basic concepts and divert them from aggressive behavior. But I also recognized, as did the teachers there, what a tremendous struggle it is for working-class parents to translate the child-centered pedagogy's emphasis on expression, freedom of movement, and exploration into the more confined, crowded spaces and circumstances—and the limited budgets—of working-class family life. When good parenting is defined as the provision of an appropriate environment for child development, class oppression expresses itself in children's everyday lives through deprivation, through the absence of material goods.

I was especially struck by the poignant way these children treasured toys. They came to school clutching G.I. Joes and My Little Ponies as though they were the most precious possessions on earth. I noticed how a T-shirt with a favorite television character could prompt a stream of talk from an otherwise reticent kid, and how a conversation on the playground about *Ghostbusters* could make children who were normally silent and withdrawn extremely animated, even garrulous. I noticed how proudly their parents spoke of being able to put a play kitchen on layaway for their daughter or rent a VCR for the weekend to play *Sesame Street*. In this book I often try to move back and forth between two perspectives: that of privileged children like my own, with money to spend and confidence that their desires really count and deserve gratification; and that of children—like those at the nursery—whose circumstances do not resemble those of the media world, who participate much more marginally in the consumer economy of childhood, and who have faced at a very young age the frequent and abrupt denial of their desires.

It is a middle-class delusion—though one often propagated by child experts—that children can be shielded from consumption, that proper parenting will nip children's interest in toys and television in the bud. Rather, I believe that we need to accept that contemporary parenthood is always already embedded in consumerism, although the scale, the size of the market, and the prestige associated with the goods vary greatly from class to class. Too often, women and children have been blamed by scholars—most of them men—for their interest in shopping and consumer goods,[1] while scholars believe themselves to be unimplicated in consumer culture and rarely examine their own consumption activities critically. Intellectuals tend to think of consumer culture as something to be censored, to be overcome. In the most common formulation of all, buying is a bad habit the masses pick up from watching too much television. But all members of modern developed societies depend heavily on commodity consumption, not just for survival but for participation—inclusion—in social networks. Clothing, furniture, records, toys—all the things that we buy involve decisions and the exercise of our own judgment and "taste." Obviously we do not control what is available for us to choose from in the first place. But consuming offers a certain scope for creativity. The deliberate, chosen meanings in most people's lives come more often from what they consume than what they produce, and these meanings are not individual but social and deserving of much more attention from academics interested in culture.

In researching this book, I surrounded myself with all kinds of media related to children, television, advertising, and toys. My sampling methods have not been scientific, but my samples have been sizable. Because my training is in criticism, I have relied heavily on description and case study rather than on social science methods. I read parenting magazines and women's magazines—both contemporary and bound copies from the 1920s to the present. I subscribed to toy, advertising, and television industry trade publications. I interviewed toy store managers, toy-manufacturing executives, advertising researchers, and casting agencies. Everywhere I took my children I listened and watched: at toy stores, fast-food restaurants, supermarkets, playgrounds, day-care centers. I silently inventoried the gifts at every children's birthday party I went to—or observed at the local pizza parlor. And everywhere I went I talked with parents and teachers about toys and television programs and the importance of these in their children's lives.

I also turned to sociologists, anthropologists, and social historians for help in understanding the growth of children's consumer culture, and I summarize this work in the first chapter. Consumerism needs to be placed in the context of larger social changes—in domestic work, in mothers' labor force participation, and in patterns of child rearing. While television was offered in the 1950s as a relief from mothers' child-care responsibilities, a sort of taboo on children's television, stemming in part from the unfounded belief that viewing is passive, began to appear in the advice of child experts. Children's consumption—of television and of snacks and toys— poses special problems for adults, who tend to damn kids' consumer desires as hedonistic. I examine hedonism and emulation as explanations for consumer behavior that have special relevance to the conflicts of parents and children over consumer goods.

In the chapters that follow I describe children's consumer culture as it exists in magazine ads, television commercials, toy stores, and animated television programs. I place these things in the context of marketing and advertising as institutions that confer meaning on media texts and commodities and speak to audiences and consumers in particular ways. Toys serve different goals for children and parents. Toys have been sold to parents through advertisements in print media based on claims for educational value at the same time that toys have been sold to children in television commercials based on their "badge appeal" to peers. Chapter Two looks through back issues of *Parents* magazine from the 1920s to the 1980s to trace the ways that toy advertising aimed at parents has vacillated between pitches emphasizing the toy's capacity to make children happy and the promotion of an instrumental view of play in which a child's every waking moment is deemed an opportunity for cognitive development and educational advancement.

In Chapter Three, I examine the controversy over television advertising to children and compare the images of the audience put forward by Action for Children's Television and by the producers of children's shows and commercials. What commercials for children look like and why children find them entertaining are examined through an analysis of commercials in Chapter Four. Here I borrow from critical models developed in feminism and cultural studies that have argued that television—like most forms of U.S. popular culture—is utopian and open to a variety of interpretations by different viewers. The constraints on this utopianism are evaluated in my discussion of racial representation in children's commercials. I focus on gender representation in the series *My Little Pony* (Chapter Five) and *Slimer and the Real Ghostbusters* (Chapter Six). Through a close description of these animated series, I establish a basis for children's pleasure in television while highlighting the ways in which commercials and videos borrow and adapt adult genres of U.S. popular culture. Chapter Seven takes to the aisles of toy stores. I compare the mass-market chain store Toys "R" Us with upscale, educational toy stores in terms of a clash of values—and social aspirations—between classes, and between parents and children.

I have chosen to work with the lowest forms of children's television and culture: Saturday morning commercials and animated commercial series. Their appeal is more complex and they are more self-conscious about consumerism than most adults realize. I feel it is important to defend children's television from its most vociferous critics for two reasons. First, children's television has all but disappeared from the network (noncable) mornings and afternoons, leaving only Saturday morning, and access to children's television has increasingly become a matter of money—of being able to buy cable and home videos. As media researcher Patricia Palmer has argued, "poor programs"—and I would add here a lack of programs—"are also the consequence of holding low expectations of the television medium for its child audience."[2] Second, millions of children and their families are written off by teachers and social workers—by intellectuals—as television zombies. It is necessary continually to attack the smug self-satisfaction of educated middle-class people who believe themselves to be cleverer than those who do not attempt to monitor, mask, or deny their own television viewing, who believe that other people's children are already ruined by "exposure" to television. Poor children may rely on television to acquire knowledge and experience unavailable to them in other ways, but the downgrading of this knowledge in the formal educational system punishes them.

I believe it is necessary to defend U.S. consumer culture against many of the elitist moral judgments against it; at the same time, I think it is absolutely necessary to criticize the gross economic inequities that are expressed in, negotiated through, and created by advertising and marketing. I believe that commercial children's television is better than some parents think it is, but I also believe that parents and children need to be very conscious of the ways television organizes, distorts, and expresses gender and race difference. Ultimately, my goal is to better understand childhood and parenthood as they are expressed through and mediated by television, advertising, and consumer goods.

1

CHILDREN'S DESIRES/ MOTHERS' DILEMMAS

THE SOCIAL CONTEXTS OF CONSUMPTION

Goods are for mobilizing other people.
—MARY DOUGLAS

Toys, commercials, and animated programs are the lingua franca of young children at babysitters' and grandmothers' houses, day-care centers, and preschools across the United States. Most children leave home long before they enter the public school system, to spend their day away from parents and with other children their own age. At the snack table they admire one another's T-shirts and lunchboxes emblazoned with film and television characters. At show-and-tell or "sharing" time they proudly present the Ninja Turtles, Barbies, Batmen, and My Little Ponies purchased at Toys "R" Us and given them at birthday parties. Most children know the same commercials, television programs, movies, and music. By wearing their media preferences on their sleeves and carrying their most prized possessions everywhere they go, children make visible their identifications with those more ephemeral objects of consumer culture—namely, films, videos, and television programs.

Consumer culture provides children with a shared repository of images, characters, plots, and themes: it provides the basis for small talk and play, and it does this on a national, even global scale. Outside the house, children can bank on finding that nearly every other child they meet will know some of the same things—and probably *have* many of the same things—that they do. Thus very young children are now sufficiently immersed in a consumer culture to be able to strike up a conversation with one another about a character imprinted on a T-shirt or a toy in hand, to spot one of their kind—a fan of My Little Ponies or Ninja Turtles—across the aisles of Safeway or Toys "R" Us. Mass-market commodities are woven into the social fabric of children's lives: they are seen on sleepovers, at show-and-tell in school, on the block or in the apartment building, on the T-shirt. Young children's consumption holds an ambiguous position between domestic space and public space. Young children are only in the process of learning the distinctions between public and private and the activities appropriate to each. In a sense, this is why their consumption activities are so interesting compared with the more restrained and compartmentalized behaviors of adults.

Within the family, children's taste for certain television shows and certain toys can set them apart from their elders. Sometimes young children feel their knowledge and mastery of consumer culture to be a kind of power: something they know, but of which adults are ridiculously ignorant. Young children cannot make purchases or watch television without adult assistance, however, so parents—usually mothers—are implicated in their consumption and often disapprove of their desires. Thus the battle lines between parents and children over toys and media are drawn when the child is very young. Many mothers, and nearly all middle-class intellectuals, view popular toys and children's television as an alien culture with which they are uncomfortable to varying degrees. Adults often perceive TV and toys as dumb and sexist, or depraved and violent. Many parents find the television shows hard to watch, the commercials offensive, and the toys kitschy. Among the upper middle class the conflict between parents and children over toys and television is not based on affordability but on ideological and aesthetic objections. Upper middle-class parents want their children to like things that are "better to like";[1] they struggle to teach them the tastes for classic toys, the aesthetics of natural materials, and the interest in self-improving "educational" materials favored by their class—and to spurn children's consumer culture as mass, TV based, commercial, and plastic.

Mothers may object to children's consumer culture, but they usually give in to it as well, largely because of the usefulness of television programs and toys as convenience goods for caretakers of children. While giving in, adults often harbor profound doubts about the effects of children's consumer culture today and worry that their own children are learning from the mass media an ethic of greed and a proclivity for hedonism.

I believe it is a mistake to judge children's desires for toys and television programs exclusively in terms of greed and individual hedonism. Children's desires are not depraved. In wanting to have toys and see television programs, children are also expressing a desire for a shared culture with their schoolmates and friends and a strong imagination of community. Moreover, observing children's use of consumer goods and popular media can remind adults of the importance of material culture in their own lives. Adults as well as children invest intense feeling in objects and attribute a wealth of personal and idiosyncratic meanings in mass-produced goods.

It is true that young children do not originate any of the symbols of this subculture; rather, a group of professional adults designs toys and TV shows for children that—when their market research tells them it will be appealing to children—deliberately violate the norms and aesthetics of middle-class culture. Market researchers seek children on whom to test their ideas on colors, cuteness, humor, and heroism, but children participate passively in the design process. Girls may love ponies, but they did not make them a cultural symbol on their own. Toys are made in certain ways using certain materials dictated by the availability of cheap labor, usually in China. Similarly, children's television shows are appropriated into young children's culture on a large scale, but adult scriptwriters devise the stories. What children get is limited by the professional ideologies of advertising and entertainment industry workers, the capabilities of industrial production and design of children's goods and media, and the influence of manufacturers and television producers on governmental regulation and broadcasting policy.

It is a mistake, however, to see marketers as evil brainwashers and children as naive innocents, as they are so often depicted in journalists' accounts of the toy industry. The toy and television industries defense against their critics is that children are the ones who make or break the toys and television programs offered to them, that they vote with their remote controls and their dollars. This belief must be treated as more than cynical apologism. Children's desire for toys and media is more than the direct fulfillment of the designs of manufacturers and marketers, however attractive this notion may be in its simplicity. The industry's characterization of the children's audience as fickle and discriminating must be taken seriously. We know that children make meanings out of toys that are unanticipated by—perhaps indecipherable to—their adult designers, who are often baffled by the success of toys like Teenage Mutant Ninja Turtles. Children are creative in their appropriation of consumer goods and media, and the meanings they make with these materials are not necessarily and not completely in line with a materialist ethos. Children create their own meanings from the stories and symbols of consumer culture.

By emphasizing the creative processes of consumption, I am also suggesting that a more useful approach to toys and children's television programs is to insist that they *are* culture. As the British anthropologist Daniel Miller argues:

> Mass goods represent culture, not because they are merely there as the environment in which we operate, but because they are an integral part of that process of objectification by which we create ourselves as an industrial society: our identities, our social affiliations, our lived everyday practices. The authenticity of artifacts as culture derives not from their relationship to some historical style or manufacturing process—in other words, there is no truth or falsity immanent in them—but rather from their active participation in a process of social self-creation in which they are directly constitutive of our understanding of ourselves and others.[2]

As cultural objects, toys and children's television deserve much more careful analysis and attention than they are usually granted. They deserve to be studied as complex, hybrid manifestations of adult culture, which are engaged with in various and contradictory ways by different children under different circumstances. To study children's toys in this way demands the suspension of adult judgment for a time. I believe that we need a break from the blanket condemnation of children's consumer culture in order to understand it; we need to identify clearly the resemblances as well as the differences between children's and adults' culture; and we need to clarify the elitist aspects of many critical disparagements of children's mass culture.

Toys and children's television programs are cultural products that mimic adult culture by imitating popular entertainment genres and borrowing from them characters, plots, locales, and costumes. Action-adventure stories, science fiction, musicals, soap operas, and melodramas contribute a store of themes and symbols to children's television. In some cases, children's toys and television characters copy themes of the adult culture but present them in exaggerated versions unacceptable to adults. Gender roles are a notorious example of this. Female characters are marked by exaggerated aesthetic codes: high-pitched voices, pastel colors, frills, endless quantities of hair, and an innate capacity for sympathy. Male characters appear as superheroes with enormous muscles, deep voices, and an earnest and unrelenting capacity for action and bravery. Children's commercial television is also what we may call utopian, universally appealing to children in its subversion of parental values of discipline, seriousness, intellectual achievement, respect for authority, and complexity by celebrating rebellion, disruption, simplicity, freedom, and energy.

Attention to the utopian aspects of popular culture—a type of analysis originated by the Marxist philosopher Ernst Bloch—has been advocated by literary theorist Fredric Jameson as a useful antidote to manipulation theories of the mass media and the tendency to see television as nothing but false consciousness. Film critic Richard Dyer has also identified an element of utopianism in a wide variety of entertainment forms from musicals to comedy to television news: "the image of 'something better' to escape into, or something we want deeply that our day-to-day lives don't provide. Alternatives, hopes, wishes—these are the stuff of utopia, the sense that things could be better, that something other than what is can be imagined and may be realized."[3] In this tradition, certain aspects of mass culture are seen to relate to "specific inadequacies in society": abundance replaces scarcity and the unequal distribution of wealth; boundless energy replaces exhaustion. Dreariness is countered by intensity—"the capacity of entertainment to present either complex or unpleasant feelings in a way that makes them seem uncomplicated, direct and vivid, not 'qualified' or 'ambiguous' as day-to-day life makes them."[4] Transparency replaces manipulation; community replaces fragmentation.

The kind of utopianism found in entertainment is severely restricted, however. Although they see positive sides to utopianism, Jameson notes a "profound identity" between "utopian gratification and ideological manipulation," and Dyer warns that the consideration of problems is typically limited to those for which capitalism itself offers remedies—through consumption. Too often, entertainment "provides alternatives *to* capitalism which will be provided *by* capitalism."[5] Still, the concept of utopian sensibility can help to explain much of the appeal of children's cartoons and commercials. They portray an abundance of the things most prized by children—

food and toys; their musical themes and fast action are breathtakingly energetic; they enact a rebellion against adult restriction; they present a version of the world in which good and evil, male and female, are unmistakably coded in ways easily comprehended by a young child; and they celebrate a community of peers. Children's mass culture rejects the instrumental uses of toys and television for teaching and self-improvement preferred by parents.

The contemporary mass culture of childhood can be found in magazine ads and television commercials, toys and toy stores, and television programs aimed at children. How do these reflect differing and conflicting viewpoints between adults and children? How do contemporary advertising, toy sales, and commercial television programming create and reflect the gap between adults and children? How are race, gender, and class differences highlighted or submerged in children's consumer culture? How do children's media borrow and transform popular genres in adult entertainment? How has the market of affluent parents been targeted by "alternative" toy and video makers? The differences as well as the resemblances between children's and parents' consumer cultures form the topic of this book.

With a clear understanding of the limitations of utopianism in mind, I want to consider how children's consumer culture and the promises it makes grew as big as they are today. The history is complex, involving changes in parents' workloads, the dominance of developmental psychology and the way it has formed our attitudes toward toys, and the impact of television on the nuclear family. I believe it is necessary to place children's popular culture in the contexts of historical changes in households and in the work mothers and fathers do, attitudes toward child rearing encouraged by experts and marketers, and the widespread present perception that television is bad for children. I also wish to examine hedonism and emulation, explanations for consumerism from sociological theory, in light of their special relevance to the predicament of parents' and young children's differing perceptions of children's consumer culture.

Household Histories

Children's consumerism is usually discussed in the narrow terms of the relationship between the child as an individual and the advertiser. In that interaction, mothers appear only as shadowy figures of neglect. Mothers presumably are most culpable when they leave their children alone to watch commercial television. But young children's consumption of television and mass-market goods must also be understood in the context of child care, as mothers' work. The growth of the market for toys and children's convenience foods depends as much on the mother's vulnerability as on her children's. The increasing labor and time intensity of mothers' work through the century set the stage for the proliferation of children's consumer goods. Typically, critics of the toy industry attribute its growth since the 1950s to the increasing sophistication of advertising directed at children—especially through the medium of television. This is only one part of the story.

In order for the volume of toy sales to have increased, families had to move to houses with space to keep the toys, and children had to have mothers who were so busy that they needed new ways to keep children entertained. These mothers often did not have traditional child-care support networks in place, as increased mobility meant that more families lived far away from their relatives. A rapid growth in income and the extension of credit in the 1950s and 1960s gave mothers the means to buy toys.

Feminist historians and sociologists argue that mothers now have more work to do than they used to.[6] Such a claim seems counterintuitive: didn't modernization and the rise of consumerism reduce the workload for each household? The explanation for this paradox lies in the social history of household technology, the increase in consumption as a form of work necessary for the maintenance of households, and the changing standards of child rearing propagated by experts. Each of these factors has played a major role in increasing the work that mothers must do. The rise in consumerism in the twentieth century has coincided with a redistribution of household labor and an increase in the work that adult women living in nuclear families are expected to do.

Throughout the twentieth century, U.S. households experienced an overall improvement of domestic well-being: more clean clothes; more varied diet; cleaner, larger living spaces; more heating. These improvements in the standard of living were brought about by broad-scale economic development initiated in the 1920, and, after a brief but severe hiatus during the Great Depression, were fully realized in the 1950s: the extension of utilities, the diffusion of household appliances, the building of single-family homes (usually in the suburbs), and the availability of mass-produced commodities in supermarkets and shopping malls. Family members expected a greater

Now... my children entertain themselves

" I have more time for myself, thanks to Capitol children's records. And the children keep busy and happy. We *all* have more fun when they get out the Capitol record albums.

We join in the spirit with jolly Bozo the Clown, h circus music and animal sounds. And Bugs Bunny and Walt Disney cartoon characters give hours an hours of merry listening. Capitol's Record Readers are picture books that talk... pages of thrilling drawings in full color, timed to the records. It's wholesome entertainment, helping children's eager minds learn good taste and appreciation for finer things.'

Capitol makes records on **SUPERFLEX**, *virtually unbreakable*. Bend 'em, drop 'em. Just right

1. Toys offered to provide mothers with some free time.

variety and quantity of goods "in stock" in the pantry and refrigerator. Thus women often felt obliged to make frequent, lengthy trips to a grocery store that was now self-service and located farther from home. Women living in families also faced new kinds of chores, transportation of husbands and children, for instance, became a bigger part of the job, as suburban sprawl required driving to work, stores, schools, playgrounds, and swimming pools.

Changes in household technologies can be divided into three periods.[7] In the early decades of the nineteenth century, some of the domestic work that men traditionally performed for the home, such as chopping wood and raising food, was eliminated for (some) men, freeing them to assume jobs in factories and offices. Some of women's work, such as spinning and weaving, was also eliminated, but women's work in the home—cooking, sewing, laundering, child care, cleaning—was still arduous and time-consuming (notwithstanding the fact that working-class women in larger numbers throughout the century did factory work in addition to these chores, making up 20 percent of the wage labor force by 1910). The second stage began in the 1920s as mass production, retailing, and advertising developed rapidly on a broad scale. At the same time, the home was increasingly mechanized, and municipalities and public service industries laid down sewer lines and gas and electrical supply systems that would determine the locations of future residential building. Historian Ruth Schwartz Cowan has underscored the fact that the planning for these foundations of modern household technology was based on an assumed sexual division of labor: women shouldered the hidden costs of these changes with their household labor.

A third stage extended through the post–World War II period. During this period, domestic standards of living improved on a mass scale, and modern domestic technologies became common to working-class as well as middle-class homes. By 1970, two-thirds of the population owned their own homes: single-family, detached homes in low-density neighborhoods located far from urban centers. These "dream homes" were not available to everyone; single white women, the white elderly working class and lower middle class, minority men and women, and the minority elderly were often excluded from home ownership.[8] With soaring real estate prices and mortgage debt, the dream of home ownership has slipped out of reach for increasing numbers of white baby boomers as well. Nevertheless, since the 1950s, children have been central to the dream of home ownership: suburban homes—pictured continually in television sitcoms and magazine advertisements—were to be filled with everything the parents had not had. Family and recreation rooms were big enough to accommodate train sets and to provide a place to sit for everyone in the family while watching television or listening to the stereo. Ranch-style houses provided separate children's bedrooms that could be filled with toys. Driveways, broad side-walks, and little traffic provided safe places for bicycling and roller-skating. The dream houses were located in safe, homogeneous neighborhoods far from the city and were designed to facilitate a new style of child-centered family life. Child care and consumption were to be managed by the mother, now increasingly isolated from urban life and even other relatives.

Cowan argues that the material advantages of the new domestic technologies were such that they produced a kind of social revolution in which women living in families—even the mothers of small children—could enter the paid work force in the 1960s and 1970s without an intolerable decline in material comfort. Between 1950 and 1986, the number of women working outside the home rose from 30 to 55 percent; the number of married women in the paid labor force also had children under six rose from 23 percent to 54 percent. More mothers have paid jobs (or are seeking work) than childless women.[9] Although the comfort of children and husbands might not have suffered a blow, another price has had to be paid. The labor cost of the transition to two-income or female-headed households with small children has been borne almost entirely by women, who work a staggeringly long week in the home and on the job outside the home. Surprisingly, women spend about as many hours maintaining the household today as they did in the 1920s (whether they are employed outside the home or not). As feminist scholar Dolores Hayden argues, the work of homemaking has become extremely complex, averaging about sixty hours a week by 1982 and involving complicated negotiations between the commercial sector (stores, banks, credit institutions) and the public sector (hospitals, doctors' offices, welfare offices, schools).

> Part of homemaking involves seeing that each family member's myriad personal needs are fully met. The new dress must be the right size; the new fourth grade teacher must understand a child's history of learning difficulties. Sometimes relationships with stores or institutions turn into adversarial ones. If the new car is a lemon; if the grade school isn't teaching reading fast enough, if the hospital offers an incorrect diagnosis, if the social security benefit check is late, then the stressful nature of the homemaker's brokering work between home, market and state is exacerbated.[10]

Households differ in terms of how much work women do to maintain them. However, the most important factor in predicting the

2. Advertisers for household goods acknowledge the arduousness of mothers' work.

workload is not income, or education, or paid employment, but the presence of children in the home. A time study expert has found, in a breakdown of household tasks, that the addition of an infant increases the total number of tasks done in a household by 412 such tasks per month; when families have children aged two to five, the workload increases by 295 tasks over childless households. When measured in terms of time spent rather than number of tasks performed, a baby adds about ten days' worth of tasks to the household per month; a small child, about five days' worth to the norm for monthly levels of household work. "Any other influence exerted by the characteristics of the home, characteristics of the members, or their preferences pales in comparison with the influence of children on the household." [11] If children increase the amount of housework women do, it is reasonable to assume that a lower birthrate would also reduce women's work. This has not happened, in part because experts advocate more elaborate and time-consuming ways of caring for and entertaining each child, who now has fewer siblings to play with. As one scholar put it, being a working mother in the United States today is "virtually a guarantee of being overworked and perpetually exhausted." [12]

When mothers enter the paid work force, do fathers do more housework and child care? Most studies of men's contribution to housework have answered no. In the 1970s, two major studies concluded that men did no more housework when their wives worked than when they did not and that they often did less work overall because the wife's extra income meant that the husband could put in fewer hours on the job. A study conducted in 1985 found that employed mothers averaged eighty-five hours of work per week, compared to their husbands' sixty-six hours. The "leisure gap" between mothers and fathers has been estimated at eleven to thirty hours per week. Arlie Hochschild averaged the results of several studies to estimate that women worked fifteen hours more each week than men. "Over a year, they worked an *extra month of twenty-four-hour days a year*" (emphasis in original). [13] Hochschild's ethnography of shared housework and child care among working parents found that of the time men spent at home, more of their time was devoted to child care than to housework: "Since most parents prefer to tend to their children than clean house, men do more of what they'd rather do. More men than women take their children on 'fun' outings to the park, the zoo, the movies. Women spend more time on maintenance, feeding and bathing children, enjoyable activities to be sure, but often less leisurely or 'special' than going to the zoo." [14]

Hochschild found no correlation between class position and the likelihood that a father would do a larger share of housework and child care. Interestingly, she noted that working-class fathers—who held traditional notions of women's work—shared the work in practice and underestimated their participation in interviews, while middle-class fathers—who espoused egalitarian notions about housework and child care—shared less and overestimated theirs. The divorce and unmarried pregnancy rates have dramatically increased since the 1970s, in many cases eliminating fathers' participation in child care altogether. A study completed in 1981 found that only 26 percent of divorced fathers had seen their children for three weeks in the past year; only 20 percent of fathers had paid court-ordered child support regularly.[15]

Mothers have fewer helpers than they used to. Throughout the twentieth century, working-class women switched from domestic work for middle-class families to other kinds of work when it became available. In 1870 there had been one servant per eight households; by 1920 there was one per eighteen.[16] Other domestic helpers, such as older children in the family or neighborhood children, were less available, because childhood was increasingly defined as a time of learning and playing, not working. Thus, Cowan argues that since World War I there has been a leveling out of class differences in the kind and amount of domestic work all women do; middle-class women are as likely to scrub their own bathrooms as are working-class women, but working-class women are likely do the chore after an arduous day of wage labor. Phyllis Palmer has described some of the subtle changes in the image of the middle-class housewife that accompanied the loss of domestic servants:

> The years from 1920 to 1945 may be viewed as a transitional period during which middle-class homes changed from being *directed* by a lady-housewife to being *served* by the wife. . . . Both at the beginning and end of the period the housewife's existence was to be devoted to her home and family. By the end of the era, however, she was less able to hire another woman to take over many of the physical tasks such devotion entailed. As a consequence, housewives lost some benefits of the angelic image of the middle-class wife, which derived from their attachment to the home but was enhanced by the contrast between the housewife and the domestic servant. With declining access to servants, the housewife not only did more work, she also felt herself to be a drudge. Without a servant to emphasize her superiority, this wife found her role considerably less tolerable.[17]

From slavery to this day, African American women have routinely worked long hours outside the home *and* cared for their own families. Media and scholarly attention to the plight of the working mother only increased when large numbers of white, middle-class women found themselves working the double shift. Today, increasing numbers of immigrant women—many of them Central American or Southeast Asian—are hired by two-income professional families as housekeepers and nannies. Arlie Hochschild has noted the widening split between "women who do jobs that pay enough to pay a babysitter and the women who baby-sit or tend to other home needs." [18] Hochschild notes the gender dimension of this split as well: "[As] more mothers rely on the work of lower-paid specialists, the value accorded the work of mothering (not the value of children) has declined for women, making it all the harder for men to take it up." [19]

Of course, all mothers do not carry the negative image of their work as drudgery. Helena Z. Lopata found, in a study conducted in the 1970s, that variations in the housewife's role based on race, ethnicity, and class led women to evaluate their labor differently: "While some women are overwhelmed by the isolation, the repetitiveness of tasks, and the double burden of the employed wife, others work out a life style which they find satisfying . . . helping to explain why working-class women may be tempted to leave the labor force—housewifery *is* creative and autonomous, compared with most jobs which women are likely to fill in the labor force." [20] Although advertising and television denigrate domestic work as something to avoid or do as rapidly as possible, this work carries greater significance for women from strong ethnic traditions. Beatrice Pesquera found that Chicanas working outside the home feel a special responsibility for preserving domestic culture as a part of their cultural heritage, teaching Spanish songs and stories to their children, teaching their daughters to cook traditional foods; but she also noted that this creates tension because it adds on another task to their already crowded schedule.

The enormous demands placed on women's time—exacerbated when mothers work for pay outside the home—make children's goods appealing, even necessary, for mothers. Videos provide tired mothers time to cook dinner, feed the baby, or clean the house. Toys keep children entertained while they tramp along with their mothers on errands to the bank, the doctor's office, the post office—or the welfare office. Snacks and toys and videos make children happy: no matter how fleeting the joy, it is an important goal for mothers in a culture in which childhood means happiness. It is easier to take care of happy children than bored, restless ones. Consumer goods offer mothers what one ad agency researcher called "the chance to be a hero for ten minutes" by buying cereal or candy in the grocery store.[21] Children go shopping because mothers go shopping, and mothers have few alternatives but to take them along. Young children could never have been exploited as a market if they were not already visiting stores with their mothers. Urbanization, the automobile, and a rising crime rate have left few safe public areas where children can play or where children are even allowed. Grocery stores and malls are among the few places where mothers accompanied by their children can go and find they are welcome. The increase in children's consumption of television and toys, then, has been caused in part by the increasing difficulty in the job of caring for children.

Advice about Child Rearing

Ideas about child rearing changed at the same time that mass-market goods were first disseminated and domestic labor patterns shifted. Advice literature defined the job of mothering as complicated, difficult, time-consuming—and serious in the consequences for the child if the mother did not perform well. In her classic analysis of housework, feminist sociologist Ann Oakley observed that "the discovery of the child's importance has affected women more than it has men." [22] While the upgrading of children's lives, the emphasis on early education, and the campaign against physical abuse have brought great improvements to some children's lives, these gains have been won through an increased burden on mothers. Throughout the twentieth century, authoritative knowledge about children has been taken over by specialists—childhood experts, psychologists, psychoanalysts, social workers—thus undermining women's authority as rearers of children.

I use the term "advice literature" for any form of journalism and nonfiction writing that purports to solve the problems of everyday life and proffer a set of behavioral guidelines for women in the roles of wife and mother. These forms share an address to the "average" woman and usually a sympathetic, soothing tone, especially in the hands of women writers. Class differences are normally elided in advice literature, which tends to assume a middle-class or upper middle-class norm. Advice literature includes bestsellers dedicated to these topics (by writers such as Benjamin Spock, Penelope Leach, J. B. Watson); problem columns in magazines that publish letters from readers seeking advice; similar columns by agony aunts such as Ann Landers and Dear Abby in newspapers; expert columns such as the pages written by doctors and psychologists in parenting magazines (*Child, Working Mother, Parents, American Baby*) devoted to children of a particular age; and, most recently, cable television talk shows. These programs—such as *What Every Baby Knows* and *Growing Up Together* on Lifetime and *Healthy Kids* and *American Baby* on the Family Channel—feature familiar experts such as Penelope Leach and T. Berry Brazelton as either guests or moderators offering advice on parenting problems. The shows are sponsored by companies such as Procter and Gamble—traditional sponsors of daytime soap operas and the makers of Luvs and Pampers disposable diapers. They adopt a developmental perspective on children, emphasizing shared stages in mental, physical, and personality development against a backdrop of dream houses and professional couples. Much academic research on children in the social sciences finds fairly immediate translation into advice literature.

Since the 1920s when J. B. Watson (father of American behaviorism and advertising consultant) published his best-selling book on infant and child care, U.S. advice literature has stressed the paramount importance of early experience and the malleability of the infant through behavioral conditioning. Such beliefs meant that a mother's role (and it was always assumed in this literature that it was the *mother's* role) entailed a grave new responsibility, one much more demanding than the mere hygienic imperatives of early twentieth-century advice literature. Watson and others in the 1920s and 1930s increased demands on mothers' time by stressing not only the need for health and hygiene but also the imposition of strict daily schedules on children's activities and the permanence of psychological formations of early childhood. Expert advice about child rearing picked up momentum after World War II, and book sales soared with the baby boom. Throughout the 1940s and 1950s, Piaget's model of cognitive development was selectively borrowed from in order to emphasize the importance of environment and the child's "active" achievement of growth. Anthropologist Martha Wolfenstein found that the emphasis on parental control in the 1920s and 1930s gave way in the 1940s and 1950s to the equally time-consuming ideal of "fun morality" and the notion that mothers should play with and stimulate their babies.

Accompanying the enormous growth in the numbers of advice manuals sold after the Second World War was the radical change in the kind of advice the new generation of experts offered. Child-rearing "techniques" advocated in the postwar period emphasized intellectual growth:

> The new model baby was warmly affectionate, impulsive, dependent and (preferably) scintillatingly intelligent. Spock talked about the "daily stimulation from loving parents" which was necessary if "emotional depth and a keen intelligence" were to be fostered; Jerome Kagan identified the "two critical concerns" of American parents as "attachment to mother and rate of cognitive development." [23]

The implications of the dissemination of professional advice on child rearing are many. Advice on child rearing now came from experts rather than from family members, neighbors, and friends who would have a more intimate knowledge of the family's cultural and financial situation. Many of the new experts were medical doctors. Thus middle-aged, middle-class men replaced or competed with the advice of older female neighbors and relatives. Experts advised mothers to care not only for the body and its health but for the mind and its rate of development. They increased the demand for nurturing behavior in constant supply. The new child psychology was a child-centered model. Implicit in its proscriptions was a disavowal of maternal authority and an upgrading of the child's own desires as rational and goal directed. Because early life events for the child were of supreme importance, caretaking responsibilities expanded. As historian Christina Hardyment comments: "[B]eing a constant reassuring presence, considering one's child's every need, creating a stimulating environment exactly suited to its current developmental stage—all these take up a great deal of time." [24]

Advice literature's assumptions do not change, even when mothers work outside the home for pay. Media critic Janice Winship has pointed out that such advice encourages women to do it alone, simultaneously acknowledging the insurmountable odds against them, and remaining unremittingly cheerful about women's chances for success. The ways that women's magazines refer to the stress experienced by a working mother while presenting her image as vital, daring, and exciting, rather than as a drudge, are epitomized in *Redbook*'s "juggler," its ideal reader/consumer depicted in ads and referred to in editorial material who enjoys an affluent lifestyle, a rewarding career, and unproblematic relationships with her husband and children.

As experts advocated increased attention to children, product designers moved in to assist mothers in their tasks with new tools. Expert advice about child rearing exists in a complex relationship to marketing. The lines between advice and advertising are blurry. Advice literature in its dedicated form, such as the paperback book or magazine column, cannot be easily distinguished from "advertising" versions, that often include a letter from a mother requesting advice or a discussion of infant nutrition. Advertisements tend to repeat the same advice found in books and proffer the same solutions—often involving the purchase of a commodity or service to ease the woman's workload. As I noted earlier, ad copywriters for everything from baby food to crayons borrow from the unsponsored writing of the experts and do much to popularize and disseminate their work. In toy advertisements from *Parents* magazine, Piaget's ideas about "stages" of development and the separability of skills (cognitive, motor, social) abound. Yet editorial advice about buying things for children can be contradictory: sometimes encouraging restraint and saving; warning parents against spoiling and the use of bribes; encouraging do-it-yourself alternatives to store-bought items.

During the 1920s and 1930s advertisers increasingly forecast and directed the turn that advice literature took. Social historian Roland Marchand found that when advertisements promised that a product would provide a woman with more leisure time, one of the most commonly suggested uses for the product was spending time with children. In contrast to the vision of didacticism and moral guidance common to nineteenth-century ideals of child rearing, parents and children were to spend a new "companionable leisure" together. This leisure had as its goal more than mere pleasure, however; it was a way of fostering the child's personal development. Choosing the right product immediately rewarded the mother with "increased attention and companionship."

Advertising advocated covert forms of parental regulation by suggesting that parents win the child over rather than assert authority punitively. One axiom disseminated through advertising, especially for medicinal and food products, was that "children would inevitably choose the wrong diet or acquire undesirable habits if left to themselves." [25] Yet advertisements encouraged the view of some child experts that children should not be forced or coaxed or nagged into compliance. Marchand uses the example of Campbell's soup advertising campaigns developed during this period—and widely used today: "It's not vegetables to them [which they would naturally reject] it's just good food." Marchand dubs such techniques "the parable of the Captivated Child." [26] In a more negative form, some of these ads portrayed more overt conflict between parent and child. "Drink that milk or go straight to bed," scolds an angry mother towering over her daughter; the addition of Cocomalt can remove such trials. In another ad, a little girl sulks at the kitchen table, flanked by mother coaxing on one side and father reaching into his pocket (for a bribe?) on the other: this under the caption "Must you wheedle your child into eating?" Wheatena offers the "delicious whole wheat cereal" that could answer the parents problems because "children love Wheatena!" Advertisers offered commodities as the means to achieve the new ideals of child rearing and to banish conflict entirely from the parent-child relationship.

As Marchand suggests, the type of psychological child-rearing advice disseminated in advice literature and in advertising coincided with the "rising enthusiasm for professional 'personnel management' in industry in the 1920s and 1930s," with its attempt "to mold people's behavior and facilitate their 'adjustment' by psychological manipulation rather than authoritarian coercion." [27] Sociologist Nancy Chodorow has noted a similar connection between child-rearing techniques and the needs of an industrial, capitalist society: "Socialization is a particularly psychological affair, since it must lead to the assimilation and internal organization of generalized capacities for participating in a hierarchical and differentiated social world, rather than to training for a specific role. . . . Production, for instance, is more efficient and profitable when workers develop a willing and docile personality." [28] The parental strategy of material rewards and coercions advocated in advertising mimics the adult worker's saving and striving for the material rewards of consumer culture.

During this period, advertising for products to be used for children reproduced ideas from bestsellers on child rearing, probably because the advertisers as an elite, upper middle-class group were themselves early initiates into the new child-rearing philosophies. There were some important emphases, however, added to this material in copywriting:

> For obvious merchandising reasons, the ads advocated parental indulgence with far less qualification than the experts. Sensing that family democracy meant earlier and wider participation in the joys of consumerism, advertisers enthusiastically endorsed the

idea of family conferences and shared decision-making. Advertising tableaux surpassed even the child-rearing manuals in placing total responsibilities on the parents for every detail of the child's development, thus magnifying the potential for guilt. And they exaggerated the ease with which children might be manipulated. Psychologists occasionally argued that the mother might need to assert her domination in a direct contest of wills with the child, but the advertising parable portrayed a parent-child relationship in which open conflict was always unnecessary.[29]

These four features of advertising to parents—the encouragement of indulgence in parents; the democratic rights of children in the family; total, exclusive responsibility of mothers for children's development; and the possibility (the promise through consumer goods) of the indefinite deferral of open conflict with the child—are all features that we find present to varying degrees in advice literature, advertising targeted at mothers, and the popular culture of childhood today.

Television

Given the extraordinary amount of unpaid work required of women maintaining households with children, it is unsurprising that television sets—with their potential use as a babysitting machine—were purchased so fast by so many families in the 1950s and that families with children were the first to want them.[30] Television offered mothers a break. Television historian Lynn Spigel has documented the ways that television was at first hailed as a medium of family togetherness, a source of increased domestic harmony and intimacy in the dream home, an alternative to the mother as a source of learning for children at home. But watching television also increased the potential conflicts with children over wanting more than mothers were able or willing to buy for them, and it offered idealized images of the happy housewife and mother fulfilling her job with ease. Worries over television's effects on children—ranging from facial tics to passivity—soon came to the fore, and experts assigned to mothers the job of censoring, monitoring, and accompanying the child's viewing. If a mother heeded the experts' advice, she lost the free time television provided; if she did not, she used television as a babysitter only at the cost of feeling guilty about it.

In social discourse, various portrayals of television compete with one another, each informed by and representing a specific set of

3. Ads mimicked the form and substance of parental advice columns, here focusing on problems at the table: "Even though food shouldn't be used as a toy, there's no reason why food shouldn't be fun."

4. The "Ideal Child's Food" promises to defer open conflict between parent and child indefinitely.

If Children
Served the Breakfast

Do You Think That Any Table Would Lack Puffed Wheat or Rice?

Most homes, of course, would serve these dainties if children had their way.

Not for breakfast only, but in bowls of milk at night. Also dry, like nut meats, for between-meal foods. These toasted grains, puffed to eight times normal size, are fascinating tit-bits to the young.

To grown-ups, too. A big dairy lunch room found that four out of five men who took ready-cooked cereals chose either Puffed Wheat or Puffed Rice.

Why Not Please Them?

Yet these food confections—these bubbles of grain—are better than they taste. Never were whole grains so fitted for food as they are by this Anderson process.

Here they are toasted for an hour. Here they are steam exploded. Here every food granule, for ease of digestion, is literally blasted to pieces. Every authority knows this to be the hygienic form of grain food.

Don't you think that children who like Puffed Grains should enjoy them to their hearts' content?

5. *The family democracy: "If Children Served the Breakfast . . ."*

TELEVISION
has changed our Lives

By ELLA APRIL CODEL

THE CHILDREN counted the days until our television was installed. They had been identifying television antennas on the roofs of homes in our neighborhood as enthusiastically as they played their favorite game of identifying auto licenses from different states.

Our preparation took the outward form of a household upheaval under the guise of redecorating. Television to me meant comfort, easy groupings of friends and family, with definite emphasis on ability to watch the screen without moving from a normal conversation group. In other words, I wanted everyone to be seated as usual, but should anyone suggest, "Let's see what's on television," I wanted no pushing and scraping of chairs—I wanted just one person having to get up to tune in.

We had a family conference. All agreed they didn't want a new arrangement of furniture, yet they reluctantly agreed to tolerate an experiment. For several weeks there was lots of criticism about this or that shift in furniture. While the living room seemed to be the logical place for the console type, we finally chose the den because it was cozier and lent itself to smaller groups; also, it was closer to our kitchen and more accessible for the youngsters and myself when preparing food or refreshments. Moreover, our piano was in the living room, and we wanted no conflict with television. However, for many families with children, the playroom or rumpus room may be best because the children and their friends can then be completely at ease away *(Continued on page 64)*

While family activities go on as usual, television both enriches and entertains.

6. *In the early days, television was seen as promoting family harmony and "togetherness."*

interests. In writing about children's television, competing and contradictory positions are advanced by industry producers, consumer protection groups such as Action for Children's Television; academic "childhood professionals," such as educators, pediatricians, psychologists, and social workers; and academic media researchers.

Each of these groups contributes to a discourse that allows certain things to be said and rules out other things—or makes them unimaginable. The discourse of child experts usually assumes a certain normative view of what children are like (naive, impressionable, uncritical), of what television should do (help children learn to read and to understand math and science), of what is an appropriate way to spend leisure time (being physically and mentally active, *doing* things), and of what television viewing is (passive and mindless). These ideas derive from larger medical, religious, and social science bodies of thought.

When parents and teachers read about children, toys, and television, they normally rely on journalists' accounts published in newspapers and women's magazines. The tone of such articles has been frequently alarmist, fueling mothers' fears about commercial television's long-term effects on children and inspiring guilt over taking advantage of television's convenience. Warnings from child psychologists about television's effects have been curiously out of step with much mass communications research, which has stressed a view of media consumption as active rather than passive and enumerated the variety of "uses and gratifications" to be gained from the media. Nonetheless, blaming television for everything that's wrong with children is a rhetorical strategy for which the print media seem to have a special attraction. The most quotable and attractive sources for journalists—the story makers—are people who will say in the simplest possible terms that children are unwitting victims of the devil television. It is a satisfying notion: to find a single source with direct, casually observable effects to blame for all that is wrong with children today.

The most widely held belief about television among parents and educators is that television viewing is passive. This notion circulates regularly in media targeted to parents: pediatricians' pamphlets, magazines, agony columns, advice literature. "There is a powerful, idealised image of childhood as a time of activity and doing that reinforces some of my misgivings about television," explains one parent.[31] Complaints about children's TV viewing—such as those voiced by media critics Marie Winn and Neil Postman—are backed by a nostalgic mourning for an idealized vision of a "lost" childhood: a childhood that was a time of doing, of direct experience.[32]

Why is passivity the attribute so often used to condemn children's television viewing? In sharp contrast to eighteenth- and nineteenth-century Anglo-American notions about children, in which submission, obedience, and docility were prized, today passive is about the

7. *Toy advertisers capitalized on escalating fears about television's bad effects on the child. Here record players and walkie-talkies are proposed as better ways to "help him grow" than a "steady TV diet."*

worst thing a child can be. As I have noted, developmental psychology is now the dominant model of childhood in teaching, psychology, social work, and medicine. Passivity is especially problematic, even pathological, according to this model.[33] The notion of children watching television offends the widely held belief in the importance of the child *actively* achieving developmental tasks. Child experts, television critics, and protectionists are convinced that television deters children from achieving normative agendas of child development: direct interaction with peers and parents, "large motor" skills, socialization, cognitive and physical development. Television is excluded from the list of activities that can "stimulate" growth—and stimulation is something that parents are supposed to provide in endless supply from infancy onward.

Experts regularly advise that the less television viewing, the better; videotapes are preferable to broadcast television because they have no commercials; if you must let your child watch, make it PBS; no viewing is best of all. As one media researcher pointed out: "The amount of television children watch is still quoted in a way which presupposes adult amazement and disapproval. We speak of 'heavy' or 'light' viewers as if there is indeed a measurable 'amount' of the thing called TV viewing which has entered into the child's system and stays there like a dead weight."[34] Child experts can be exacting taskmasters when they advise parents to monitor children's viewing: "Establish ground rules, prevent TV from becoming an addiction," say Dorothy and Jerome Singer in *Parents* magazine: no TV before school, during meals, during daytime hours, or before homework is done. "And don't suggest that the child 'go watch TV' whenever you are feeling overwhelmed or need privacy."[35] Obesity, violence, and poor school performance are continually held up as the threatened results of television viewing.

The first major North American study of children and television, based on data collected between 1958 and 1960, was adamantly neutral about television viewing.[36] Among preschool children, those who watched television started school with larger vocabularies and more knowledge about the world than children who had not watched television. For older children, television was found to be neither particularly beneficial nor harmful. The physical effects of television viewing were negligible, and any correlation between viewing and passivity depended on other factors in the home life of the child. The researchers, Wilbur Schramm, Jack Lyle, and Edwin Parker, noted different attitudes among parents toward television: blue-collar parents were more grateful for television's convenience and less critical of its programs; whereas middle-class parents held stronger reservations about television. In every aspect of the relationship between television viewing and a child's worldview, IQ, social class, and social relations were powerful determinants.

What filtered down to advice literature from this and other early studies was a tendency to urge mothers to work harder at their children's television viewing: by censoring, accompanying viewing, and discussing programming with the child, thus losing the free time that television might offer. Certainly television has changed children's lives. But it has done so in complex—and not necessarily negative ways—demonstrated in a wealth of sophisticated research in the 1970s and 1980s by scholars such as Jennings Bryant, Suzanne Pingree, Ellen Wartella, James Anderson, Daniel Anderson, and Elizabeth Lorch.[37] Recently, a number of mass communications researchers employing qualitative methods to study children's viewing habits have again challenged the notion that children are passive in relation to television. Unfortunately this work has gathered little attention outside academic circles.

Two recent studies based on parents' reports of their children's viewing have sketched a more active—and interactive—picture of children's viewing. Patricia Palmer, in an observational study of Australian children watching TV at home, has charted the great variety of ways children behave when watching television—from intent viewing of a few favorite programs to distracted viewing combined with other activities, such as playing with toys or pets, chatting, drawing. Palmer found that children had a propensity for performing, reenacting, and reinterpreting the material—especially television commercials—often as an affectionate interaction with parents, siblings, and friends. Children spend a lot of time discussing television, arguing about it, and criticizing it, both on the playground with friends and at home with parents and siblings. Palmer's work is important for simply listing the enormous range of children's response to television. Television goes on in the lives of children long after it is seen, and it is constantly subject to discussion and reinterpretation. Palmer reminds us how rich a source of material for social interaction television is, something denied by the persistent image (and I mean this literally, as in magazine and newspaper illustrations) of the child alone before the television set.[38] Far from passive, children, Palmer argues, are a lively audience for television.

The best research on children and television conceives of children's cognitive skills as embedded in a social world and developing at an early age. Dafna Lemish's study of children under two indicates how very early television viewing skills develop, and how babies' experience of television is tied to the everyday world of the family. Lemish's U.S. study, based on parents' recording of their children's behavior, chronicles the rapid changes in babies' attention to and selective perception of television material. Well before the age of two, children were able to monitor television at a glance for interesting material and had mastered a host of audiovisual signs that they used to distinguish among programs and genres. As reported in so many studies of children and television, the toddlers in Lemish's study found television commercials (which *Sesame Street*'s short, dynamic sequences deliberately resemble) especially appealing. Their appreciation of television material progressed rapidly from recognizing familiar objects (children, animals), to selecting favorite animated musical sequences, to attending live-action "story" segments. Young children could distinguish at a glance adult material, such as the news, from children's programming. The children seemed to enjoy teasing parents about their control of the set, manipulating the television as a toy (volume and channel controls) while parents tried to watch adult programs. A study by Paul Messaris found, as did Lemish, that mothers were fascinated by their children's rapid development in relation to television and enjoyed discussing it—but the specter of expert advice hung over them: they wished not to be badly thought of for expressing an interested enthusiasm over their children's viewing.[39] Most adults watch television and most parents let their children watch television, but many mothers feel compelled to apologize for it and see regulating children's consumption of television as part of their job.

The most theoretically sophisticated work on children's television is that of Robert Hodge and David Tripp, who analyze a single episode of an unexceptional 1978 cartoon called *Fangface*.[40] Their project benefits from the contributions of semiotics, structuralism, ideological analysis and post-structuralism; it is a good example of the kind of work currently identified by the term "cultural studies." Cartoons have only occasionally been subject to any kind of literary analysis—and never to the kind of painstaking attention Hodge and Tripp expend on *Fangface*. Instead, child psychologists and media sociologists have tended to use the methods of quantitative content analysis to "measure" the children's cartoon during a fixed block of hours during the broadcasting schedule. Content analysts count how many acts of violence occur, how many males and females there are, how many minority characters appear, how often villains speak with a foreign accent, and so on. The virtue of a structuralist/semiotic analysis is that it focuses on the combinations and structures of meaning. This level of understanding tends to be lost in content analysis, in which the meanings of discrete units of information in a television program are not related to the context in which they appear.

Hodge and Tripp argue that cartoons—widely considered one of the lowest forms of television—are surprisingly complex. Children are fascinated by them not because they have been turned into television zombies but because they are understandably engaged by the complex blend of aesthetic, narrative, visual, verbal, and ideological codes at work in them. Although cartoons are characterized by a great deal of repetition and redundancy, Hodge and Tripp argue that their subject matter, as well as their way of conveying it, is complicated stuff. Children use these cartoons to decipher the most important structures in their culture.

In their analysis, Hodge and Tripp demonstrate "the enormous complexity of what is often taken to be a very simple and straightforward message structure": *Fangface* negotiates the categories of nature and culture, the central myth of society in Lévi-Strauss's terms.[41] Hodge and Tripp grant that the meanings they find in *Fangface* may not be thought of as "residing" in the text at all, but are a product of their own interaction with the text. They allow for the options of chaotic or idiosyncratic meanings in the children's decoding of *Fangface*, as well as the possibility that children will ignore many elements in the cartoon simply because they are irrelevant to them.[42] Hodge and Tripp stop short of relativizing all "decoding" or arguing that "anything goes" in interpreting cartoons. Yet they emphasize the limited and partial nature of the responses that children (and adults) will make about television: how these will be created by the context—the classroom, the home, the laboratory—in which children are speaking; how gender, race and age differences within the group will influence the discussion.[43] Researchers such as Hodge and Tripp, Palmer, and Lemish share my position that children are not passive in their use of television, and their work enumerates the diversity of children's viewing as it is practiced in the living room. The actual behaviors of TV watching can be construed as more active than advice literature normally allows, and I would argue that children's television—even the most banal cartoons—adequately challenges children on a cognitive level.

Despite heavy reliance by mothers on the medium, the middle-class belief in the badness of television content is very firmly entrenched. Complaints and fears often involve its moral reductionism, its lack of reality, its racism and sexism, and its violence. One kind of complaint is based on the types of stories children's television presents, as Peggy Charren of Action for Children's Television put it: "It's all cartoon characters—no real people, no character development. The story is always a simple good-versus-evil, with no complexity and no human emotions: this battle, that crash, this one triumphs, that one fails, and it's all over. History, science, mystery, the arts—these are scarce because they haven't been presold to the 32.5 million children in America's TV households." [44] I agree with critics that the content of children's television warrants serious attention, and I focus on these issues in my discussion of commercials and toy-based programs—the most despised of children's TV genres. The charges directed at children's shows, however, are based on adult attention that is casual and erratic. When adults look more closely at children's television, they will seldom find that it delivers a single, unambiguous message to children. Instead, children's television, borrowing and adapting long-standing adult genres of U.S. popular culture, tends to reproduce familiar stereotypes, settings, and plots.

A more valid basis for faulting children's television is its store of words and images that are loaded with histories of oppression—based on class, gender, race and ethnicity. Children's television—like much of children's literature—places white boys at the center of the action. Children of color and girls of all races are dispersed to the sidelines as mascots, companions, victims. A child's identification with television is at best problematic when that child is Asian American or Black or Latino, or working-class or female—to name just a few examples. What needs to be untangled in the discussion of children's television are the aesthetic norms of high culture from the political critique of race, gender, and class stereotypes.

Hedonism and Emulation

As any mother can tell you, television is good at inspiring one form of activity: requesting toys, drinks, cereals, candy—and more television programs. Thus television provides mothers with a break but hardly a free lunch, as they must grant or fend off requests in the grocery store for cereals and candy as well as demands for toys. *Working Mother* magazine quoted one mother on the subject: "Commercials tend to put ideas in children's head of what they must have, and our lives become unbearable when we refuse." The popularity of video over broadcast television stems in part from the desire to shelter children from television commercials. A thornier complaint about commercial television, then, is that it makes kids want toys and foods. One dimension of this complaint is the painful experience of working-class parents who must repeatedly deny their own children the goodies that surround them in stores and that other children seem to have so many of. But the growth of children's consumer culture has made some things cheap enough that poor parents can provide them, at least occasionally: the two-dollar McDonald's Happy Meal with its Barbie or Hot Wheels toy, the four-dollar Ninja Turtle.

The other dimension arises from parents who have the money to grant a child's product request but feel a profound discomfort with the very intensity of children's wanting. Children's consumption is now the focus of a protective, paternalistic concern that previously focused on women and the working class. Children's desires for consumer goods trigger fears of a decline in morals and the emergence of a narcissistic personality type. Adults condemn children as hedonistic and believe that television and liberal child-rearing practices have produced children gravely lacking in self restraint. Parents are baffled or revolted by their children's taste for mass-market goods, while they fail to recognize their own use of consumption for status purposes.

The stigmatization of children's consumer desires deserves analysis in its own right. To begin that analysis, I turned to sociology for more general explanations of consumers' motivations and their relationship to morality on the one hand and the social structure on the other. Historians, anthropologists, and social theorists explain consumer behavior with the concepts of hedonism and emulation, concepts that pertain to children's consumption as well, and the special problems children's requests cause for adults. The concept of hedonism figures prominently in academic research on the subject and in common-sense explanations of the growth of consumerism. It identifies a hedonistic personality bent in the American public as the enabling condition for the growth of a consumer economy. Emulation, on the other hand, associates consumption with social aspirations, arguing that commodities are the primary means of expressing social ambition and social differentiation.

The hedonism explanation attributes increased levels of spending to new personality proclivities and a degeneration in morals. On a mass scale, citizens seek pleasure through commodities and hold less concern for the public good. Individual gratification is the primary motor behind mass consumption, according to this argument. In his writing on the subject, historian T. J. Jackson Lears has placed the change from a Puritan ethic of restraint and self-denial to a new kind of hedonism in the period 1880–1930. The increasing secularization of U.S. society, the growth of individualism, and the relaxation of family and community ties made this possible. Lears's thesis is that "to thrive and spread, a consumer culture required more than a national apparatus of marketing and distribution; it also needed a favorable moral climate. . . . [T]he crucial moral change . . . was the beginning of a shift from the Protestant ethos of salvation through self-denial toward a therapeutic ethos stressing self-realization in this world." [45]

Social critics on the right and the left have found much to condemn in hedonistic consumerism and the particular brand of individualism it apparently expresses. Conservatives have tended to see consumers as greedy, immoral, and destructive of spiritual life, as in Daniel Bell's account, *The Cultural Contradictions of Capitalism*. Marxists have criticized the way consumer activity detracts from political activity that might change the fundamental economic and social relations of society, an argument best known from Herbert Marcuse's *One-Dimensional Man*. Social critics on the right hold advertising responsible for promoting the new hedonism by emphasizing material satisfactions in the here and now. Social critics on the left blame advertising for masking the exploitative nature of capitalist production behind a veneer of attractive, affluent—and mythical—lifestyles. Daniel Miller has noted that a common theme in the left-wing critique of mass consumption is the

> tacit and covert implication that those people who have to live in and through such an object world are equally superficial and deluded, and are unable to comprehend their position. This implies a rejection of any activities undertaken by the mass of the population (always with the exception of direct revolutionary action) as a possible basis for learning about the future development of our society. The argument is that people cannot construct

socialism out of kitsch (sometimes with the equally problematic
implication that they can out of art).[46]

In both right- and left-wing versions of the critique of consumerism, the hedonism explanation blames individuals for being decadent, weak, lazy, self-indulgent; for being morally flawed; for
pursuing personal happiness rather than the public good. Consumption is often pathologized through the language of psychoanalysis.
U.S. scholars such as Stuart Ewen and Christopher Lasch have emphasized the restless narcissism of consumerism: consumers flitting
from one purchase to the next, losing the capacity to delay gratification, victims of their own unquenchable desires. The hedonism
notion has easily fit Freud's model of personality development in
which the immature, pleasure-seeking id must be brought under
control of the superego, or conscience. Thus preschool-age children, still ruled by the id, are the hedonistic consumers par excellence, and women, whose psychological maturity Freud cast in
radical doubt, are seen as highly problematic consumers, to say the
least. Critics often see women's consumption as based in narcissism,
condemning a distinctively feminine appetite for makeup and clothing—goods devalued as trivial. For children, hedonism takes the
form of more immediate bodily pleasures, especially oral gratification—appetites for sweet, fatty snack foods, goods that adults often
disapprove of.

Two important reservations have been raised regarding the hedonism explanation for consumer activity: it has usually been used to
explain the consumption of stigmatized and often relatively powerless social groups, and it often relies on an implicit, ultimately
untenable distinction between luxuries and necessities. Daniel Horowitz has usefully placed the theme of hedonism in the discourse
on consumer culture in a historical perspective. Comparing the
nineteenth- and twentieth-century critiques of consumption in the
United States, he argued that

> traditional and modern moralism both had a puritanical preference
> for self-control: the earlier group when it came to production
> and profligate consumption; the later one when it came to mass
> commercial consumption. What nineteenth-century observers had
> feared in the working class, their successors tended to see in the
> middle class—the pursuit of transitory happiness, the absence of
> self-control in consumption, the risk of corruption and the failure

to aspire to higher things. For both sets of observers, the danger was that people selected escape, not renewal; false pleasures not true ones.[47]

If the predilection for mass-produced consumer goods has often been taken as a sign of weakness, it is not surprising that critics often singled out women, the working class, and, increasingly, children as consumers most victimized by their own insatiable desires. Hedonism is something that motivates *other people's* consumption, not one's own. Intellectuals, who usually perceive their own consumption as blameless because it appears more austere (involving the life of the mind rather than the life of the body, and the purchase of things such as books, concert and plane tickets, and computers), often characterize the working and nonintellectual middle classes as plagued by uncontrollable materialism, the pleasure principle run amok.[48]

In the United States today, husbands often scorn their wives' interest in fashion; the middle class disapproves of the working class's taste for ostentatious automobiles; parents disdain the junk food and TV-advertised toys that children ask them to spend their money on. In the case of children, television advertising broke down restrictions on consumption resulting from their lack of access to printed messages. No longer do children consume only what their parents deem necessary or appropriate; rather, they have consumer desires of their own for goods that are widely held to be "of doubtful legitimacy," to use a phrase from Thorstein Veblen. As Veblen argued, the consumption of socially inferior groups has been characterized as trivial and irrational throughout history.

The hedonism explanation implicitly excludes from the phenomenon of consumerism some classes of goods: those that satisfy natural human needs, usually defined narrowly as biological and physiological necessities. Presumably, nonluxury items are used for basic nutrition, the maintenance of good health, warmth, and shelter. The distinction between goods that are natural and necessary and goods that are somehow unnatural and extravagant, however, is not so easy to maintain as it may first appear, especially in a society in which so few material goods are produced at home. The line between appropriate, healthy consumption and neurotic, compulsive consumerism is a fine one. Because material goods are involved in a system of social meanings, that is, in a culture, it is not possible to keep aesthetics, style, and socially constructed meanings out of a consideration of their use. We can translate this argument into Marx's concept of the commodity form as comprising exchange value, based on the price that a seller can get for a commodity (where the human labor that produced it is usually veiled), and use value, based on what the buyer can do with the commodity; use values are cultural, inseparably joining aesthetic and utilitarian functions.[49]

All goods are implicated in a system of communications; in the language of semiotics, commodities always function as signs. It is therefore impossible to separate form and content in a consideration of consumer goods, just as it is difficult to distinguish between "good," plain, functional consumerism on the one hand and "bad," fancy, hedonistic consumerism on the other. Coats make fashion statements (intentional or inadvertent) and keep us warm simultaneously; all goods—advertised or not—are implicated in nonutilitarian, nonfunctional cultural meanings, which may or may not have been envisioned by the producers of those goods.[50]

It is equally true that opting out of the commodity system can carry a great deal of value in terms of status relations: the activity of baking one's own bread, for example, was embraced by many members of the upper middle class as well as intellectuals and members of the counterculture in the last decade or two. The payoff for this activity comes in part from serving home-baked bread to one's guests: the cachet of opting out of the consumer economy. In a 1904 essay on fashion, German sociologist Georg Simmel remarked that it is impossible to withdraw from the system of social meanings that fashion and consumer culture impose: opting out is itself making a statement to others about one's group belonging.[51] The necessity/luxury distinction attempts to separate form from function in the analysis of the artifacts of material culture and their necessity for survival. Yet the humble loaf of home-baked bread bears the mark of a complex set of culinary and aesthetic tastes, just as much as the Big Mac. As Thorstein Veblen wrote: "[I]t would be hazardous to assert that a useful purpose is ever absent from the utility of any article or of any service, however obviously its prime purpose and chief element is conspicuous waste; and it would be only less hazardous to assert of any primarily useful product that the element of waste is not concerned in its value, immediately or remotely."[52]

The insistence on the inseparability of form and content in material culture is a useful antidote to a tendency in recent left-wing critique of mass culture to see a pathological emphasis on style and appearance, a "triumph of the superficial," in Stuart Ewen's words. Frankfurt School scholars and their U.S. successors, such as Mark Crispin Miller, Todd Gitlin, and Stuart Ewen, have argued that social identity based on consumption is regressive. The travesty of modern mass culture—and postmodernism—from a Marxist point of view is that people are defined as markets, defined by their relations as consumers rather than by their relationship to the means of production. For Stuart Ewen, the public display of "style" is based on superficial alliances, feeding "a notion of class defined primarily in *consumptive* rather than productive terms, highlighting individual, above common, identity." [53] Daniel Miller has criticized this tendency within Marxist accounts of consumer culture as underpinned by a form of "vulgar functionalism" in which "goods possess some basic 'use value' relating to a constant and evident need, and . . . stylistic diversity is mere waste promoted by the branding policy of capitalism." Instead, Miller argues that "consumer concern for style or fashion is neither the result of capitalism nor the operation of middle-class values, but simply an assertion of the nature of goods as culture. . . . [W]hen goods are treated as an element of culture itself, we find a much wider spectrum of contradictions and strategies within which objects are implicated." [54]

The contemporary British anthropologist Mary Douglas has argued that so-called luxuries are in fact social necessities; any distinction between necessary and unnecessary goods fails to account for the crucial importance of consumption for ceremonial purposes, for social cohesion, and for the maintenance of networks of support. The anthropological approach to consumption advocated by Douglas minimizes the differences between preindustrial societies and contemporary late capitalist societies by stressing the role of consumption rituals in each. Douglas's work advocates a nonmoralistic view of consumption, understood as more than a subsistence activity. In *The World of Goods*, Douglas and Baron Isherwood conceive of consumption as a means of entry into a social world, a forum for making connections with others whose services, support, and information are necessary to survival in the social system.

In contesting the definitions of poverty typically used in economic theory, Douglas argues that "unless we know why people need luxuries and how they use them we are nowhere near taking the problems of inequality seriously." [55] For example, educating children in reading and arithmetic is not enough to assure success in the social system; the child also needs to have acquired certain skills, many of which are attained through attendance at consumption events (birthday parties, holiday celebrations, visits at friends' houses, and so on).

> The child who leaves school will need a means of acquiring a wide range of useful names, access to specialized information services, a habit of seeking professional advice and means to pay for it, above all, a continual means of up-dating information as the technological base changes and everything with it. . . . [T]he theory of needs should start by assuming that any individual needs goods in order to commit other people to his projects. He needs goods to involve others as fellow-consumers in his consumption rituals. Goods are for mobilizing other people.[56]

To condemn people to a level of mere subsistence consumption is to exclude them from the basis for success and security within a social network. The organization and management of consumption events (from children's birthday parties to Thanksgiving dinners to cocktail parties) is one underrated area of women's domestic labor. Consumption events such as weddings involve a double movement of inclusion and exclusion: they promote bonding among certain groups of people, implicitly excluding others; they serve to "mark" goods (such as foods and gifts) as especially valuable and superior to other classes of goods.

Douglas's work has been criticized on the grounds that it completely ignores the forces of production, the distinctive features of contemporary capitalism, and the consequences of the astronomical scale of multinational production and distribution. Communications scholar Sut Jhally has stressed—following Marx's discussion in *Capital*—the importance of recognizing the distinctive nature of "commodity fetishism" under capitalism, where "the appearance of things in the marketplace masks the story of who fashioned them, and under what conditions. . . . What commodities fail to communicate to consumers is information about the process of production. Unlike goods in earlier societies, they do not bear the signature of their makers, whose motives and actions we might access because we knew who they were."[57]

For Marxist critics, goods are fundamentally misunderstood, because consumers have no information about the human labor that produced them. People misperceive commodities as having an inherent value, failing to comprehend that the value of commodities is produced by labor. Advertising contributes to this process by pushing the relations of production out of the picture and replacing them with symbolic use values related solely to consumption. As Sut Jhally describes it, after Marx, "only once the real meaning has been systematically *emptied* out of commodities does advertising then *refill* this void with its own symbols." [58] The anthropological study of consumption can legitimately be criticized on the grounds that it poorly integrates the study of production and consumption. But Douglas and others insist that the meanings that advertisers associate with commodities in media representations and that consumers grant to commodities through appropriation *are* real, as authentic as the meanings that stem from the sphere of production and deserving of study in their own right.

Sociologist Colin Campbell has argued for the continued usefulness of the concept of hedonism while providing a more nuanced and historically based definition of it. Explicitly positioning himself in opposition to those who "regard wanting as an irrational, involuntary and 'unworthy' form of behavior," Campbell sees modern hedonism as rooted in Romanticism, with its assumption that "people could be morally improved through the provision of cultural products that yielded pleasure" and its stress on the power of "dreaming about a more perfect world." Campbell defines modern hedonism as a "preoccupation with 'pleasure,' envisaged as a potential quality of all experience." Modern hedonism "explains how the individual's interest is primarily focused on the meanings and images which can be imputed to a product, something which requires novelty to be present." Clearly, modern advertising plays a significant role in hedonism by continually associating images with products. Campbell argues for a model of modern hedonism that "makes it possible to understand how a consumer creates (and abandons) 'wants,' and why it is that this has become a never-ending process, but also directs attention to the character of consumption as a voluntaristic, self-directed and creative process in which cultural ideals are necessarily implicated." [59]

The concept of emulation links consumption to the behavior, tastes, and styles of one's social betters and the desire for upward social mobility. The emphasis has been on the extent to which consumption involves not just keeping up with the Joneses but getting ahead of the Joneses. The emulation analysis stems from the work of Thorstein Veblen and Georg Simmel and has taken a new direction in the work of contemporary French sociologist Pierre Bourdieu. As in the hedonism explanation, social emulation is seen as creating an unending cycle of consumer desire because consumers are spurred on by the consumption spectacles of the upper classes.[60] As Thorstein Veblen, who coined the term "conspicuous consumption," wrote, "the standard of expenditure which commonly guides our efforts is not the average, ordinary expenditure already achieved; it is an ideal of consumption that lies just beyond our reach, or to reach which requires some strain. The motive is emulation—the stimulus of an invidious comparison which prompts us to outdo those with whom we are in the habit of classing ourselves."[61] The emulation hypothesis, like the hedonism explanation, rests on a somewhat pejorative view of the consumer's motivations, but it emphasizes the transient and cyclical nature of fashion and human desire rather than the personality of the consumer.

The upper classes create value in particular fashions that are then imitated by the lower classes. Anthropologist Grant McCracken has dubbed this the "trickle down theory of fashion." McCracken, following on the work of Georg Simmel, notes that emulation creates a kind of "chase and flight" pattern, in which the upper classes, once imitated, must change fashions to re-create the distinction of rarity. As Simmel himself described it, "The very character of fashion demands that it should be exercised at one time only by a portion of the given group, the great majority being merely on the road to adopting it. . . . As fashion spreads, it gradually goes to its doom."[62] Emulation is only possible in a social universe large enough—as in the city—that most people are strangers, so that it becomes possible to mistakenly place an individual as a member of a higher social class. Emulation occurs only when people believe social mobility is a plausible possibility.[63] Equal opportunity through education is one of the primary vehicles for upward mobility, so it is not surprising that claims for the educational value of consumer goods such as toys dominate advertising to parents. Emulation can be seen as a malicious behavior, where the motivation is snobbish display and putting down others; or it can be seen as a strategy most members of society engage in to achieve the utopian dream of sharing in a society's wealth and privileges.

In *Distinction*, Pierre Bourdieu focused attention on the role of education and the influence of "cultural capital" on taste, the selection and valorization of certain categories of consumer goods: "Taste classifies, and it classifies the classifier. Social subjects, classified by their classifications, distinguish themselves by the distinctions they make, between the beautiful and the ugly, the distinguished and

8. Playmobil toys, a "Pre-S.A.T. Training Kit," to promote toddlers' future collegiate success.

the vulgar, in which their position in the objective classifications is expressed or betrayed." [64] These distinctions are used to legitimate the privileges of those with more education and more money, who envision themselves as superior to those whose tastes differ from their own. Bourdieu emphasizes that these distinctions are just as present in the selection of novels to read and pictures to hang on the walls of one's home as they are in choices of food or hairstyle.

Bourdieu's account focuses on the relationships among types of goods and argues that the meaning of any given commodity derives from its similarities to and differences from other commodities in the society.[65] Increasingly society requires consumers to understand and manipulate complex meanings and connotations attached to consumer goods, so that they may choose to make the right impressions—and so that they may avoid mistakes. Recent anthropological work in consumer culture has emphasized the complex negotiations involved in the linking of commodities to social status. Emulation involves a double movement: imitation of those richer and differentiation from those poorer or less "refined."

Bourdieu's concept of cultural capital needs to be modified to suit the United States. Sociologists Michele Lamont and Annette Lareau have predicted that American legitimate culture is "less related to knowledge of the Western humanist culture, is more technically oriented (with an emphasis on scientific or computer information), and more materialistic."[66] While Bourdieu found that the possessors of cultural capital exhibited attitudes and personal styles such as "aloofness, originality, non-profit orientation, brilliance," Lamont and Lareau note that "some evidence suggests that aggressiveness, competence, entrepreneurship, self-reliance, self-directiveness"— qualities cultivated by the forms of child-rearing encouraged by child experts—are valued in the United States. They suggest that *purchasable*—rather than *culturally acquired*—signals of legitimate culture may be more acceptable and may be granted more weight in the United States than in France; this would seem to allow for greater ease in upward social mobility, but at the same time "fewer valued signals are likely to be inexpensive."[67] Financial capital may be more important, although cultural capital may be easier to acquire. Thus there is a greater possibility in the United States for parents to buy a social status for their children higher than their own, or to believe that this is possible, although the large number of children—especially African American children—living in poverty narrows the likelihood of that happening.

As an explanation for consumer behavior, social emulation involves a reduction to a single axis of differentiation that may be inadequate to an understanding of contemporary consumer culture. In the case of children's goods we can see that several different axes are at work in social emulation: adults may emulate bourgeois norms, but children, oblivious to the benefits of adhering to their parents' taste, may be set upon imitating older children—as in the fascination of young children with teenagers—or members of their

9. Designer baby clothing for fashion-conscious parents: such as Baby Guess.

peer group who are not necessarily "higher" on the social scale by adult standards. For example, young middle-class children often prioritize gender over class identifications, preferring the extreme forms of He-Man and Barbie, which their parents consider distasteful, and thereby violating the middle class's stylistic norms of gender coding. Interpreting consumer goods in terms of their status value is a skill that must be learned; the hierarchy one uses is hardly a universal scheme but varies widely based on one's social group of reference and must be studied empirically. Children value forms of "cultural capital" that are frequently scorned by adults, who possess forms of cultural capital legitimated by grown-up society.

Young children have good reasons for liking television and wanting toys, and mothers have good reasons for providing them. Children's interest in consumer culture involves much more than greed, hedonism, or passivity: it involves the desire for community and for a utopian freedom from adult authority, seriousness, and goal directedness. As a mass culture, toys and television give children a medium of communication—this is why I have described it as a lingua franca. Consumer culture does, however, limit children's utopian impulses. When engaged with consumer culture, children promote some identifications—those of a same-sex peer group—while demoting others. Peer groups offer a limited basis for social alliances when considered apart from other aspects of social identity—race, ethnicity, gender, class, region. But consumer culture changes through use, and it is inflected by children with surprising originality in everyday life. The basis of my approach is that toys and television must be placed in the larger culture of childhood, the relations between parents and children, the links between consumption and social identity, and the intersections of media reception and material consumption.

2

BUYING HAPPINESS, BUYING SUCCESS

TOY ADVERTISING TO PARENTS

> Dear Santa—Please make me happy with an Uncle Sam's Savings Bank and Cash Store Register. (1928)

> Christmas is for Kids. . . . and kids have their own ideas about Christmas. What small tots really want is lots of *color* . . . lots of *action* and lots of *toys*! That's why Christmas is *more fun* with toys made of Styron (Dow Polystyrene). (1948)

> They're not just toys. They're playthinks. (1971)

> Are they teachers? or are they toys? (1978)

Since it was founded in 1926,[1] *Parents* magazine has offered advice to mother about children from "crib to college." *Parents* and its advertising have made concrete an idealized vision of childhood and of the relations between parents and children, thus inflecting the discourse of child-rearing experts in significant ways. For decades, *Parents* has been the leading specialty magazine about children and the largest seller of advertising pages and subscriptions. Today the field is crowded with highly similar competitors, such as *Working Mother, Child*, and *Parenting* magazines, but *Parents* represents the mainstream of American views on child rearing. In its advertising and in its editorial copy, *Parents* provides a catalog of the way toys have become a central preoccupation of the culture of early childhood in the United States, and of the conflicting emotions and dreams toys have come to symbolize for many parents.

When *Parents* magazine was founded in the 1920s, children's sentimental value had been skyrocketing for several decades: in historian Viviana Zelizer's words, children were in the process of becoming "priceless." Zelizer identifies the period from 1870 to 1930 as the time when "a profound transformation in the economic and sentimental value of children" took place: "[A] child is expected to provide love, smiles, and emotional satisfaction, but no money or labor."[2] One sign of the sentimentalization of childhood was the proliferation of idealized images of children on household decorations in the late nineteenth century[3]—images that were commonly used in advertising in the twentieth century. While the expenses involved in caring for children increased dramatically (today estimated to be well over $100,000 by the age of eighteen), the new cult of childhood set children apart from the economic. Childhood was "sacralized," invested with religious and sentimental meaning.

> While in the nineteenth century, the market value of children was culturally acceptable, later the new normative ideal of the child as an exclusively emotional and affective asset precluded instrumental or fiscal considerations. In an increasingly commercialized world, children were reserved a separate non-commercial place, *extra-commercium*. . . . Properly loved children, regardless of social class, belonged in a domesticated, nonproductive world of lessons, games and token money.[4]

The sentimentalization of children throughout the culture set the stage for advertising pitches that stressed the incomparable pleasure of making children happy by presenting them with toys. As children were divorced from the commercial world as producers, parents were increasingly approached with a widening range of consumer goods for children's leisure. But toy advertisers were never wholly content with hedonistic pitches, and social emulation has also played a role in the development of the toy market. Since the 1920s, advertising has vacillated between promises to make children happy and promises to make children social and intellectual achievers.

Parents magazine assumes its reader to be a mother with money to spend, a dedication to improvement, and a large capacity for guilt about the fulfillment of her maternal role (despite the title, there is little indication that a male parent is an anticipated reader). *Parents* has consistently addressed itself to the affluent reader: like many women's magazines, it appears to address the socially aspiring reader by describing lifestyles in its editorial material that are far wealthier than her own. In the 1920s, *Parents* offered advertising for boarding schools, for trips to Florida during the winter, for governesses; in the 1990s it features cruises to Disneyworld, advice on buying a home or investing money. One of the attractions of the middle-class women's magazine is its promise to teach women skills that they may not have learned as children. *Parents* promises a better life for one's children through wise consumption decisions. This is one of the optimistic, egalitarian sentiments of the American mass media, and advice literature in particular. Women's magazines promise to make up for any deficiencies one might have in education, in social etiquette, or in material wealth by offering self-improvement and self-education schemes.

The women's magazine offers a remedy for social distinctions. It promises to teach everything one needs to know and thus eradicate what Pierre Bourdieu has described as one of the most indelible marks of social class in more aristocratic, European societies: ". . . [N]othing perhaps depends more on early learning, especially the learning which takes place without any express intention to teach, than the dispositions and knowledge that are invested in clothing, furnishing and cooking, or more precisely in the ways clothes, furniture and food are bought."[5] This is what *Parents* is largely about: to learn how to buy the best for one's children and thus prepare them for a life of material success and happiness.

Contradictory positions toward consumerism abound in the editorial and the advertising copy in *Parents* magazine today. Curious about the development of these contradictions, I began looking at old issues to try to inventory the various ways in which advertisers have tried to inspire parents to buy and determine whether toy advertising to parents has changed in the past sixty years. I have found consistent conflicts related to parental spending on children, and a few proposed resolutions to these conflicts that reappear from decade to decade. Because toy advertisers compete fiercely with one another, contradictory arguments often appear in different advertisements in the same issue.

Toy advertisers have focused on a handful of motivations for parental toy buying in developing their pitches. Readers—implicitly mothers—are addressed as parents who share a set of desires for their children. These include that children have fun, that children get ahead in life, that children achieve in school, that children grow up to resemble their parents, that children be active rather than passive, that children amuse themselves without adult attention. These desires are translated into various product claims, such as toys create happiness; toys teach skills; toys bring parents and children close together; toys keep children busy; toys inspire activity. These claims have been presented with varying frequency throughout the publication of *Parents*. Some motivations, such as the desire for high achievers, are more dominant and more acceptable as direct statements than others, such as the desire for children to entertain themselves. Often two claims are interwoven; for example, the notions that toys are fun and that toys teach have been combined in the same pitch hundreds of times. Toy advertising has used hedonistic pitches—just make your child happy—as well as pitches based on social aspirations—make your child a superior competitor in school and in the workplace. Increasingly, parental advice literature and toy advertising have sought to erase any differences between the two, repeating the somewhat dubious promise that toys can make a child smarter and more competitive without losing any of their capacity to generate fun and happiness. The contradiction between a puritanical history and the new consumerism is summed up in the often-repeated phrase that play is a child's work.

Toy advertising in the United States has addressed parents as people who want their children to get ahead in this world, and it has suggested that certain kinds of toys will assure their success while usually avoiding explicit appeals to snobbery. At the same time, advertisers carefully guard against objections to toy buying as spoiling, negatively associated with hedonism. In many ways, toy advertising has conscientiously followed the ideal of "virtuous consumerism" that social historian Elaine Tyler May associates with the postwar period. Virtuous consumerism stressed "pragmatism and morality, rather than opulence and luxury."[6] Advertisers proposed "family enrichment" as an essential ingredient of a good and healthy consumerism. May points out that "the commodities people bought were intended to reinforce home life and uphold traditional gender roles."[7]

Toy advertisements place children in social tableaux, Roland Marchand's term for advertisements "in which persons are depicted in such a way as to suggest their relationship to each other or to a larger social structure."[8] As Marchand describes it, "the social tableau advertisement usually depicts a contemporary 'slice-of-life' setting." Such ads "often enhance social scenes through their brilliance of imagery and intensity of focus."[9] The social tableau advertisement represents race, gender, and class differences in vivid forms and ascribes to different children a range of "effects" of toy play: including having fun, learning skills, and rehearsing adult roles. *Parents* magazine's vision of happy children was restricted for decades to affluent children—most often boys, and normally whites. Girls were depicted very differently than boys. Children of color did not appear in toy advertisements in *Parents* until the 1960s. Most advertising images of children available today depict white children at play.

In the twenties, thirties, and forties, toy advertisements made up less than 20 percent of the advertising in *Parents* magazine: books, medicines, cereals, and soups predominated. Most advertisements related to parents' concern for children's health, echoes of a time of higher child and infant mortality rates and a period when advice literature concentrated primarily on questions of hygiene and health.[10] Although the concern with health continues to play an important—not to say obsessional—role in *Parents* magazine today, concern with toys and with children's media has steadily increased. The amount of toy advertising in *Parents* first jumped dramatically in the late 1940s and 1950s as the baby boom began, the toy industry expanded, and new kinds of plastics were readily and cheaply available to toy manufacturers.

The Merriest Christmas Ever!

The oldest convention in toy advertising has been to stress the child's joy upon receiving the gift and the favor that will immediately befall the adult giver: "Make them smile." "Thrills your children won't forget." "Fun—loads of it!" "For his most EXCITING Christmas." ". . . the *most wanted* gift of all." "Christmas is for kids—make it merry with toys made of Styron." "If you aim to delight . . ." Thus, the child's pleasure—and nothing more—was often the basis of the pitch.

Advertisers in the postwar period frequently pictured children unwrapping presents with delight written large on their faces. One technique was to vocalize the child's response. A 1948 ad for Acme cowboy boots read: "OOOH! Know any youngsters who wouldn't be big eyed and breathless at the sight of Acme Cowboy Boots on Christmas morning?" "OOOH! A real Singer sewing machine that's

**For the "Best Christmas Ever"
Give Shiny New COLSONS**

*Want to make this a really <u>special</u>
Christmas for your children? Buy them
COLSONS—the gift that <u>stays</u> exciting all
year round, year after year. For three
generations COLSON vehicles have
been providing Christmas joy in
American homes. If you recall
the thrill of <u>your</u> first bicycle
or velocipede, you'll agree
there's no surer guarantee
for that "starry-eyed look" on
Christmas morning.*

10. *The Christmas tree scene, with parents looking on. "Make it a Colson Christmas!"*

just my size," reads the title of a 1950 ad showing a drawing of a girl's excited face, her mouth forming an "O." [11]

A favorite scene of the late 1940s and early 1950s was the white family at the Christmas tree. Typically, the image includes a boy and a girl in pajamas rushing forward toward presents under the tree in the foreground while the smiling parents, dressed in robes, touch each other in the background. Sometimes, the brand name itself describes the type of Christmas the child wants: "Make it a Colson Christmas for the best Christmas ever!"; older brother and younger sister are pictured with hands thrown back, their mouths open in an "ah," the glow from the tree shining on their faces as they behold their bicycles." [12] The social tableau of two parents and two children in a modern ranch-style living room was repeated often in all kinds of ads. The Christmas tree scene mimicked the home movies and snapshots that families were encouraged to take of the same event in their home. It is one example of what Elaine Tyler May has called the ideology of "domestic containment": the home as a site of fun and family togetherness, where each member of the family can pursue a range of leisure activities—distributed by age and gender—and where modern conveniences appear to have done away with the problem of domestic labor. [13]

The Christmas tree scene is the only image of fathers as spectators to children's play that can be found in *Parents* magazine. Mothers, on the other hand, are often pictured in an idle, contemplative moment, seated, gazing at a child (often her daughter) at play. In the Christmas tree scene, the father's posture and his expression suggest his satisfaction as the benevolent provider of material riches. The father here plays a different role from that of the mother watching or listening in, where the emphasis is on the sentimental regard of children's play. The mother as passive observer of her daughter's play is still used today, as in a recent ad for Madame Alexander dolls in which the mother watches her daughter's tea party.

Toy advertisements conscientiously avoid any scene in which the child might appear demanding. In a few toy ads from the late 1920s and 1930s, a child is given a "speaking part," as product spokesperson: "I'll say you ought to have a new Flexible Flyer," reads the caption of a boy mounted on his sled, "but I haven't time to tell you ALL about it now! I want to take my own Flexible Flyer out on the hill—and let the other fellows see some speed" (1935). More typically, a neutral, third-person product spokesperson addresses parents about the merits of toys or their children's desire to have them,

11. Simple hedonism: "Christmas is More Fun *at our house with toys made of Styron."*

rather than having children report directly to parents. Letters to Santa were especially popular in the 1920s and made the communication from children to parents indirect, if coercive nonetheless. "Dear Santa," reads a boy with a crowd of others reading letters behind him in the background, "Please make me happy with an Uncle Sam's Savings Bank and Cash Store Register." A 1928 ad for Effanbee dolls pictures the curly-haired doll with the caption "Please, Santa, bring me this new Bubbles."

12. The mother quietly observing her child's play.

When toys began to be advertised on television, and children could ask for toys before even entering a toy store, children were pictured dreaming about toys they had seen in commercials, rather than announcing their desires aloud. "He's dreaming of a Kenner Christmas: with the exciting toys he saw on TV," explains a 1966 ad with a close-up of a boy smiling in his sleep. "While visions of Tonka Toys danced in his head," read the caption of a picture of a boy asleep, a Tonka catalog lying open beside his pillow. "And

Dear Santa -
Please make me happy with an Uncle Sam's Savings Bank and Cash Store Register

Children *everywhere* are
writing letters like this
to Santa Claus.

EVERY boy and girl likes to play store—it's so much fun making believe you are grown up and buying things and saving money in the bank.

When your Uncle Sam's Bank is filled with money it opens up as if by magic and all your riches pour right into your lap to be used by you for anything you want. Isn't that nice? Girls and boys all over the U. S. think so— that's why there are over a million Uncle Sam's Cash Store Registers and Savings Banks now in use.

Just imagine all the wonderful things you will be able to do with the money you can save when you have *your own* Uncle Sam's Bank!

Ask Mother and Dad—they probably played with Uncle Sam's Cash Store Registers and saved in Uncle Sam's Banks when *they* were children.

GROWN-UPS! Start your youngsters in the habit of thrift and saving and you'll be surprised how quickly it will take hold. Teaching them through play, when they are young, is so much easier! Let the children see you use an Uncle Sam's Savings Bank yourself—

NICKELS·DIMES·QUARTERS
AMOUNT DEPOSITED
DOLLARS-CENTS
UNCLE SAM'S 3 COIN REGISTER BANK
6¼"x 5½"x4"
Weighs 2½ lbs.

**Uncle Sam's
3-Coin Register Bank**

13. Letters to Santa offered an indirect, if nevertheless coercive, means of communicating desires.

visions of Transogram danced in their heads," reads the copy over a drawing of two boys smiling in their sleep, presumably dreaming of the Yogi Bear and Huckleberry Hound games that they "saw on TV." "What do you suppose he's thinking?" asks another Tonka ad over a "daydreaming" boy with his head resting on the car itself as his pillow.

In all these ads, the suggested motivation for adults to buy toys was a simple desire to please. Today this strategy has been increasingly replaced by claims for the educational value of toys. The delight in ownership is a form of persuasion that has migrated almost entirely to television advertising directed at children, where it is deemed unfair by critics of children's commercial television. The "Oohs" and "Ahs" of print ads have changed to the continual exclamations of "Wow!" and "Totally rad!" on the audio tracks of children's commercials. Children are expected to do their own bidding for promotional toys they have seen on television: when toys are advertised to parents today, the parents are usually exhorted to loftier motivations than mere delight on Christmas morning. Because television advertising, frequent visits to stores, and contact

What

do you suppose

he's thinking?

What do children think of at times like this? You have to be a child to really know.

It's usually when a child is playing with a favorite toy that he gets into this world of his own, "a million miles away. Quite often that toy is a Tonka Toy, the famous scale-model that looks and works like a real truck.

Children have cherished Tonka Toys for years because Tonka Toys are built for years of play. They're ruggedly made of automobile weight steel and protected by 2 coats of non-toxic real truck paint. All of the edges are rolled for safety and the tires are so strong they'll probably outlast the toy—and that's really saying something

Make Tonka Toys part of your child's world. There are 66 different ones that come in three different sizes (Regular, Mini and Mighty) because boys come in different sizes too.

14. Daydreaming about the toys he wants, rather than nagging.

with peers through preschool have provided children with enough product information to pressure parents at an early age, the "aim to delight" pitch has lost its innocence and is relatively rare in toy advertising to parents today. Of course, parents still buy toys to make children happy, but this impulse is nearly always accom-

15. Squeals of delight were the gift giver's reward.

panied by claims for the improving potential of the toy. Toys are praised for their instrumental value, for what they make of children. Fostering learning, activity, and creativity—rather than providing thrills and fun—has come to dominate advertising directed at parents.

Loftier Goals

Pleasing children with toys first sounded a sour note in advertisements for encyclopedias and pianos, which set parental concern for future achievement in direct competition with the thrilled squeals of children rewarded with toys on Christmas. "Beyond the dollhouse," reads an advertisement for Steinway pianos that appeared in *Parents* in the late 1920s. Encyclopedia advertisers—among the most loyal of *Parents* magazine's sponsors—fed parental anxiety during the Depression. "Are you preparing your child for fame or failure?" "The average child in fifth grade, according to Government statistics, has only one chance in 50 to complete a college education—one chance in 50, really, to avoid failure. Fame comes usually only to those who have a working knowledge of many subjects."[14] "What do you want your children to be?" reads the heading of a 1930 ad for *Compton's* encyclopedia, as the illustration portrays the career aspirations parents hold for their children. Surrounding the headline are pictures of adults: a man sitting at a desk with the sign "Vice President" clearly in view; a woman in evening dress playing the piano for a listening man dressed in a tuxedo. The copy paints a grim picture of competition:

> America has twenty million children between the ages of five and fifteen. Twenty years from now your children are going to find themselves in the severest competition against those twenty million, not only for money, for power, for position, for happiness, but for everything that makes life worth living. . . . [T]here is only one way to compete with the accumulated money and power. And that is with accumulated knowledge.[15]

These campaigns resemble one of the standard advertising narratives of the Depression identified by Roland Marchand: the parable of the Unraised Hand.[16] The parable scolded parents for their child's poor performance in school—something that could be attributed to everything from a poor breakfast to the absence of a typewriter in the home.

By the 1950s, encyclopedia sellers openly reproached parents for spending freely on toys while neglecting to spend on books. Encyclopedia advertisers countered toy ads with a more ominous view of the scene at the Christmas tree and attempted to persuade parents that Christmas giving entailed more serious obligations. In one such ad, a happy girl and boy are seated on the floor, surrounded by toys, and look smilingly toward the camera, as in a Christmas day family snapshot; the text poses the question "Have you given them what they REALLY need?" The copy goes on to explain to parents: "[T]he big-league fielder's glove, the baby doll that drinks from a bottle, the shiny new bike . . . they're your way of telling your children 'We love you.' But happy youngsters need more than love alone if they are to become happy and successful adults. They need the thoughtful, intelligent atmosphere only you can provide . . . with the remarkable Book of Knowledge." [17] The *Book of Knowledge* anti-toy campaign continued throughout the 1950s and 1960s. In 1956 an arty close-up of a doll upside down accompanied the scolding caption "will your gift last a day or a lifetime?" The question is repeated in 1957, with a picture of a boy unwrapping a new football. In 1961 the decision to buy an encyclopedia becomes a parental declaration of independence: "Let Santa give them what they want, you give them what they need"; now the toys are abandoned under the tree, and the boy of six or so sits in his pajamas reading the encyclopedia, his toy train ignored in favor of the book.

The anti-toy motifs in many encyclopedia ads indicate the contradictory and ambiguous nature of advertisements published in the same magazine. As competitors for the same share of disposable income, encyclopedia publishers tried to persuade parents *not* to buy so many toys, while the toy manufacturers and many of the authors in the magazine routinely endorsed toy consumption. *Parents* has consistently expressed a mainstream, business-friendly view of spending on children—but this view has not played a single function or emanated from a single cause. It is actually full of mixed messages: give children toys because they are important for development; books are more important than toys; be sure to give children what they want; be sure to demonstrate to them wise consumer spending. When the experts disagree, it puts a bigger burden on the mother. No matter what she does, it may be wrong!

Toys That Teach

A convivial relationship often exists between advertising copy and advice in the form of columns and feature articles in women's magazines. Although, as the title indicates, *Parents* addresses mothers and fathers, its editorial content and advertising copy have consistently assumed that women will be the primary caretakers of children and the readers of the magazine. As in most women's magazines, the advertisements in *Parents'* are often as important a source of information as the articles, columns, or features, and women often buy magazines to look at the ads. *Parents* magazine propagated "new" ideas about child psychology, child-rearing techniques, and expert opinions, most of which encouraged the consumption of equipment, books, foods, and amusements of all kinds designed specifically for children. *Parents* helped to spread the word on the developmental model of child psychology and to popularize the idea that childhood is divided into discrete, observable stages. This notion alone proved to be an especially useful one to advertisers. *Parents* encouraged mothers to see weekly and monthly changes in their children's development. If toys are so closely tied to a child's abilities, no parent would want to hold her son or daughter back by waiting for Christmas or a birthday before replacing old toys with new ones better suited to a child's developing abilities. The division of the child into a package of separable abilities (cognitive, large motor, fine motor, communication)—each of which could be improved through practice and play with specially designed objects—has provided the basis for endless product differentiation. All consumer goods for children (including books and videos) can be specially merchandised according to age. When it has come to advice on toy buying, developmental psychology's insistence on the importance of a stimulating environment (well stocked with toys) has dovetailed nicely with *Parents* magazine's need to coddle the advertisers on whom their revenues have depended.

In the 1920s and 1930s, feature writers in *Parents* magazine took up the cause of toy purchasing and ferreted out possible objections or sources of resistance to the new consumer ethic, such as overaccumulation or spoiling. A handful of core notions about children's play and the role of toys in development have been repeated in *Parents* magazine with only slight variations for sixty years; attitudes about spending and wise consumption have been more variable. Some of the thoughts on children's play were the truisms of developmental psychology: that children will express different interests in their play at different ages; that play fosters development; that this development can be broken down into compartmentalized skills—cognition, coordination, the senses. Toys are conceived of in this scheme as essential components of the child's environment, and parenthood brings with it the obligation to supply toys. *Parents* magazine continually advised about the best kinds of toys, and this advice tended more and more often to be supplied not just by "writers" and mothers but by Ph.D.'s and M.D.'s. Toys should be safe, unbreakable, and educational, should inspire activity in the child rather than passivity, should develop both the mind and the body—and should be fun, too.

Before 1950, columnists typically encouraged some restraint. A 1928 article warned parents, "Buy few but good toys. . . . Don't buy too much: an overabundance fosters carelessness, greed and indifference." [18] In the fifties, parental resistance (from a generation who grew up during the Depression) was tackled head on: "Toys are a necessity of life to youngsters. Few of them can ever receive too many." [19] If Christmas day was overstimulating for children because of too many presents, *Parents* helpfully suggested that presents could be parceled out over a few days (a piece of advice *Parents* regularly offers today): "A youngster can, of course, get confused and overwhelmed on Christmas day because he is not jurist enough to face more than a few choices happily all at once (It's better to do some of the giving at other times.) But in general, a toy thoughtfully and willingly given with the child's desires in mind is reassurance—a parcel of love. And children need much reassurance in a world of giants." [20] The concept of being spoiled was itself redefined as a lack of emotional response from parents rather than a surplus of material goods: "A spoiled child is often one who has been given everything except love. But toys can be an evidence of love; authorities today are not much sold on the old theory that having plenty of playthings will spoil a child." [21]

Parents continually repeated the platitude that play was educationally valuable. Often this was tied to the metaphor of play as work for children. Thus every minute of childhood, every hour of recreation, was recruited in the service of future earning power. Anthropologist Brian Sutton-Smith has argued, rather pessimistically, that

> the rise of the toy as a child's gift in modern society can also be seen as the rise of an instrument that would accustom children to . . . solitary preoccupation and solitary striving for achievement. . . . [T]he toy is a model of the kind of isolation that is essential to progress in the modern world. . . . With the toy we habituate children to solitary, impersonal activity; and this is a forecast of their years to come as solitary professionals and experts. [22]

Before child labor was formally outlawed in 1938, a new strain of the Puritan work ethic reasserted itself in the notion that play was work and that all play could pay off in the future. Thus the growing consumption ethic accommodated itself to existing ideologies— sometimes in contradictory ways. In advertising and in advice literature, toys held out one of the most attractive promises of all consumer goods, and this is perhaps why the postwar baby boomer growth of the toy industry was so enormous. Toys could guarantee joy yet be instruments of hard work and achievement. What more could anyone ask from a commodity?

"Toys That Teach" was a common title for articles appearing in *Parents* in the 1920s and 1930s. "Why need toys be educational? . . . [T]his makes toys and playing sound like no fun at all, but of course that is not the case," reassured Janet M. Knopf, "toy consultant" in 1930.[23] There was to be no problem in combining pleasure with learning, although the onus was on the parents—read "mother"—to keep things fun by selecting the correct toy for the child's level. *Parents* warned against the dangers of buying toys that frustrate a child: "A child should be protected from the discouragement of failure. . . [W]e do not want him to have an inferiority feeling."[24] The same advice held in 1953, and it is often repeated today: "Keep the child always in mind—his age, sex, stage of development, natural inclinations. A toy too advanced can be defeating; psychologists talk with great respect today of the 'habit of success.' "[25] Paralleling the combination of fun with learning was the successful merging of mind and body. Toys offered the means to solve mind-body dualism: "Thoughtfully chosen playthings help a child to grow and mature—not only in physical ways but mentally and emotionally as well," wrote Helen Thomson, "mother and psychiatric social worker,"[26] "The plaything you choose is a magical thing. . . . [T]he child is changed and as if by magic grows, as each new toy he plays with brings knowledge, skill and pleasure to his mind and hand."[27]

Grandiose claims for the educational benefits of toys have been around since the nineteenth century, and the middle-class children's market for toys has been exploited for at least two centuries. Marketing of children's goods to middle-class parents coincided with the rise of the bourgeoisie and the birth of consumer culture in Europe.[28] Historian J. H. Plumb found that children's jigsaw puzzles, card games, mechanical toys, toy theaters, and miniature printing presses—nearly all of these advertised for their educational value— proliferated in Britain in the eighteenth century.

Plumb attributes the success of eighteenth century toy sales to the popularity of Locke's expanded notion of children's educability—

something accompanied by parental anxiety over children's success. "Society required accomplishment, and accomplishment required expenditure. The children's new world became a market that could be exploited. Few desires will empty a pocket quicker than social aspiration—and the main route was, then as now, through education, which combined social adornment with the opportunity of a more financially rewarding career for children." [29] Historian Mary Lynn Stevens Heininger, in a study of children's goods in the United States between 1820 and 1920, traces a similar growth in toys available for children. "By the early nineteenth century, there were almost as many educational toys available as there are today," and through most of these "ran the theme of self-improvement and self-education." [30] "Target" marketing to an educated class of parents was not a twentieth-century invention, although it was tailored in *Parents* magazine to balance conflicting feelings toward consumption and its hedonistic and emulative aspects in the United States throughout the twentieth century.

When *Parents* magazine first began publishing in the 1920s, educational claims were usually limited to desks, toy typewriters, or chalkboards and to specialized educational toy manufacturers such as Playskool. Educational toys promised to "speed the child's education." Playskool adopted the slogan "Learning while playing" in the 1920s and claimed that its toys provided "valuable benefits in mental stimulation, coordination of mind and muscle, and general sense of training." All its products were designed by "the Playskool Institute, a group of child educators constantly at work developing new toys." With the proper furnishing, the home could rival the school as a place of learning. A desk was advertised in 1928 as "PLAYSKOOL The Home Kindergarten"; "Playskool playing is pre-schooling," another ad explained as a boy sat at his desk working while his sister looked on. The rival Chautaqua Equipment Company advertised desk sets in the late 1920s by claiming: "A child is educating himself through his play in the home just as surely as he is being educated in school." A blackboard manufacturer offered, "Early childhood is the formative period that molds the future of your children. Make these happy play hours profitable in the future development of your child with a LITHO PLATE educational blackboard" (1930).

Parents magazine and its advertisers struggled to persuade its readers of the importance of fostering the child's intellectual capacities from birth onward. Occasional reservations were expressed by the experts, who were not entirely comfortable with the solitary

16. Desks as educational gifts for children, providing Mother the time to read.

nature of play with toys, however intellectually stimulating. In a 1936 article, the author, Beatrice Gelber, outlined four kinds of play: physical, manipulative and sensory, imaginative, and intellectual. Gelber, in talking about the fourth kind of play, warned, "Most intellectual occupations can be indulged in by the individual alone. This may lead to atrophy of social tastes, which should be guarded against"—an argument similar to the rigorously repeated taboo on masturbation in children in J. B. Watson's work (and by many other experts).

This point has been made more recently by Brian Sutton-Smith, arguing that in most cultures for most of history play meant playing with other children, not with things. A further problem was to reconcile the notion of intellectual play with the ideal of fresh air and exercise that many child experts had focused on in the early decades of the twentieth century. One strategy was to reassure parents that toys were now *scientifically* engineered to match the child's exact needs. The toy manufacturers joined the corps of childhood experts and were presented as avid researchers of childhood: "With all the emphasis of late on the educational aspect of toys, perhaps you are uncertain that your choice will perform that function and also contribute fun and play value. The fear is an unnecessary one for the toy field is well guided by scientific standards and toys are designed and sold according to age appeal." [31]

In the 1940s and 1950s, claims about the educational nature of

17. In the 1960s, educational claims became more overtly competitive: "Educators have found that a creative environment can raise a preschooler's I.Q. as much as 20 points."

toys increased, although the emphasis was still placed on play value and children's delight. Transogram, which formerly stressed the joy-on-Christmas-morning pitch, dubbed children's toys "tools to express their creativeness." In the 1960s, educational claims became more competitive, and ad copy became preoccupied with intelligence and IQ scores. Playskool's slogan in 1966 was "Toys that build kids." "How do you want your kids built? Intelligent? Aware?

Sharp? These are the kinds of kids Playskool toys help build. Creative. Imaginative. Inquisitive." Scientists had "proven" and quantified the positive benefits that children incur from a home well stocked with toys: "Educators have found that a creative environment can raise a pre-schooler's I.Q. as much as 20 points." The setting of toy ads moved out of the home and into the classroom, a more competitive atmosphere. The photography suggested a preschool "class picture." Lofty intellectual claims were made, as they are today, about every toy, not just ones involved in literacy. "They're not just toys. They're playthinks. Every playthink is designed to make a pre-schooler think just a little harder while they're having fun," claimed an ad for Romperroom toys such as blocks, a dump truck, and a gingerbread game in 1971. Time spent at home could be usefully put toward the educational process as toy manufacturers built "a little school into every toy."

Lego won prestige for its lucrative line of building blocks introduced in the sixties, by associating their brand of "creative play" with professional success while condemning other kinds of play—the kind boys do with television-advertised action figures.[32] In 1966, Lego offered parents the bonus of a quiet house while stressing the intellectual benefits these products afforded children.

> Peace[:] There is, in this nervous world, one toy that does not shoot or go boom or rat-tat-tat-tat. Its name is Lego. It makes things. . . . That is what Lego brings to the children of 1966. Concentration. Imagination. Patience. Pride. Let somebody else's child get his kicks tracking a little kid through a gun sight. War isn't very adventurous anymore. There's more adventure in a medical lab, or at the U.N. That's why we make Lego. And why you should buy it.[33]

The message here, appearing in 1966, is both anti–Vietnam War and anti–G.I. Joe, which had been introduced in 1964 with great success. Another 1966 Lego ad emphasized height as a metaphor for status, attainment, achievement, with an extremely low angle shot of a boy standing on a step stool building a gigantic elephant construction twice his size (his younger sister plays on the floor below him, looking down). "Lego . . . the thoughtful toy."

Imagination, creativity, and activity became the buzzwords of toy advertising in the 1970s, as play with toys was deemed superior to television watching, imputed by toy advertisers to be passive and

18. Lego toys on the offensive against toy guns advertised on TV: "Let somebody else's child get his kicks tracking a little kid through a gun sight."

unimaginative. Activity was simultaneously physical and mental. An ad for Discovery toys in 1971 announced: "A new series of 20 preschool toys that relate to a child's real world—they combine color, feel, dimension, sound, motions and basic cause and effect. They're fun—and help children learn by doing." "Now your kids can do more than watch Sesame Street. They can play with it." Kusan airplane toys were offered "for every child who already has

19. *Lego emphasizing lofty achievements through play.*

the most precious gift of all—the precious gift of imagination."
Arts and crafts were renamed "activity toys" within the industry,
promising "the happiness that develops through a sense of accomplishment from playing with Ohio art toys . . . from being involved
rather than remaining spectators." Toy manufacturers posited play
as a favorable alternative to media consumption: "Fisher-Price believes there's too much push-button entertainment today."

The newer definition of play as activity was not to be confused
with the busyness promised in the occasional toy ads of the thirties
or forties, the toy as a fun distraction—a mere pastime—that was
convenient for mothers because it allowed them time to cook and
clean or talk on the phone. Supplying a toy just so a mother could
win time to herself did not jibe with the increasing emphasis on a
mother's constant monitoring and stimulation of her child. But the
emphasis on activity and learning, the idea that toys—as well as

mothers—could also teach, solved this problem nicely. Now activity was an end in itself, the sign of achievement of developmental tasks, evidence of work in progress. Toys were good for children and could replace and perhaps surpass the mother's need to teach the child. Ads depicting a four-person nuclear family or pairs of siblings or mothers at play with their children nearly disappear as the educational pitches heated up in the 1960s. As increasing numbers of mothers entered the paid work force and young children entered preschools and day-care programs, the scenes of play switch from the home to the school or bare studio set.[34] Increasingly children were pictured either in a classroom setting with peers or alone, in a medium shot, glancing up to look into the camera—interrupted for a moment from their educational pursuit with the toy, the mother now absent. This change may reflect increased uncertainty since the 1950s on the part of ad designers over ways to depict the ideal or even the normal domestic arrangement.

Girls at Work

Mothers have continued to make appearances in advertisements for girls' toys, however. Advertisements for girls' toys have undergone fewer changes than other toys in the past fifty years because they continue to depict girls' play as a miniature version of their mothers' domestic work. The product categories of girls' toys have remained remarkably stable since the twenties: vacuum cleaners, ovens, strollers or shopping carts, kitchen sets, doll houses. Girls' toys continue to be described in terms of their aesthetic appeal more often than for their educational value. Susan Willis has pointed out that these kinds of toys become possible only when children are no longer relied upon to carry out chores with real household tools, but they also represent an "institutionalized" form of play because they replicate the specific historical forms of women's domestic labor.[35] Toy advertisements portray girls' play as much closer to the real world of work—housework and child care—than they do boys' play.

Advertisements for girls' toys have tended to emphasize the realistic nature of dolls and home furnishings. Dolls are usually advertised on their own merits, often with an emphasis on their helplessness, crying, shivering, trembling, hunger, and need for a diaper change. The dolls themselves are blond and blue-eyed, like the girls in the ads. A *Parents* feature article describing the toys of the 1948 Christmas season boasted:

20. *"Just Like Mother's"*: *girls' play is a miniature version of their mothers' domestic work.*

Baby dolls are so life-like that their soft, plastic skin feels almost real. They can be bathed, fed from a bottle and they wet. One doll coos softly and cries when she is squeezed; another cries when a pacifier is placed in her mouth; and still another actually "burps" after her feeding. Imagine the endless hours of play and tender loving care that little girls will give these new baby dolls! Also awaiting the little girl is almost every conceivable household appliance she can dream of and all of them are workable and many are even electrified. There is the washing machine, vacuum cleaner, pop-up toaster, waffle iron, clear plastic pitcher and drinking glasses that look like crystal but are unbreakable. Doll houses and doll house furnishings reflect colonial or modern design. [36]

Toy advertising copy often sounded the same as descriptions of adult appliances, stressing the product's fashionability, "smartness," and convenient features. In addition, toy ads emphasized the valuable training in home economics that came from contact with such toys. A 1928 toy kitchen ad described the "smooth glistening porcelain table top and the little roll front" that could be raised or lowered. The ad continued: "Behind the swinging doors below is ample space for pans and bowls 'just like mother'—the little housekeeper will learn as she uses this little cabinet that there is a 'Place for everything and everything in its place.'"[37]

The resemblance between girls' play and mothers' work was made literal in one tableau that appeared in both toy advertising and advertising for household products (such as cleaners and appliances). The picture was of mother and daughter "side by side" in housework, the only difference between them the scale of their equipment. This is not an image of collaboration, as with fathers and sons building the same project together: the girl pretends to do exactly what mother is doing for her own, separate household "just like mother's." The cultivation of discipline and education in home economics were stressed in ads from the twenties to the fifties. This was a different kind of educational value—a more old-fashioned, moralistic sort—than the stimulation of intellect promised by educational toys. Girls needed to learn how to get things done around the house, not how to excel in matters of the intellect or the imagination.

Girls' play has always been depicted as closer to mundane—that is, domestic—reality than boys' play. In toy ads, a girl likes to work: it makes her happy. "When you buy a kitchen cabinet for your little girl—you buy years of playday happiness. You buy playdays that are habit-forming days—playdays that will remain with her always." In a 1928 ad for a "playroom equipment" company, the girl is approaching the table as a server while a boy sits waiting. The Tootsietoy dollhouse furniture suggests that "the child is taught to play house and do as Mother does at the age when impressions begin to mean so much"—with a detailed description of the house "living room, dining room, two bedrooms, kitchen and bath" and the furnishings: "8-piece bathroom set in the new colors, green, orchid or white." The girls are featured with heavy makeup and curled hair. In the 1950s, photographs depict a girl playing alone, isolated in her fantasy home just as her mother was in the suburban dream house. In one ad the same model is pictured putting baby in a high chair, with carpet sweeper, with shopping basket, with dishes, pouring batter into a frying pan, and bathing a child. Girls' toys were updated so that the toys were miniatures of what their mothers were actually using, inculcating brand loyalty in household purchasing at an early age. Consumption and shopping became an ever more important aspect of the play.[38] "Doll dishes and every-

21. *Mother and daughter look alike, dress alike, and work side by side in the kitchen.*

thing to wash them! Vel, Ajax, Brillo, Dupont Sponge, Cadie Cloth, Rubbermaid, Morgan Jones dish towel." There was more emphasis on consumer training: "They love to play 'grown up' with DOLL-E-TOYS and KIDD-E-TOYS . . . made from the same Mirro Aluminum mother uses." "Little girls can do their own cleaning with this safe, practical vacuum that hums just like mother's."

Who is Suzy Homemaker???

She's every little girl who wants to be just like her mother. That's why all the Suzy Homemaker appliances look and work just like yours. They're big and beautiful—and work like real. The Suzy Homemaker Oven bakes cakes big enough to serve six! Top burners really heat. And it's completely safe! Oven door automatically locks when in use and won't open until oven cools. The exclusive new Topper Safety Plug protects against electrical shock.

The same kind of quality and care that goes into the Suzy Homemaker Oven (A) is in all Suzy Homemaker appliances. The Washer-Dryer (B)

really washes clothes with agitator action, jet spray—and even spins dry! The Vacuum Cleaner (C) actually vacuums up dirt, comes complete with attachments. The Iron (D—with ironing board) has a jet spray sprinkler and it really heats! Completely safe with a red warning light and safety plug.

Never before could your little girl learn homemaking skills with appliances so big, so safe, so real! Every Little Girl Wants Suzy Homemaker™ Appliances!

22. *Mother and daughter compete, rather than collaborate, on their separate appliances.*

23. *Dollhouses copied the latest in home fashions and design.*

24. A solitary girl plays at child care, cooking, cleaning, and shopping.

Thus girls' play through the 1960s was restricted to child care, cooking, cleaning, and shopping or to the kind of work that goes into appearance and fashion. The role of play in gender socialization was explicitly praised in ads for girls' toys. They were set in domestic space and normally portrayed the girl alone or with her mother. When girls were not engaged in miniature acts of housework, they were often pictured dressing up in their mothers' clothes, gazing into the mirror. The self-absorbed gaze in the mirror has a

3 LITTLE MISS SHOPPER

She'll play "store"
every day with her
Amsco Doll-E-Shopper!
All-steel shopping cart,
miniatures of famous
packages. Doll seat
with movable tray.
DOLL-E-SHOPPER

25. Girls' toys cultivated brand awareness and emphasized shopping.

long history in the pictorial representation of adult women; in the 1950s this is transferred to little girls. Overall, the image of girls is sexualized in the 1950s: in front of the mirror girls are dressed in panties or negligees; even while doing housework they are frequently posed with their buttocks sticking out, a posture that revealed their panties. "Tinkerbell won't rush her," claims a cologne manufacturer selling a "complete vanity set up," as though to deny the obvious overtones of adult sexuality. Thus toy ads combined a number of postwar feminine ideals: the wife as expert shopper, happy keeper of a dream home, and sexually attractive woman who brought honor to her husband in all these things.

In toy advertisements from the 1950s and 1960s, ads for what are today considered gender-neutral or nonsexist toys (such as construction sets, bicycles, board games) feature a single boy or a girl together with a boy, often with the girl watching the boy play. While nearly all the advertisements stress the active nature of children's play, girls were included in an ambiguous way in the tableaux of play in the fifties and sixties. Within the family circle, mother and daughter often take the place of observers of the action, spectators to the male bonding of father and son at play.[39] The father's and son's poses match, as do the mother's and daughter's. This was made explicit in the long-running campaign for Lionel train sets. "It's

for particular people like me and you...
only facial quality Chiffon will do!

You and Mommy just couldn't be any other way, Angel! You're both
fastidious about your skin care, your clothes, your hair. So naturally you're just
as particular about your toilet tissue. You like facial-soft Twin-Ply Chiffon
...especially made for special people. It's multi-rinsed in pure Cascade
snow-water for added softness, greater purity, extra absorbency.
Snowy-white, special quality Chiffon...featured at stores everywhere.

26. *Advertisers used the pretense of dress-up play to sexualize the image
of young girls.*

27. *Girls' toys emphasized attractiveness, as well as mothering and home-making skills.*

"The Gift that makes me a Boy again!"

TRAINS — Powerful, swiftly-moving trains. Smoke-puffing, whistling Trains—the famous scale-detailed LIONEL TRAINS. What better gift than a Lionel for that boy of yours?

LIONEL TRAINS

MANY a dad has said, looking at LIONEL TRAINS under the Christmas tree—"Yes, this is the gift that makes me a boy again!" What fun he and junior will have with their LIONEL model railroad. Years and years of FUN—because LIONEL

TRAINS last a lifetime! The new LIONEL locos and cars and accessories for 1948 are wonderful. But—do send for the catalog today and read all about them. Then ask your dealer to show you all the new LIONEL TRAINS. (Priced as low as $15.95.)

Send for Catalog-Special Offer

28. Train sets claimed to rejuvenate fathers while drawing them closer to their family.

good for a boy to use his hands building a Railroad. . . . It's good
for Dad to shed the years and join in. And it's good for mom to see
the boy in her man and the man in her boy." Model railroads were
expensive and took up a great deal of space, factors that placed a
certain ceiling on the market; but in the striving to increase market
share, little attempt was ever made to bring girls into the action.[40]
The girl, like the mother, sits outside the circle of the train set,

29. *Mother and daughter are appreciative spectators to the play of father
and son.*

pointing and commenting on the action, while father and son hold the switches. Similarly, board game ads stressed family unity and togetherness as promoted by toys. The father and son are typically poised in the middle of action, discussion, or exchange (arguing over a move, playing a card), while the mother and daughter look on delightedly. A 1956 advertisement for a plastic building set features a father putting the crowning touch on a skyscraper while mother and daughter stand aside. The girl appears delighted just to watch.

The advertising for traditional girls' toys has undergone very little change since the 1950s, although references in advertising copy to

They learn
while they play–
with wonderful DYLENE® plastic toys

30. Mother and daughter are delighted just to watch the fun and learning take place.

girls' play as training in home economics have gone out of fashion. On rare occasions, boys do play housework in toy ads. Fisher-Price advertised its toy vacuum with a picture of a girl seated on the couch reading the *Wall Street Journal* while a boy vacuumed the floor under her feet. But this kind of ad is very exceptional, and the role reversal is itself a joke.

Children of Color

Historically, the advertising image of childhood has a color, and it is white. This is why it is easier for whites to pick out children of color in advertisements than it is to see their absence in all-white ads. Images of white children are remarkably stable: most of the models—usually blond and blue-eyed—bear a striking resemblance to one another. According to Mary Lynn Stevens Heininger, this type of child emerged in portraiture, decorations, and illustrations in the middle of the eighteenth century: "Perhaps with their roots in portrayals of Renaissance cherubs, these images depicted children as wide-eyed, chubby cheeked, and, especially toward the end of the century, fair-skinned and fair-haired." [41] Thus the glorification of blond, light-skinned children as a type coincides with the historical trend toward a sentimentalized childhood. Richard Dyer has argued that whiteness *as a norm* informs all media representation—and I would add here media representations of childhood, "as if it is the natural, inevitable, ordinary way of being human. . . . White is not anything really, not an identity, not a particularising quality, because it is everything—white is no color because it is all colors. This property of whiteness to be everything and nothing, is the source of its representational power." [42]

Children of color first appear in *Parents* in the 1960s, more often in illustrations than in advertisements. Usually the child of color is a token, one of a crowd of children in the classroom. Target advertising to Black and Latino parents for children's products has been slow to develop: it is still very rare for toy advertisers to make up print ads depicting Black children for publication in African American magazines such as *Ebony* or *Essence*, although diaper, drug, and cosmetics manufacturers do so routinely. Even when these magazines run Christmas season articles advising readers about the selection of children's gifts, major toy manufacturers rarely buy advertising space. Instead, a handful of ads for small specialty manufacturers of dolls and board games depicting Black children and Black dolls appear in these magazines—rarely in *Parents*. Mattel began manufacturing African American Barbies in the mid-1960s, but only in the 1980s did the company develop a multiracial series of dolls, companions to Barbie, and adult and child members of the Heart Family. No print ad campaigns were devised for women's magazines until 1991.[43]

The makers of preschool-age toys are more likely than other manufacturers to use Black and white children together in their general market ads—occasionally an Asian child appears as well. School desegregation is one factor in this change in representation. Another is that the icon of preschool education since the 1970s, *Sesame Street*, has created an association between racial integration and educational value that advertisers attempt to use to their advantage. Yet advertisers follow slightly different rules than *Sesame Street* does. While *Sesame Street* frequently has Black or Latino children in single, starring roles, advertisers still tend to use children of color in a crowd. If a single child is shown, it is usually a white boy. Mostly, when an advertising scene takes place in the kitchen or on the front porch or in the backyard, all the models are white. When advertisers do use children of color, the scenes are usually set out of doors, on city streets, or most often in the limbo of a photography studio cyclorama.[44]

There are probably more racially integrated ads for children's products because of the advertisers' growing consciousness of minority parents as a market. Advertisers are interested in attracting the Black market if they can do so without offending the white one. The solution to the problem of including children of color without alienating white parents has been to express the dominance of white children nonverbally. Typically, ads reveal an implicit hierarchy of race relations. Anglo children are the stars, African American children the bit players. Erving Goffman has noted how characters' "placement relative to one another will provide an index or mapping of their presumed **social** position relative to one another."[45] In toy advertisements, the superiority of white children is reinforced through visual composition and through gestural codes.

A four-page spread for the preschool manufacturer Today's Kids (printed frequently in many women's magazines, including *Parents*, for three years in a row) features four different toys played with by a racially and ethnically diverse group. The integration helps to convey the sense of the modern that Today's Kids wants to suggest: "We don't make the same old toys. Because they're not the same old kids." On the first page, five children of different ages direct their attention to various "activity centers" on the circular Busy Center. Only the Black child has his back to the camera, his face turned away. On the second page, girls play with the stove, the play phone, and the vanity of the Sweetheart Playhouse. Seven children appear, all of them white, with long, curly hair. On the third page, the Merry-Go-Round features three children playing. Again, it is the blond child, who smiles and looks directly into the camera, while

31. *Busy Center: the white children face forward, the Black child faces back.*

the Black child's head is turned, so that the child's face is completely out of view. Finally, on the last page, three boys play All Star Basketball, and the Black boy is shown full face. His two white playmates are somewhat blurred as they go up for a shot, and they are twice the size and twice the age of the Black child. To its credit, Today's Kids 1992 ad campaign features an image rare in toy advertising: a lone African American boy seated at a writing desk.

32. The blond child smiles and looks directly at the camera; the black-haired child has her head completely turned.

All Star Basketball™

Our real challenge was to create a toy that's a real challenge.

Superstars aren't made by watching sports on TV. They're made by playing the real thing. That's why we designed All Star Basketball. It's all the excitement of the actual game. Scaled down to his size (and adjustable, so it grows as he grows). It even has a break-away rim that lets him slam dunk. Just like the pros. And it's tough enough to stand up to years of rugged play. Long enough for your future star to discover that playing the game is infinitely more fun than watching it. To find the store location nearest you, call toll-free 1-800-258-TOYS.

today's kids™

We don't make the same old toys. Because they're not the same old kids.

33. The African American boy is clearly visible, but the Anglo boys tower over him and dominate the play.

When ads for educational toys feature a multiracial group of child models, the copy often suggests competitiveness between races: the language used—that of success, of power, of getting ahead—creates a not-so-subtle pressure. "It's time children took education into their own hands." "Presenting the first of life's little challenges." "Power Play." "Moving Up." Thus racially integrated ads can operate in different ways for African American and for white parents: as a flattering inclusion in the dream that your child too can be a

34. A rare image of an African American boy in a scholarly pursuit rather than an athletic one.

genius, an image that was restricted to whites until recently; as an image of cooperation and friendship between whites and Blacks; or as an anxious reminder of the need to stay ahead, to be sure your child does not fall behind (especially does not fall behind his Black classmates). Most ads allow for both kinds of interpretations: in a 1986 ad for a musical computer called Little Maestro, a white boy reaches over the shoulder of his Black friend to assist him in pushing the right button on the musical computer. The body language is reinforced by the fact that the blond boy is a head taller and dressed in a button-down collar shirt and tie, while the Black boy is dressed in a sports shirt.

The representation of children of color resembles what happened with white girls in relation to games and building toys; and it may eventually change. At first white girls were largely excluded altogether or were pictured in the same space playing separately with different toys (usually dolls or animals). In the 1950s and 1960s, girls were often present, as observers of two male playmates, but passive. In one example, the girl is blurry, slightly out of focus, positioned in the background, not touching the toy, just watching, while the boy is in the foreground touching the pieces. Such passivity relative to the white male's action is what typifies the representation of children of color in toy advertising today.

Today white girls have been incorporated into ads in some more active poses—with some notable modifications. The solution for including girls as active participants indicates the extent to which the image of the female as active is difficult to reconcile with traditional notions of maleness. Advertisers were unable to reverse roles and place girls in dominant positions or to include girls as equal partners in scenes with boys. Rather, they developed "his and her" versions of the same campaign: girls posed actively in ads where they appeared alone; but a boy version of the same ad was also printed, often in the same magazine.[46] It seems that only in this "separate but equal" way could the same kinds of claims be made for girls as for boys. Two such companion ads for Lego ran in the mid-seventies. The ad copy is typical in its tendency to flatter mothers about their child's abilities, carefully phrasing everything in the language of developmental psychology: "She's bright, She's expressive, She's unique. And Lego's preschool helps her show it." "He was born curious. It's his natural curiosity that gives birth to creativity and imagination." Although the themes are largely similar, the girl is associated with "expression," the boy with the more exalted "imagination."

In its celebration of consumption and the home as a focus of leisure activity, toy advertising in *Parents* conformed to far-reaching trends in popular culture over the past sixty years. Toy advertisers alternately celebrated expansive consumerism and the nuclear family or conveyed a somewhat grimmer sense of competitive individualism in the sixties. As the toy business expanded, more and more toy advertisers joined the few explicitly educational companies by changing from promises of fun and enjoyment to much grander claims about educational value, claims that were fueled by the dominant vision of childhood offered by social scientists and psychologists. Magazine columns and feature articles laid the groundwork for the explosion of spending on children in the 1950s and 1960s: carefully convincing mothers of the need to buy toys, of the wonders that could be accomplished—and taught—by merely providing the right commodities in the home. While developmental psychology could be interpreted as a model that emphasizes the basic similarities among all children, advertisers and childhood experts tended to promote a version that stressed the measurement of differences among children, the need to achieve, to make progress, to get ahead.

At first, the vision of the active, achieving child was reserved for white boys in the popular imagery of advertising. In the past twenty years, some subtle changes have taken place in these social tableaux to expand membership (and of course the market) in the cult of the creative, discovering, active child. White girls now lead a double life in toy advertising for parents: in the pink and flowery world of doll ads and in the coed, "gender-neutral," primary-color world of educational toys. Children of color continue to be granted only a partial, second-class citizenship in the idealized play scenes of toy advertisers: dwarfed by their white contemporaries. Like many other manufacturers of consumer goods, toymakers have normally assumed that white parents are their ideal market. Why this is so— whether it is because they adopt a stereotyped notion of pervasive poverty, or their ad budgets are too limited, or they believe that Black and Latino parents will be as charmed as white parents by the blond and blue-eyed child models who populate most toy ads—is difficult to say.

When we scrutinize advertising's representations in terms of class, gender, and racial ideologies, we find that they change over time and will necessarily be subject to different interpretations by different social groups. In general, advertising seems to suggest that everyone can have it all, that consumption guarantees success and happiness. But advertising also produces and reproduces images of being white and being affluent *as a norm*. Above all, advertising, like most of popular culture, is "leaky" in terms of ideological function. It fosters ideals, such as the happy childhood, on which it cannot deliver. Even limited participation in the ideal of a hedonistic childhood became a possibility for working-class parents only after World War II. Although the postwar baby boom was accompanied by a rapid rise in income, and while the extension of credit made possible increased spending on children, today the dream of a childhood rich in toys is slipping out of reach for millions of parents—especially single mothers—living at or below the poverty level. As Terry Lovell reminds us: "Capitalism generates desires and makes implicit promises some of which cannot be made good for anybody and most of which cannot be met for all people and classes under capitalism." [47] For this reason, the precise "effects" of toy advertising cannot necessarily be inferred from advertisements alone. Certainly ads have helped to circulate the vision of a happy child surrounded by toys. This ideal plays a powerful role in shaping common-sense notions of the emotional value of childhood and surrounds parents in the form of thousands of advertisements each year.

There has already been a mutiny against the notion of play as work, as getting ahead, as aiding the learning of ABCs. That mutiny has taken place in a different medium—television—and was staged for a different audience—children. The conventions and values of children's television advertising bear little resemblance to the ways parents have been urged to buy. Television advertising to children seems oblivious to social aspiration or educational goals in its dedication to good times and the pleasure of the here and now. In comparison with ads for parents, children's television commercials seem more crass and even more hedonistic and rely on a different set of cultural references entirely. Separate advertising to parents and to children has fueled the tendency for parents and children to have different and mutually exclusive motivations for selecting toys, thus spawning many of the objections to children's television commercials that I examine in the next chapter.

3

THE REAL POWER
OF COMMERCIALS

QUESTIONING THE TERMS OF DEBATE

[T]o kids, commercials *are* the entertainment.
—PAUL AUERBACH, VISION MARKETING

P eople fighting for increased regulation of children's commercial television view children as passive, naive, and
easily duped by advertising. People who work for advertising agencies view children as active, discriminating—even
fickle—consumers. Those interested in selling things to children
have an amoral but probably better-informed and more accurate
view of young children as a television audience than do protection
groups and educators. The problem is not that children do not
understand commercials—as the protectionists would have it—but
that they do. To put it another way, young children may not have
passed researchers' tests on the comprehension of "selling intent,"
but they obviously understand a great deal about commercials—and
like them very much.

In the United States the major voice of protest against children's
commercial television has been the well-intentioned Action for
Children's Television (ACT). Throughout the 1970s and 1980s,
newspapers and magazines publicized ACT's cause vigorously.
Journalists found that the young child haplessly exploited by television advertising is an image that incites a lot of outrage; at their
worst, they promoted the notion that children who watch commercial television are the victims of parental—again this usually meant
maternal—negligence. The arguments that ACT used to convince
the Federal Trade Commission (FTC) and the Federal Communications Commission (FCC) to regulate children's television, however,

are unhelpful if we want to understand what children's commercials are, why they are successful, and how they speak to a children's culture distinct from and in many ways repellent to adult culture. ACT's position actually forestalled attention to the content of children's television. My quarrel with ACT is with its idealist vision of childhood, its simplistic advocacy of "good" culture—as universal and self-evident—over mass culture, and its facile distinctions between the commercial and the artistic, the worthwhile and the merely sensually pleasurable. ACT's discussion promoted simplistic behaviorist models of media's effect on children, encouraging teachers and parents to ignore the uncertainty of researchers' results about children's television viewing and stubbornly believe that children are brainwashed by TV.

Action for Children's Television

Founded in 1968 by a group of women in Massachusetts, ACT achieved high visibility throughout the media as a lobbying group committed to monitoring the content of children's television (especially commercials) and to increasing regulation of the television industry through parental pressure on television producers as well as and on legislators, the FTC, and the FCC. ACT sought to accomplish two objectives: increasing choice in children's programming, and stopping the "overcommercialization" of children's media. The founder and spokesperson of ACT, Peggy Charren, maintained high visibility throughout the television trade press (*Variety, Advertising Age*) and popular weeklies (*Time, Parade*). For twenty years Charren has offered herself as an authority on children's television (self-taught, but motivated by her own experiences as a mother): tirelessly granting interviews, giving speeches, writing editorials. ACT practiced sophisticated public relations. It organized national symposia on children and television featuring media celebrities and nationally recognized child experts; it lobbied Capitol Hill by hosting wine and apple juice parties for members of Congress with appearances by Big Bird and Mickey Mouse; it gathered an impressive list of corporate sponsors (including Hallmark, HBO, and Nickelodeon) and an honorary advisory committee including Senator Edward M. Kennedy and T. Berry Brazelton, M.D. (author of best-selling advice books for parents). ACT selectively borrowed from media effects research to stress the need to protect children from television advertising. Throughout the 1970s, ACT petitioned the FCC and the FTC for an outright ban on commercials during children's programming. In 1981, however, after a series of political limitations had been imposed on it, the FTC concluded that "the only effective remedy would be a ban on all advertising oriented towards young children, and such a ban, as a practical matter, cannot be implemented."[1] The aggressive lobbying efforts of manufacturers, advertising agencies, and broadcasters had won out with a Republican administration and a "hands-off" regulation policy, backed by the provision that all FTC rules would be subject to a congressional veto. Today, political protest about advertising to children is largely limited to complaints about "deceptive" advertising campaigns (specific charges of a false or misleading communication from an advertiser to a future seller) and attempts to reduce the number of minutes commercials are broadcast per hour, as in the Children's Television Act of 1990. ACT itself disbanded in 1992 after setting the agenda for public discussion of children's television for more than two decades.

Stressing the results of social science research of the 1970s, ACT claimed that young children have difficulty separating programming from commercials and that they cannot comprehend the selling intent of commercials. The group argued that advertising to young children was unfair because children have not attained the cognitive skills necessary to understand the premises of advertising. It worked to ban selling by program hosts, deceptive toy advertising, all commercials for vitamins (on grounds that vitamins were involved in poisoning deaths among children), all commercials for sugary foods, and toy-based programs (also called program-length commercials). In a 1979 "Speaker's Kit," for those interested in giving public lectures on the need for regulating children's television, ACT offered the following facts: "The average child watches over five hours of advertising each week and sees over 30,000 commercials each year. Advertisers spend over $700 million a year selling to children. The child becomes the advertiser's sales representative in the home." ACT's objections are that "children cannot distinguish programs and commercials, children believe that commercials are true, do not understand selling intent, don't understand advertising techniques (premiums, disclaimers, camera techniques, exotic settings, happy spectators), TV brings children into the marketplace before they have developed the emotional and intellectual maturity to understand it."[2]

ACT justified most of its platform with research using a limited developmental model that strives to protect young children from the onslaught of commercial messages until they have reached an appropriate stage. Essentially this work poses an ethical question about communication situations in which the receiver is in some way deficient compared with an assumed norm of understanding. Thus the primary issue became one of age appropriateness and developmental level, an issue we have seen repeatedly in advertising and advice columns directed at parents.

Such complaints drew on social science research from the 1970s into the effects of television advertising on children, many of which were included in the National Science Foundation's (NSF) report filed as part of the FTC's consideration of a ban on advertising to children. The NSF report stated two of its primary concerns as whether children "comprehend the difference in purpose between commercials and programs" and whether children recognize the selling intention of commercials. Media researcher Scott Ward concluded in his review of U.S. research on television advertising and children that research into age-related differences in the cognitive abilities of children, along with the effect of these on their comprehension of selling intent, has been the dominant concern in U.S. research.[3] Studying children's comprehension of commercials is a complicated matter, however. Children may often be confused by the interviewing methods used by researchers, so that those who are unable to verbalize "selling intent" to the satisfaction of an adult may yet perceive differences between commercials and programs. When adult researchers hold the view dominant among those with a great deal of education that commercials are trash, they may misinterpret a child's different evaluation of commercials as a failure of understanding. For example, Dafna Lemish found that children seem to classify television into two categories—programs and commercials—when they are still toddlers, often paying more attention to the commercials.[4]

Whatever its scientific or moral worth, the notion that children do not understand the selling intent of commercials has been the most widely publicized "fact" about children and advertising, repeated in hundreds of newspaper and magazine articles and widely cited in academic writing today. Every newspaper article, magazine feature, or editorial I have ever read on the subject of children and advertising objects to the practice of television advertising to young children primarily on the grounds of young children's inability to understand selling intent. The appeal of this idea probably has to do with the centrality of the cognitive development model to contemporary understandings of childhood. In focusing on what children do *not* understand about commercials and by assuming that children are deficient compared with adults, academic researchers have excluded questions about what children *do* understand and make of commercials. The assumption has been that children's immaturity accounts for their interest in commercials, along with the implicit—and dubious—notion that children will lose interest as soon as they achieve a normal, adult state of rationality.

One practical advantage in the focus on children's ability to distinguish programs and commercials was that it provided a clear-cut ameliorative solution (one that would leave the business practices of children's television untouched). For example, all networks developed "separators," five- or ten-second video inserts broadcast between the program and the commercial break on Saturday morning television. Typically, animated characters or singing and dancing children deliver the message "after these messages we'll be right back." The production and broadcast of such separators remain standard industry practice despite the fact that the NSF report was forced to conclude that the effectiveness of separation devices—in actually drawing the children's attention away from the screen during commercial breaks—remained an "open question." (Some parents have observed that these separators actually spark preschoolers' interest in the TV.) At the outset, the NSF had listed its priorities as "issues which were of the greatest interest to the parties involved (researchers, public interest groups, advertisers, networks), were amenable to empirical testing, and offered some prospect of concrete policy action based on empirical findings." [5]

The kind of research described in the NSF report—and cited in ACT's bibliographies on children and advertising—usually deals crudely with television content. [6] Quantitative studies have established that most of the commercials on Saturday morning television advertise sugary foods or toys; show the food eaten and the toy played with, and link fantasy elements with the products advertised. [7] Some U.S. research on the effects of TV advertising on children only considers content to the extent that representations are "misleading, deceptive." This research follows from the restrictions imposed in the political struggle over the Federal Trade Commission. In the 1980s, the FTC restricted further regulations to those "based on the advertising being deceptive rather than being unfair." [8] The attention usually focuses on "audio-visual techniques" that are actionable violations of the industry code (the Children's Advertising Review Unit of the National Advertising Division of the Council of Better Business Bureaus started in 1975): toys that seem larger on TV than they really are or can move on their own, or products seen together that must be purchased separately. These kinds of problems have been handled with disclaimers by the manufacturer, while other issues such as drug advertising to children or violent or dangerous acts in commercials are regulated by an advertising industry group.[9] The criticism of deceptive advertising falls within the narrow confines of the advertising industry's traditional concern for self-regulation and self-censorship. Thus research agendas have fostered vigilance about a narrow set of concerns that the advertising industry has historically agreed constitute poor public relations.

Implicit in ACT's characterization of the child consumer in need of protection is the rational adult consumer cool to advertising's persuasive whims. ACT essentially issues a call for fair play, based on middle-class faith in rational consumerism, defined in terms of calculated purchasing that maximizes satisfaction. Adults should not allow children to be duped into impulse buying and wanton desires for goods before they have been initiated, preferably by parents, into the practice of wise and rational consumption. One of ACT's stated goals is to protect the child from disillusionment with the consumer marketplace: "While some suggest that advertising trains children to be consumers, does advertising tell our children that deception is an approved strategy in the marketplace, and that they are entering a world where manipulation and misrepresentation go hand in hand with making a profit?"[10] In acting to prevent such learning on the part of children, ACT shares one of the advertising industry's own public relations goals. The dominance of ACT's characterization of the problem was faulty for two reasons: it underestimated children's understanding of commercials and thus avoided the thornier issue of why children liked them; and it overestimated adult immunity to and distance from advertising.

Charren justified ACT's strict opposition to boycotts and censorship—positions that make her rather popular with the networks—in terms of the need to encourage the production of children's programming. As Kathryn Montgomery has argued about public interest groups protesting prime-time television content, such limited goals are typical of the advocacy groups that have remained friendly with the television networks. Industry outrage at consumer boycotts on First Amendment grounds is a legacy of the struggles with the

Moral Majority of the 1970s and 1980s, when the industry effectively equated boycotting with censorship.[11] But ACT not only recommended more palatable tactics, they supported the industry's favorite response to protesters: if you don't like it don't watch it. ACT emphasized in much of its publicity and educational material that the single most significant act available to parents is turning off the television set. In doing so, it placed the burden squarely on the shoulders of mothers.

ACT's emphasis on publicity, benign paternalism in the form of corporate sponsorship, and "reasonable demands" is a symptom of the way the organization is limited by a liberal reformist ideology. Its moral agenda goes only so far as a concern to protect children from being openly cheated, to foster normative agendas of child development, and to inculcate a taste for middle-class culture. ACT's limitations were those of a consumerist perspective: the provision of expert advice and product ratings; the monitoring of blatantly unfair business practices insofar as they create consumer dissatisfaction; the facilitation of model consumer behavior and the cultivation of middle-class values in consumer behavior (durability, saving, good taste, restraint, delayed gratification, wholesomeness, good health). Direct political action through boycotting or interest group protests was discouraged and monitoring by expert professionals offered in its place.

The discourse set by ACT limited public discussion of children's television in certain ways. Its antiboycott position effectively limited protest against specific representations, thus limiting political struggles over race and gender ideologies on television. When television consumption is defined as a quantifiable problem in which the ultimate goal is *less*, discussion of television content seems pointless. ACT's protest and its publicity created pervasive feelings of guilt among parents over commercial television viewing and in some ways silenced mothers, who could hardly discuss commercial children's television openly if they were supposed to have watched as little as possible.

The Industry View of Children

Within the television and advertising industries, children are characterized as a market not very different from others: as potentially lucrative, as prone to fads and to disasters, but also as particularly volatile and difficult to predict. Like women, they are exceptionally attractive to marketers because they spend so much time shopping.

Because they accompany and influence mothers on shopping trips, children constitute an especially appealing market. Their capacity to make purchase requests of adults is just one aspect of their "three in one" appeal.[12] Children influence adults (on cheap items and on major consumer durables, such as appliances and cars), they will soon spend a lot of money themselves, and they provide an opportunity to inculcate brand loyalty at an early age, thus ensuring future markets. While the young children's market is somewhat difficult to measure, and often gets lumped together in a package of children from age two to eleven, the keen interest in early impressions and the lure of brand loyalty make young children appealing. From Levi's to Reebok to Seven-Up, traditionally adult advertisers are increasingly approaching children.[13] Nickelodeon has extolled the appetites of children, as well as their influence over parents on consumer purchases from dog food to cars, to its potential advertisers in a series of ads appearing in *Advertising Age*.

In the early 1950s, broadcasters provided children's programming without commercials in an attempt to convince families to purchase television sets. Lynn Spigel has documented the ways that arguments related to children, such as educational and therapeutic value as well as family togetherness, were continually used to sell television sets.[14] (Today these same claims are regularly used in advertising for cable stations such as the Disney, Family, and Discovery channels.) In 1954, Disney sponsored the series *Disneyland*, with advertisements for Disney tie-ins, and demonstrated to the rest of the industry the potential profits in appealing directly to children. By the 1960s, the U.S. television industry established a system in which networks produced TV programming, and sponsors, rather than producing their own shows, bought commercial time from the networks. Hanna-Barbera's invention of limited animation techniques in the late 1950s made animated half-hour programs inexpensive enough to be profitable for the networks. Thus Saturday morning television was created and became the focus of marketing efforts directed at children.[15] Brian Young explains the desirability of "demographic purity" in Saturday morning programming:

> One of the principles of selling this type of specialized market is to seek a relatively high response rate from a smaller, selected audience. . . . This means that only a certain type of audience should watch a particular programme and advertisements as the impact of the sales pitch would be wasted on non-target groups.

Demographic purity was the aim of Saturday morning programming, where different age groups of children were attracted selectively at different times in the morning. The aim was to build a continuous audience flow through the morning, moving from programmes for younger children early in the morning to those appealing to older children later. [16]

Television commercials for children were developed in this context of "demographically pure" programming: they are not made to be watched by parents, who use Saturday morning television to gain time to sleep in, do chores, go to work, or read the newspaper. Advertisers treat Saturday morning as a time when children can be spoken to in the terms of a peer culture, with little concern for adult values or intervention.

Saturday morning represents the most intense concentration of children's television advertising during the week, but it has many competitors. With the growth of cable programming and syndication, many of the same commercials are broadcast weekday mornings, afternoons, early evenings, and all day Saturday and Sunday. Advertisers of children's products have a special need for television commercials because young children cannot read and are relatively isolated in the domestic sphere. Other forms of advertising such as newspapers, magazines, billboards, and direct mail are unavailable. The television industry also needs children because they are the only audience available during certain "dayparts," the industry term for blocks of hours during the broadcasting day. The children's market is large enough to lead advertisers to invest very heavily in it: expenditures exceed $500 million per year, with revenues increasingly split between network and syndication. In 1989, network revenues from advertising were $180 million; $160 million for syndication. In 1990, all-network advertising revenues shot up as high as $500 million, according to one estimate. [17] Buying of commercial time has become so specialized that many of the major advertisers employ a separate firm that specializes in the children's market. The business can vary greatly from year to year; competition from Fox network, Nickelodeon, and other cable networks has made the market increasingly complex. One recent tendency has been for girls' toys to advertise more heavily on Saturday morning, which has a majority of girl viewers; more syndicated ad space on boys' shows is purchased for the sale of boys' toys. [18]

In taking as their business a concern with what children like, the television industry has always concerned itself more than media effects researchers with children's readings and understandings of television (and allowed that these may be very different from adult readings and understandings). Advertisers recognize the ways that children live in a media culture of their own and are highly conscious of the social nature of children's lives outside the nuclear family. Advertisers encourage peer influence in the creation of a separate fashion system. Ad agencies treat children's tastes as complex, changeable and hard to manipulate. They encourage the identification of younger children with teenagers and teen fashions. One advertising agency, for example, conducts ongoing research—apart from specific ad campaigns—to monitor trends in clothes, hairstyles, musical tastes, and slang on the West and East coasts, especially among Black and Latino youth, attempting to screen for "outgoing, trendsetting kids" in junior high and high school.[19] Teen clothing, hairstyles, and language are then mimicked in commercials aimed at much younger audiences.

Advertising today avoids the appeal to rationality, which is why so much of 1970s research on children and advertising that focuses on deception fails to represent the aesthetic complexity of children's commercials or their potential as a source of entertainment. Television commercials deliberately attempt to avoid giving very much product information: "reason why" advertising, in which the commercials explain why the consumer should buy one brand over another, has nearly disappeared as consumers recognize how standardized packaged goods have become. Increasingly, advertisements offer themselves as entertainment, as enjoyable for their own sake. Media researcher Cedric Cullingford found, in a qualitative study of children's attitudes toward British advertisements, that "in nearly all children's favourite advertisements the product advertised is not as important as the style of the presentation. . . . Most children, when asked why they like an advertisement, say nothing about the product at all."[20] The four main reasons children give for liking certain advertisements are "the personalities, the gimmicks, the humour and the songs." Cullingford's study rightly places commercials in the realm of entertainment, not consumer information as most comprehension studies have done.

In their relentless cultivation of "brand awareness," advertisers rely on repetition to keep the names of soft drinks, snack foods, and toys on children's minds. One reason for this is that market researchers characterize the children's audience as fickle, lacking in product loyalty and ready to switch brands or television channels at whim. But children's ability to recall commercials is often better than their ability to recall other programs—not surprising given how frequently commercials are repeated on U.S. television and their shorter length. Children demonstrate an awareness of products, especially "in their ability to repeat jingles and catch phrases." Cullingford's interviews revealed that

> children's taste for advertisements showed an appreciation of the fantasy element; the cartoons and the gimmicks of style. Thus children appreciate what advertisers set out to offer in what [Raymond] Williams calls a magic system of inducements. In many ways advertisements offer a microcosm of what children like about television; given the slight public bow towards the value of information, they actually present repetition, songs, humour, recognisability, and stunts.[21]

Variety cited the frustration of ad executive Cy Schneider, author of an industry textbook on children's television: "Acknowledging that consumerist groups want TV advertising to kids banned under the assumption that they are 'malleable, innocent and unable to cope with advertising,' Schneider points out that research indicates children become 'more cynical and selective' as they age and start to discriminate at age four or five."[22] Giving a high rating to children's discrimination is, of course, a defensive, public relations tactic: children don't need protection if they are already so smart. Just as ACT characterized young children as bewildered and innocent in order to argue a case for regulation, the advertising industry helps stave off regulation by characterizing young children as sophisticated, discriminating viewers. As Brian Young has noted, the advertising industry prefers to present "the advertiser as friend and equal to the child who, in this scenario, is a streetwise, robust kid with abilities that academics have underestimated."[23]

I believe the advertising industry's image of the savvy viewer is much closer to reality than ACT's image of the innocent child. One reason that ad researchers have produced a more accurate image is that their marketing efforts have forced them to tie the content and the aesthetics of commercials to their relation to children's everyday experience. The image of the discriminating audience of children is more than a cynical excuse for questionable business practices: it guides the ad industry's own research practices with children in the audience. The smart, active child viewer is the image behind much of the advertising industry's own research. The *New York Times* reports that "children can turn a very cynical eye on commercials. . . . Most children are very sophisticated about advertising," according to Arlyn Brenner, the director of Child Research Services, which conducts market research for corporations. "They've been exposed to a lot of ads that overpromise what products such as toys can deliver, so they can be very hard to persuade." [24] Ad researchers view children as a very critical audience indeed: cynical about the advertiser's intentions, and ready to complain of poor production values or the misuse of slang. In the research tradition ACT drew upon, the child is presented as baffled, confused, overwhelmed by television; in advertising research, the child is presented as a media aficionado. For example, a researcher specializing in children at Leo Burnett, an advertising agency, describes his subjects this way:

> They're very media wise. They know that somebody is putting together this ad with the intent of getting them to try to buy the product by using their language. They're aware of some of the stuff that goes on. When you listen to kids in the focus groups, you find there are bunches of kids who will use words that are so sophisticated that you wonder whether they've got parents in the business. But they don't, they're just very sophisticated. They're *into* the media. We've done some copy research and if it's a rough version, we'll have *young* kids using very sophisticated production kinds of comments, like "you're using cheap video" or "the colors are kind of crummy." . . . Expectations have changed a lot. It used to be a passive audience for commercials but now the kids have become interested in media as media. [25]

While academic researchers have tended to use crude quantitative measures of media content, the producers of commercials employ qualitative interviews and focus groups to test many detailed aspects of their campaigns, such as casting, costume, palette, and storyboards. In their attention to image and sound and children's perceptions of them, advertising researchers have come to understand children's experience of television better than the well-intentioned effects researchers. The industry's approach should alert academics to the ways media sophistication is increasing with successive generations of children.

Some of the protest against children's television was that it offered cheap, shoddy productions. But in the 1990s, the production values of Saturday morning television are high. Television commercials provide a type of media experience unavailable elsewhere: their extravagant budgets, their enormous shooting ratios (number of takes for each scene that appears in the final version), and their frequent use of special effects and animation mean that they offer some of the highest "production values"—the slickest images—on television. So confident are advertisers of children's desire to watch television commercials that a company called Vision Marketing put together videotapes consisting entirely of commercials and passed them out for free at shopping malls, in the belief that the video will be watched over and over again. According to the company's senior vice president Paul Auerbach, "Kids are a much different market than adults, who don't generally like to watch commercials. But to kids, commercials *are* the entertainment. Our research shows that kids like watching commercials, and they'll watch this kind of video over and over." [26]

Much academic research on children and advertising has been informed by a strong sense that children should not like commercials and has tried to elicit from children critical statements about them. As research subjects, children pose a special challenge because we can never entirely discern the distance between their thoughts and what they say to please the researcher. A critical distance from commercials and a distaste for them have been taken as the signs of successful cognitive development. Thus the aesthetic judgment held by one segment of the population—that television commercials are trash—influences the more "scientific" evaluation of children's developmental abilities. The affluent children of well-educated parents are probably most familiar with the antitelevision and antiadvertising feelings of their parents. Many children are aware at a fairly early age that adults often disapprove of commercials and of the products they advertise. For example, three- and four-year-old children commonly speak of "junk" food versus healthy food, having learned this distinction from the doctor, the dentist, the preschool teacher, and often parents. In laboratory research, I suspect that children have often tried to please the adult researcher by offering negative statements about commercials, so that children's liking for them has been underreported. Thus children may catch on to the way remarks about television are evaluated by adults and learn to emulate the higher-status, negative opinions regarding television of their parents or teachers.

There is some research outside the advertising industry that suggests that children like commercials a great deal. Studies based on parents' observations of their children's television viewing at home in "naturalistic" settings report that children enjoy commercials enormously. Commercials are many toddlers' favorite kind of television. They are in many ways ideally suited to young children's abilities: they are short, lively, and frequently repeated. Usually, children are thought to develop a distaste for commercials as they grow older, but Barbara Brown has reported that when carrying out a research project on *The Cosby Show* that involved showing tapes to third and sixth graders, children of all races begged that they be allowed to see the commercials as well. In an important insight into preschoolers' relationship to commercials, Young has suggested that commercials are in some ways more appealing to children than television programs because commercials are "about" familiar objects:

> the television commercial shows a brand that quite possibly the child will have touched, examined or consumed, that will probably be available in local shops or supermarkets, and that is possibly on the kitchen shelves in the child's home. The television commercial is an occasion for showing the child parts of his or her familiar world. The rest of television is not. The rest of television is a "window on the world," a world of people he or she has never met and places he or she has rarely been.[27]

Most children become very keen on joke telling by the age of four or five, and commercials are an important source of humor for them. Patricia Palmer's qualitative research with school age children has shown that commercials are frequently reenacted, memorized, parodied, and included in children's jokes. While these examples involve older, school-age children, commercials also provide tag lines, songs, and jokes to four- and five-year-olds. The humorous aspect of television commercials (and cartoons) may be especially important to young children, since their resources for the production of humor are lacking, as a group of psychologists explained: "[T]hey lack fluency and articulateness in speech, and they have only gross control over their interpersonal styles. Such factors, coupled with their general inexperience of life, render them ill-equipped to inject germane humour into social interaction as a deliberate ploy."[28] Nevertheless, children cherish the ability to inject humor into their interpersonal relations and rely heavily on the media to supply it. In observational studies of children watching cartoons, psychologist

Anthony Chapman and his associates have found laughter at television as something deeply social, produced only by interaction with a peer.[29] Children may often be alone when they are watching television, but the phrases and jingles of commercials are repeated when they see their friends and are a primary means of joking.

Alternatives to Commercial Children's Television

For over twenty years, the public discussion of children's television commercials has been dominated by the effort to keep children away from them, whether by banning them altogether, limiting the number that may be broadcast, or urging parents—and this nearly always means mothers—to stop their children from watching. At the moment, in the political area of regulation, these battles have been lost. With the spread of cable, children may now watch children's syndicated shows with commercials all day long, seven days a week: on USA network's *Cartoon Express*, on Nickelodeon, on The Family Channel.

Pay cable has exploited the perception that children watching commercials is undesirable, and has provided children's programming on The Disney Channel twenty-four hours a day and children's shows on Home Box Office (HBO). These pay cable services stress "quality" programming and family entertainment and receive high ratings from their target market of affluent, college-educated parents.[30] To a large extent, however, "quality" has been coopted by video and pay cable marketers to mean any children's programming shown without commercials. The Disney Channel, for example, routinely shows programs such as "The Care Bears" that were attacked a decade ago as examples of toy-based programming. The absence of commercials on pay cable is a delusion. For every half-hour of Disney programming, young viewers are subjected to nearly ten minutes of promotions for Disney's theme parks, feature films, and upcoming programming. HBO broadcasts *Babar* each morning without commercials and runs ads in parents' magazines with the headline "It's 8 AM. Do You Know Where Your Child's Mind Is?" They describe *Babar* as a "children's classic with time-honored morals . . . fun, caring and entertaining programming, with no commercials." But children can find a wealth of *Babar* stuffed animals, books, and toys in most upscale toy stores.

Many parents with extra money to spend rent videotapes for their children regularly and feel virtuous doing so because it shields their children from television commercials—and ACT and child experts have widely recommended this practice. But most of these videos

35. Pay cable advertising capitalizing on parental anxiety over commercial television.

are tied in with a wealth of merchandise as well, and they include both commercials at the start (for Pizza Hut, for example, at the beginning of the quality children's movie *Land Before Time*) and trailers for other videotapes to rent at the finish. Many videos are age-graded and recommended by reviewers on this basis, who typically focus on a narrowly constructed cognitive-developmental model for children's understanding of television—as embraced by ACT—and thus use age appropriateness as the single most important criterion for judgment. PBS broadcasts children's programming (although its production of children's shows was reduced because of the budget cuts it faced during the Reagan and Bush administrations), but this is limited to a couple of hours in the morning and late afternoon and is especially impractical for working parents.

Sadly, one inadvertent result of the campaign against advertising to children has been that parents with the most disposable income purchase cable or videos without commercials and are left feeling that they are doing the right thing; parents with less money and time, who are unable to emulate the forms of television consumption preferred by the intellectual middle class and are thus dependent on commercial network television, are made to feel bad—if they care to listen to experts (and, of course, many do not). Encouraging parents to ban the viewing of TV commercials at home is typical of professional advice about child rearing directed at mothers in that it increases the burden of mothers' work and requires considerable expenditure of time and money. Alternative provisions of children's entertainment outside the limited time allotted to kids' shows on PBS involve additional expense (acquiring and maintaining the VCR, renting videos, paying for cable) and additional work (the trip to the video store, taping shows). The job of monitoring and censoring children's television viewing is extremely time-consuming, and most mothers will allow children to watch commercial television. The marketers of children's goods will always be more successful than child experts who advise against commercial television viewing so long as marketers and advertisers conceive more realistically of the constraints on mothers' time and energy.

Children's commercials have been treated as a special case in broadcasting, because organizations like ACT have accepted the developmental model. But in fact children's media are typical of the ways in which entertainment and advertising are difficult to disentangle, rather than exceptional. As commercial television establishes itself in Western Europe, the U.S. model for using television to market to children promises to become more widespread.[31] In England, the BBC channels have lost many child viewers to American animated shows on the commercial station ITV. While advertising to children may raise more ire than advertising to adults, its techniques are commonplace in the media. In the media industries as a whole, the distinctions between advertising and programming have become ever more muddied, with the international popularity of MTV, with the increasing role of conglomerates that plan before production the licensing potential of feature film plots and characters. The financial interests of producing and selling films, video and audio tapes, toys, and computer software have been combined in multinational corporations. As Marsha Kinder describes this trend, it "is helping to accelerate the redefinition of movies, television programs, commercials, compact discs, video games, computer programs, interactive multimedia, corporations, nations, politicians, superstars and toys as amphibious software—any one of which can be used to promote the other in a gigantic network of commercial intertextuality." [32]

Child experts routinely urge parents to talk to children about television, but they usually suggest that they do so in the terms of selling intent. Parents are encouraged to teach children to spot irrational or unreal content and recognize their persuasive intent. By the time children are in grade school, parents may be able to talk them out of wanting certain products by reasoning with them (that food gives you cavities; that toy will probably break), and children may develop a level of cynicism about commercials—especially if in doing so they are emulating the tastes of their elders. Adults may never be entirely successful in talking children out of being interested in advertising itself, or being entertained by it. Children, like adults, can benefit most from forms of media education that recognize the idealistic values of advertising today—their appealing presentation of peer companionship and fun—as well as their sophisticated manipulation of aesthetic codes, their use value for the audience as entertainment, and their designations of certain kinds of audiences.

A ban on television advertising to children and more public funding for children's television programming are meritorious causes, but they are unlikely to occur in the 1990s, when retail profits are falling, politicians—the majority of whom have favored deregulation—are eager to encourage economic growth, and public television's federal funding has been cut. In the meantime, it is important to face up to the cultural significance of advertising in children's lives. We need to ask why commercials are popular and interesting to children and how they inform a child's total media experience and store of cultural knowledge. To ask these questions is not to apologize for the advertising industries but rather to acknowledge realistically their power as cultural producers of complex and contradictory messages to children. The work of audience researchers such as Robert Hodge and David Tripp, Patricia Palmer, and David Buckingham suggests that whatever children think of commercials, it is likely that they are open to a range of interpretations, encompassing enjoyment and rejection, idiosyncratic interpretations and selective identifications. We need the study of children and television advertising to encompass a definition of children as more than just beings who have attained a certain "mental age," developmental stage, or level of cognitive achievement. Children are social beings with emergent yet strong identifications based on gender, race, and ethnicity. Commercials speak to these kinds of membership, albeit in superficial ways, while rendering the peer group the primary rallying point. There is much more to commercials than their selling intent or the ethics of their product disclosure information, the features of commercials that researchers have traditionally monitored. If we want to protest about the content of ads, if we want to teach our children media literacy skills, if we want to explore what children should want—what different children might need—we will have to take the commercial into account as a complex set of thematic, visual, aural, and narrative conventions, as I demonstrate in the next chapter.

4

UTOPIA OR DISCRIMINATION?

COMMERCIALS FOR KIDS

[W]hat adults esteem is made to appear ridiculous; what adults despise is invested with prestige.
—ALLISON JAMES

Most television commercials for children advertise food and toys and, in doing so, differ markedly from print ads directed at parents. They make no claims for the nutritional value of snacks or the educational value of toys. They cast no eye toward the future career aptitudes a toy might foster. Children's commercials are set in the here and now. Rather than the solitary children depicted in so many parent-directed ads for toys, children—usually aged six to ten—always appear in groups of at least three and often what appear to be dozens. Instead of the studious, scholarly play praised in so many parents' ads, television commercial play is noisy, hilarious, thrilling. Rather than the wordy copy and simple compositions of the print ads, commercials for children are rapidly paced, musical, and filled with special effects and animation. Children behave raucously, outsmarting adults and escaping the dull restrictions of home and school. Most of the products have fallen into disrepute with teachers and middle-class adults, by and large, many of whom view them with contempt: but this adult contempt for snacks and toys can be built in to the appeal itself.

Children's advertising offers an appealing vision of a world where "kids rule." Like most popular entertainments, commercials are utopian in some respects—portraying a childhood world more exciting, intense, and exhilarating than everyday life. But access to this child-centered utopia is restricted; full citizenship is denied to girls of all races and to boys of color. Commercials for children are not exceptionally racist and sexist—they follow long-established conventions within popular culture. Before turning to this downside of commercials—their casual racism and sexism—I wish to explain the appeal of commercials as entertainment to children, to spell out some of the secrets of their success. Given that commercials are such a successful entertainment form with preschool children, I think adults should shift attention from selling intent and commercial bans to the utopianism (which deserves to be appreciated) and the discrimination (which deserves to be directly criticized) that characterize children's commercials. These can only be grasped by getting closer to television commercials rather than avoiding them.

Both the values of television commercials—their lack of restraint, discipline, old fashioned puritanism—and their aesthetics run aground of the dominant, adult understanding of what is good, even on television. Children's commercials are everything educational shows typically are not: flashy, quick, energetic, pop, fantastic, humorous, catchy. Educational television, in contrast, is "earnest and worthwhile" and posits the child spectator as one who will "learn and benefit from listening and watching." According to Brian Young, there are several images here: the child as in need of education, the child as different, the child as less than adult in some way. "Commercial television, on the other hand, addresses the child as a 'kid,' a blend of potential anarchist and hyperactive maniac." [1] Disapproval of this aspect of television commercials, and fears of its ill effect on the young, are usually implicit in the often-repeated complaint that advertising to young children is unethical.

In a study of penny candies, British anthropologist Allison James argues that, in their selling strategies, "manufacturers may not be exploiting the power of the child's purse directly, but more insidiously, the power inherent in the conceptual gulf between the worlds of the adult and the child." [2] James describes penny candies as forms of food that blatantly violate the culture of adult eating, in name, substance, texture, and means of consumption. The fact that the forms of food most prized by children are held by adults to be repulsive, inedible "trash" or "junk" is a sign that children's culture inverts and confuses the rules of adult culture.

> By confusing the adult order children create for themselves considerable room for movement within the limits imposed upon them by adult society. This deflection of adult perception is cru-

cial for both the maintenance and continuation of the child's culture and for the growth of the concept of the self for the individual child. The process of becoming social involves a conceptual separation between 'self' and 'other.' This process is often described in terms of 'socialization,' a model which stresses the passive mimicry of others. I would suggest, however, that this process is better seen in terms of an active experience of contradiction, often with the adult world. It is thus of great significance that something which is despised and regarded as diseased and inedible by the adult world should be given great prestige as a particularly desirable form of food by the child.[3]

James's conception of the child's relationship to adult culture is highly relevant to children's television commercials and their relation to adult culture. Commercials seek to establish children's snacks and toys as belonging to a public children's culture, by either removing them from the adult-dominated domestic sphere or presenting these products as at odds with that world. Her analysis points to the inadequacy of the protectionist approach to children's television watching and to the reason advertisers are successful in establishing snacks and toys as extremely desirable things that children show an immense desire to know about at an early age.

A separate children's playground and street culture has existed as long as children have lived in cities and gone to school: but this was a culture produced by children and passed from child to child. A similar kind of culture is now produced by adults and offered to children through the mass media from toddlerhood onward. Advertising agencies have borrowed the themes of children's culture and redefined them with a focus on consumer culture. In James's formulation, "Adult order is manipulated so that what adults esteem is made to appear ridiculous; what adults despise is invested with prestige."[4] Adults are often the butt of television commercials' jokes. Thus commercials invite children at an early age to identify with other children (some of them peers, some of them older) rather than with their parents. Teachers and parents are subjected to various forms of rebellion or humiliation.

When advertisers address children, they ostentatiously test the model of parent-child relations presented in magazines such as *Parents*. Martha Wolfenstein suggested forty years ago that there had been a shift in the ideals of American child rearing toward an ethic of "fun morality." Commercials directed at children try many parents' patience by taking this to its limit—and beyond. Anti-

36. Nerdy teachers are humiliated or ridiculed.

authoritarianism is translated into images of buffoonish fathers and ridiculed, humiliated teachers. The sense of a family democracy is translated into a world where kids rule, where peer culture is all. Permissiveness becomes instant gratification: the avid pursuit of pleasure, the immediate taste thrill, the party in the bag. In a Kellogg's Cornflakes commercial, a red-haired girl sits at the kitchen table refusing to speak to her mother—she answers by holding up signs saying, "Yes" and "No" in a strategy to persuade her mother to let her eat her grown-up cereal—Cornflakes. In another cereal commercial, a boy of six or seven sneaks up on his father, who is quietly reading the paper on the porch, and snaps his picture (with a camera available through proof-of-purchase seals) at the very moment his toupee blows off. Occasionally white males are used in caricatured, usually blue collar roles, as car mechanics, policemen, drill sergeants, criminals, or wrestlers. Occasionally, Dad is featured in the action in a childlike role. In an ad for Circus-Os canned pasta, a father is left home alone, after his wife, son, and daughter expressly forbid him to touch the children's cans of Circus-Os. He immediately sits down with a bowl of Circus-Os nonetheless and finds himself surrounded by animated circus characters when he opens the can. Upon returning, the family good-naturedly catches him in the act, the animals giving away his misbehavior.

37. Father caught in the act of eating the kids' favorite food.

A Typology of Commercials

Commercial producers have borrowed heavily from genres popular with adults and adolescents, especially the musical, the action-
adventure film, televised sports, horror films, and, finally, the soap
opera. Although children's commercials appear to be trendy and
narrowly addressed to children (often referring within the commercial to adult incomprehension of what is happening), they actually
follow the conventions of familiar adult genres.

Like most television, children's commercials do not beat around
the bush: their gendered address, their locales, props, and narratives
are quickly—indeed, instantly—identifiable. This obviousness is
due in part to a careful mimicry of the codes of costume, prop, and
acting associated with adult film and television genres. Each product category (fashion dolls, baby dolls, cereals, candy bars, toy
cars, boys' action figures) has developed its own style of presentation, its own "genre." Compared with adult commercials, children's
commercials use smaller casts—normally consisting entirely of
children—and the action usually takes place all in a single studio
set, an enclosed space where children are on their own. Besides the
kinds of products being advertised, and the distinctive generic codes
usually associated with children's products, there are certain features that make them distinct from adult commercials but derive

from industry regulation, such as the "island shot," of the toy on its own on a bare set at the end of the commercial, included so that the child can make a realistic judgment of what the product looks like.

The description that follows is based on the state of the art of commercials in 1991. Children's commercials are nothing if not faddish, quick to emulate new trends in film and television culture; but at the same time they are stable in their gendered address and aesthetic codes. My survey of commercials has led me to classify them in the following categories: Musicals; Animals and Magical Helpers (fantasy/ animation); Explorers (adventure); Boy Genius (science fiction); Girls at Home (soap opera); Boys' Toys (Westerns and crime films); and Slice of Life (realist drama).

Musicals

Teddy Grahams cookies were launched by Nabisco with a musical spot that was shown hundreds of times on Saturday morning and afternoon children's shows. Three adult-sized teddy bears sing a version of Elvis's "Teddy Bear" ("I Wanna Be Your Teddy Graham"). They perform on a glittering stage, wearing fashion sunglasses and holding microphones. The bears are joined on stage by three chil-

38. A teddy bear as rock-'n'-roll star: merging the cultural symbols of the young with those of the adolescent.

dren representing the three varieties of cookie: chocolate, vanilla, and cinnamon. In addition to the children on stage, the commercial suggests the presence of a large crowd of noisy children in the audience, cheering them on. In a sequel, the bears on stage sing "Teddy Grahams are Here to Stay" to the beat (if not exactly the tune) of "Rock-'n'-Roll Is Here to Stay." The bears behave like rock stars: jumping on stage, rocking with the microphone stand, disappearing into dressing rooms, and finally leaving after the concert disguised in sunglasses in an attempt to avoid the cheering fans.

In these and many other food commercials, bystanders are instantaneously changed into a chorus of dancers. Children energetically perform in the halls of school buildings, on the street, and on stage. The rituals and props of rock idols make the "rock" genre instantly recognizable: sunglasses, guitar strumming, wild clothes, the white piano, the arrival at the airport, the pushing throngs of fans. Thus a genre associated with adolescent sexuality and rebellion is borrowed and transformed by an association with children's cookies. This commercial, like many others, merges the cultural symbols of the very young (cookies, teddy bears) with the icons of the more mature (rock stars, rock concerts).

In musical commercials the utopian energy of rock-'n'-roll dance stands for the euphoric sugar rush promised by snack foods. Rock musicals allow the numbers to be fashionable, adult, and up to the minute. They promise that "the party is in the bag." One ad mimics a scene from *Blackboard Jungle*: a bald, bespectacled science teacher drones on with the lesson. A boy removes a bag of cookies from his desk: the instant the teacher turns to the blackboard, the children erupt into wild dancing to a rock beat. They freeze back in their seats when the teacher, totally unaware of what is happening, turns back around. "Could you explain that again?" the boy asks, so that the party can recommence. In another commercial two children wait outside the principal's office, dressed in gray, seated beside a bookish secretary. When they take out their Surf's Up fruit snacks and rip open the bag, they are transported to *Beach Blanket Bingo*. "Surf's up!" they yell, and a beach rock beat plays over their fun in the sun. The boundless energy, fun, and enthusiasm of the musical numbers are contrasted with the strict, drab conformity of the classroom. In another commercial a boy bored by relatives at a family reunion escapes to the kitchen, where opening his Starburst candy unleashes a tidal wave of relief. In each case, escape is just a bag of candy away.

39. Classroom doldrums.

40. The cure for boredom: the euphoric rush promised by snack foods.

A variant of the rock musical uses computer animation and a repertoire of techniques borrowed from experimental film and MTV: time-lapse photography, black-and-white images retouched with color (in the style of old, retouched postcards), perspective changes, drawing on film. Usually a single male protagonist narrates over the

41. The result: the classroom as dance party.

rock or rap or punk soundtrack (one commercial presents a group of ten-year-old children playing instruments and singing à la David Byrne and the Talking Heads). The hip children of these postmodern musical numbers inhabit their own visual reality, completely separate from the everyday, the domestic, the academic.

There is humor in these commercials, and a self-conscious stylized irony, but also a strong statement of the clash of consumer culture values (fun, newness, fashion, the pleasure of the palate, of movement, of music) versus the physical and institutional restriction of school (drabness, discipline, self-restraint). Some commercials dramatize the conflict between children's use of commodities for hedonistic ends—the physical pleasures of good taste and energy bursts—and adult censure of such pleasures. Hedonism, defined in children's commercials as the thrills of playing and eating, is vividly displayed and celebrated as a kids' value. Adult disapproval of children's snacks and toys is defiantly ridiculed. Thus children's commercials openly declare generational independence and make it clear that children have no intention of emulating the consumer values of respectable adults.

Animals and Magical Helpers
Commercials have borrowed from fairy tales the character of the magical helper—sometimes animal, sometimes human—who acts

as children's aide, mascot, or playmate. Tony the Tiger, one of children's advertising's most successful mascots, appears to help children overcome various difficulties, cheering them on to "bring out the Tiger" in them through a bowl of Frosted Flakes. In the 1990s, Tony focuses on sports achievements. In a series of ads Tony appears just in time to help a child ridiculed by bigger kids or discouraged by competitors. The child goes on to perform astounding feats of hockey, skiing, soccer, or gymnastics. Often these commercials follow a simple narrative pattern familiar from fairy tales and myths: child encounters adversity; helper appears; helper provides magical agent; child uses magical agent (snack food) and vanquishes villain.[5]

Often animal characters insatiably crave cereal in commercials. The plots of these ads follow the chase-and-pursuit patterns familiar from Tom and Jerry, Bugs Bunny, and Elmer Fudd cartoons. In commercials, all characters pursue the cereal, and the winner gets it. Sugar Bear, the product spokesperson for Super Golden Crisp (formerly Sugar Crisp: the cereal's name changed presumably to lessen parental objections), has been successfully getting his hands on Sugar Crisp through various ruses for years. Sometimes these animated characters act like cartoon tricksters: the Fruit Loops parrot "dares" a dullard in knight's armor to smell but not eat the cereal. On the hundreds of McDonald's commercials seen each month on network television, the clown Ronald McDonald appears in live action or animation, often accompanied by helpers who are themselves pieces of food: Hamburglar, Fry Guy, various creatures representing Chicken Nuggets. Children's foods routinely break the taboo on eating live things, and commercials regularly present food products themselves as animate.

Fanciful "exotic" adults populate live-action ads. These figures are on loan from movies and fairy tales (Confucius, Tonto, Ali Baba). Sometimes they resemble figures from old advertising campaigns directed at women: the Ajax white knight, the strong-armed genie. Typically, these figures come upon children at play in everyday settings and act either as magical helpers or advisers. (They are always male: no fairy godmothers here.) In a Honeycomb commercial, three white children are visited by a genie: a shirtless Black man, turbaned, covered with jewelry, well muscled. He is shot in extreme close-up to emphasize his hugeness, and he appears and disappears according to the children's whim. An inscrutable Asian man, "The Wisdom Tooth," recommends Crest toothpaste. A Native American man sings in English about potato chips baked by "Pequeños Keebleros," animated Keebler elves. Men of color are relegated to the roles of supernatural companions and helpers—they never appear as parents—and their function is similar to that of animated animal figures. Their representations are fixed in "orientalist" fairy tales: in which they appear as more awe inspiring, romantic, mystical, and sexual than middle class whites.[6] Unlike the Anglo parental figures who remain ignorant of the pleasure of hedonistic consumption, these adults are placed in the service of satisfying children's appetites for consumer goods.

Explorers

This variant of the action-adventure genre portrays a forest or jungle expedition in which child-explorers "discover" a new food product. Historical exploration acts as a metaphor here for the child's discovery of new products through advertising. Typically a group of three to five children—most of them boys—in costumes of khakis, pith helmets, ammunition belts, and binoculars, makes its way through a jungle of palm fronds and encounters a few scares before coming upon the treasure: chocolate chip cookies, fruit snacks, canned pasta. The scene resembles the family camping trip—without the

42. *Consumption as an adventure: jungle explorers with binoculars, khakis, pith helmets.*

parents. The soundtrack includes "jungle" sound effects, such as animal noises, and the children's exclamations.

Like adventure movies from *King Kong* to *Indiana Jones*, these commercials rely on a traditional representation of the remote, exotic Third World and the domination of that world by a white male hero. In essence, these commercials substitute sagas of masculine adventure for the mundane routines of the grocery store and the kitchen, where the mother, rather than the boy, is likely to dominate. Consumption means suspense, thrills, and adventure; food is the bounty, the hard-won treasure.

White boys are cast as the adventurous, courageous leaders; a single girl may be included as part of the team; children of color are either excluded altogether or represented as passive, primitive, and ignorant. In a Nestle's Quik cartoon, two white children brave an arctic storm in search of a schoolhouse, accompanied by a rabbit and polar bear as their guides. After an avalanche cuts their journey short, they head into a diner for a cup of hot chocolate. A smiling Inuit (Native Alaskan), so caricatured that his eyes are drawn by straight lines, speechlessly and smilingly serves them. Silent, smiling, and in the background, this is the only Native American child I have found on contemporary television commercials.

Boy Genius

In a recurrent variety of children's commercial, a "boy genius" cleverly explains the product attributes while demonstrating his superior, precocious intelligence. Eggo waffles has run a series of campaigns since 1988 in which a young boy explains (sometimes to his science class at school, sometimes directly to the audience) the ingenious contraptions he has invented to guide waffles directly from the toaster to his own plate. This prevents his family members from eating his waffles before he can get to them: consequently he never has to "Leggo my Eggo." Boys in these kinds of ads sometimes mimic the authoritarian spokesmen in commercials for over-the-counter drugs or cars: they may be dressed in a doctor's white coat, with a stethoscope around the neck (as in the commercial for Nintendo's Dr. Mario). The boy genius often wears glasses. He is the only stereotype used on commercials where intellectual and verbal skills are positively evaluated: he is the only child who does not speak in slang and exclamations (his speech is adult), and he is shown approvingly to be "cool" in his own individualistic way,

43. A white boy genius explains his invention.

44. The cool boy genius, Dr. Mario spokesperson: the only stereotype where intellectual skills are positively evaluated.

rather than a nerd. Creativity and a desire for learning are the qualities that advertisers associate with white children. The boy genius, like the head of the expedition, is virtually always cast as a white boy. When Black boys are cast in this kind of role (the bespectacled spokesman for Bubble Yum, for example, who explained the gum's value for teaching arithmetic), they are surrounded by the vivid graphics and animation typical of the musical and often "rap" their pitch to a musical accompaniment.

Girls at Home

Commercials for girls' toys are closer to the print advertisements appearing in *Parents* than is any other form of children's TV advertising. Typically, these commercials feature two or three girls dressed in pastel colors playing in what appears to be an upstairs girl's bedroom, also furnished in pastel colors or in white. These commercials are always shot in a style known in the industry as "warm and fuzzy": soft-focus photography in which the light is very diffused and yellowish, like sunlight coming through a window. Everything is coded for maximum femininity: the girls have long, curly hair elaborately done; they wear frilly dresses; the room is furnished in pink tones and ruffles. Like the girls, the doll has lots of hair and pink clothes.

45. Warm and fuzzy photography typical of doll commercials.

Girls' commercials use facial close-ups of the girls or the dolls. Basically, the visual style of these commercials is very similar to that of the television soap opera. Typically, one girl speaks in admiring tones to the other girl, who presumably owns the doll. The doll's owner is the star, enjoying her one-to-one moment with the doll: whispering "I love you" or "I'm going to be a ballerina just like you." A chorus of girls' voices sings about the doll. Their song extols the virtues of the toy in cheerful, high-pitched tones. "Cherry Merry Muffin, she looks great and smells great and bakes so great." But the song also reinforces the personal nature of the exchange, as do the dolls' names, which usually include "My" in the title. "Don't shiver, Newborn Baby Shivers, my love will keep you warm." "You wash your hair, I wash mine too. No other doll makes me feel like you do." "You're this small but I love you this big." "When I give you a hug, you light up with love: PJ Sparkles shine a light on me." "Quints, Quints, Five Times more fun. I love taking care of each and everyone." "I love my Sweet Baby This-n-That, when I love her she loves me back."

These ads take place well inside domestic space, and the play going on does not threaten to disrupt it but rather invites the girl's participation in homemaking and child care as unchallenged spheres of feminine power. An adult female voice enthusiastically explains

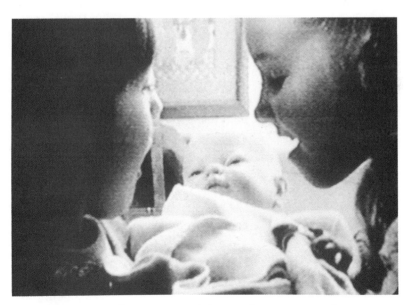

46. *Doll commercial intimacy, reminiscent of soap opera style.*

the product information and cheerfully delivers the disclaimer ("outfits sold separately," "parents put them together") at the end of the ad. A simple and unambivalent identification with the mother is put forward. Girls take the place of the mother in these commercials; the mother herself is usually offscreen. This is the primary difference between ads for dolls directed at parents, where the mother is included in the picture, fondly watching over her daughter's solitary play. The visual codes (pink and lace) and the settings (the girl's bedroom) of doll ads for parents and doll commercials for girls are the same: but the focus on peer relations in the absence of adult surveillance is typical of all children's commercials. Doll commercials express far less open rebellion against adult consumer values than do other types of children's commercials. However much some parents may object to some of the aesthetic codes (the girls' and the dolls' appearance being too pink and frilly), doll commercials focus on the traditional arenas for female consumption—care of "family members," clothing, and homemaking.

Boys' Toys

The commercials for boys' action figures (G.I. Joes, Teenage Mutant Ninja Turtles, Ghostbusters) and for cars and trucks are based almost entirely on filmic conventions of the car chase or the shootout. Close-ups of the toys in action are the rule, rather than shots of children playing with them. On the soundtrack we hear boys' voices making sound effects (engine noises, weapons) and providing speaking parts for the characters: "You're finished, Joker!"; "Slimed Again!"; "Wash down that pizza with *this*, dude!" A collection of toy commercials from the 1950s and 1960s assembled by Ira Gallin suggests that the style of boys' toy commercials has changed little, with the exception of the adult male voice-over or on-camera product spokesman, who has virtually disappeared. This style is relatively inexpensive and quick to produce, factors that are particularly important in toy advertising, which is shown to buyers at the annual toy fair long before it reaches Saturday morning television. Toy buyers hold as an axiom of the business that one should never put a girl in a commercial for a boys' toy. Boys' toy commercials seek to make the toys as exciting as possible without violating the Children's Advertising Review Unit guidelines. One area of frequent complaint involves the rule that toys must not be seen to move by themselves—thus a little boy's hand is always visible holding the Batman doll or pushing the Hot Wheels car along. Boys' toy commercials depict conflict, pursuit, and competition.

The boys on screen do not look at one another or speak to one another, except "in character." The backdrop for the toys is realistically connected with the toy's theme: city streets for Batman; dirt and shrubbery for G.I. Joe. Usually it is impossible to discern *where* the boys are playing. Like the boy explorers in food ads, there is no connection to ordinary living rooms, bedrooms, or kitchens. Boys' play with cars and action figures involves the boy impersonating the doll rather than interacting with it or establishing a relationship to it. Boys *become* their toys in play; girls take care of their toys. Even in ads for Barbie, girls on-screen enact the part of admiring spectators for Barbie on her date rather than assuming Barbie's speech.

Compared with food commercials, ads for dolls and for boys' toys tend to have few special visual effects. They adhere strictly to gendered codes of color, dress, and setting: the overall color scheme of the ad coordinates with the packages that will be found on the shelf of the toy store. Thus children can register primary and dark colors as belonging to boys, pink and pastel belonging to girls, and feel themselves at home in the proper aisle of Toys "R" Us. Toy marketers are so certain of their success with blatant gender coding that when a girls' toy is failing, they try "pinking it up" to make it more popular.[7]

47. Boys' play takes place in an imaginary space with no connection to ordinary living rooms, bedrooms, or kitchens.

Slice of Life

McDonald's has developed a style of commercial that deserves attention on its own. These ads are usually set within the restaurant and feature "realistic" conversation among groups of children ranging in age from eight to fourteen (marketers call them "tweens" and have targeted them for the past five years). Unlike most commercials seen on Saturday morning, these McDonald's ads forgo special effects and animation and magical helpers. The style and the settings are realistic.

Slice of life ads present "realistic" conversation and interaction among a mixed group of children: different races, different ages, boys and girls together. Children's talk is not normally a significant part of commercials. There may be exclamations and repetitions of the latest slang (as in "Radical, Dude" or "We're into Barbie!"), but the presence of songs on the soundtrack usually obviates the need for talk. In the McDonald's campaigns, however, children converse about everyday topics: being grounded; staying overnight in the hospital; having a crush on a girl in the neighborhood.

In 1990 and 1991, these ads focused on a group of five kids— centering on "Cosmo," a jovial, overweight blond with a buzz haircut, and his friends, two boys (one Hispanic) and two girls (one Black)—who go to McDonald's. The commercials are a serialized story, developing the characters of the children a little further each time. In every commercial, the kids are presented as a strong network of friends who genuinely care about each other, although this is often expressed in teasing. In one commercial, the children have set up a garage band and try to work out a song together. In another they go on a "video treasure hunt" where they must capture the items with a camcorder. They like to travel as a group—and McDonald's is either the place where they come together to meet or the dramatic focal point for their peer interactions. When they visit one of the boys in the hospital, they kid him that a pretty McDonald's employee asked about him; when Cosmo is finally released from being grounded, McDonald's is where they go to celebrate; when Cosmo is hanging around outside the house of the girl he has a crush on, kids riding by on a bicycle tell him she's at McDonald's. McDonald's comes to stand for the intensity of eating experience (much better than hospital food, for example) and the intensity of heterosexual romance, made safe by the fact that this is a unified group of friends that includes boys and girls and children of different races.[8]

The Rules of Inclusion

Children's commercials borrow conventions from many diverse popular culture genres, but they borrow from the musical most of all. Like musicals in their form and their function, children's commercials tap into utopian sentiments. In his discussion of the musical, "Entertainment and Utopia," Richard Dyer argues that much of popular culture taps into hopes and wishes for alternatives. Popular culture does more than merely depict hedonistic satisfaction: it presents the imagination of something different, something better. Entertainment offers no coherent model of a perfect society, as in the classical political definition of utopia, but instead represents feelings that embody utopian sentiments. Entertainment, according to Dyer, "presents, head-on as it were, what utopia would feel like rather than how it would be organised. It thus works at the level of sensibility, by which I mean an effective code that is characteristic of, and largely specific to, a given mode of cultural production."[9]

Entertainment works on the level of form as well as content. Children's commercials emphasize many of the utopian values Dyer identifies, including energy, abundance, and community. These are symbolized in the image and the soundtrack, as well as communicated in words. Nonrepresentational codes carry the feelings: rhythm, color, shape, movement, texture, camera work. The complaint is often leveled against commercial television for children that it is too fast-paced, too rapidly edited, too noisy and restless. On a formal level, the rhythm of the commercial represents the child's own restless energy. In the cookie commercial, for example, the drabness of the schoolroom and the lecture is transformed into a party; the teacher's monotone is drowned out by vibrant music; the gray tones of the classroom are replaced by children in brightly colored clothing; the homely adult is crowded out by attractive, dancing children. The fact that so many children's commercials borrow from the musical is one indication that similar sentiments are at work on a formal and a content level. The mad dancing erupting in a dreary classroom; the hyperfeminine world of doll play; the excitement of the superhero vanquishing the bad guy; the child turning the tables on the adult; the linkup of friendship and adventure—these scenarios are repeated hundreds of times in children's commercials. No wonder they catch children's attention and stick in their minds as images, phrases, gestures, and melodies.

Utopianism in commercials is limited and partial, however. It expresses dissatisfaction with the status quo and points to inadequacies in society, but it usually proposes buying and using commodities as the means to a solution, rather than real social change. Children can be taught to see the sales pitch in a commercial, and that is a useful lesson. Too often, however, adults expect that, once the selling intention of a commercial is appreciated, its interest for the child will disappear. But the nonrepresentational aspects of commercials—their rhythm, color, pitch, and movement—stick with children as much as—perhaps more than—their explicit sales pitch. Young children, unable to articulate their utopian longings in words, may find these non-representational aspects of utopian sensibility especially satisfying, and there is no good reason for adults to try to talk them out of their liking for them.

One feature of U.S. popular culture is that it often tries to symbolically "solve" the problem of difference. For example, the musical overcomes the problem of gender difference by uniting its male and female lead—despite their quarrels—in dance, and the couple becomes a perfectly matched and blended unity. Entertainment also erases other potentially problematic differences. Dyer sees entertainment as strictly in line with the dominant ideology in denying validity to problems caused by class, race, and sex differences. Prejudice and poverty have no lasting impact on characters in entertainment: all social inequities can be overcome or resolved. Utopianism can also serve to mask the fact that participation in the unity and community of entertainment has always been unequal, exclusionary. Entertainment's optimism about community can deny the real hardships discrimination creates. This holds true for children's commercials. Different children are portrayed with different aesthetic codes on television commercials. On the surface these commercials celebrate a democracy of goods, where membership is available to anyone who is the right age, gets the joke, and can purchase the product. However, commercials also negotiate the limitations of peer group identity for children in the United States today.

Gender and race seem to be both prominent and invisible in television commercials. The salience of gender and race will depend on who is watching the commercial. Some advertising research suggests that when African American actors are used in commercials, "blacks see more, whites see less." [10] Conventions of representation from other genres reappear in commercials: Blacks play bigger parts in musicals and sports stories; white males play all the roles in action-adventure plots; blond girls in fancy dresses play the big parts in the soap opera of doll commercials. Asian, Latino, or Native American children appear rarely: usually a single African American child stands in as the token minority. Television commercials both invite the participation of all children in the party and the play and, at the same time, carefully observe taboos by excluding African Americans from the center of the plot or the visual composition or by relegating girls to subsidiary, token roles when they appear in coed groups.

When Saturday morning commercials are set in realistic locales, they generally present a WASP, middle class world. The appearance and clothing of the child models, the frilly bedrooms and spacious kitchens, and the expansive backyards suggest the suburban dream home. In trying to investigate the advertising industry's own awareness of racial representation (not an easy thing to do given how much of the research is considered "proprietary" and advertisers' and advertising agencies' high degree of public-relations defensiveness concerning issues of both race and children), I was referred to the talent agencies that cast children's commercials for advertising agencies. Talent agents uniformly claim that they are looking for kids who are "outgoing and confident," "full of personality," "articulate, precocious and bright." When pressed to discuss the relationship between race and casting, one agent claimed that "how well kids photograph is what's important. If everyone has the same coloring, it is easy to light the set." Thus, according to that agent, lighter skin tones are chosen not for any racial preference but only for ease in lighting. For the same reason, when kids are to be photographed in groups, agents pick those who are closest in skin tones. The phrase "all-American" was used by two casting directors as a kind of code word for Caucasian looks. The blue-eyed blond and the freckled redhead were often preferred types. McDonald's was considered an unusual client in its casting calls for large numbers of ethnics, including Latinos, "Orientals," and Blacks, and for more "character-y kids," children with a flawed appearance.[11] Obviously the technical problems with lighting can be overcome when multiracial casting is an explicit part of an advertiser's strategy to reach its target markets.

As in the advertising in *Parents* magazine, when Black children appear in commercials, they are seldom seen at home. The commercials in which children of color appear are never situated in a kitchen or a bedroom; nor are the children shown interacting with their parents. Within the world of the commercial, there is no traceable source, no point of origin for ethnic differences: rather, children appear as "equals" against a backdrop of public space, and racial difference is nothing more than physical appearance; it involves no cultural differences.

In many commercials, subtle details of placement on the television screen mark African American children as different from the blue-eyed blonds. In the Teddy Graham commercial mentioned in my discussion of the musical, a white boy and girl and an African American boy dance on stage with the bears. As the children pop up behind the white piano played by one of the bear musicians, the children eat cookies and crowd into the spotlight. Throughout this action the Black boy is partially obscured from view by the piano or nearly pushed out of the frame by the other kids. He is placed in the left third of the screen—the least dynamic portion of the frame according to design theory. Like most Black models, the boy has been directed to smile broadly and act clownish, manic. (Sadness, frustration, or complaint tend to be the prerogative of whites in children's books, films, and television programs.) In a 1989 television commercial for Style Magic Barbie, one Black and two white girls appear together. All three girls marvel over the voluminous curly blond hair of Barbie. It is unusual that the Black girl is given the largest speaking part, exclaiming over the fun of Barbie, enthusiastically describing her attributes. But the Black version of the doll is seen only in the background and is never admired or played with by the Black girl. In the final shot, the Black girl stands behind a seated white girl, fixing her hair.

U.S. designers of dolls, however, have always glorified light skin, blond hair, blue eyes, tiny noses, and thin lips. When commercials are set in the upstairs bedroom and advertise the pinkest, most traditionally feminine toys—baby dolls, clay flowers, kitchens—toy commercials use only white models. When girls are really being middle class girls—wearing long hair and traditional, pastel dresses, playing with dolls and flowers—they are always *white* girls. Merchandising as well as advertising usually excludes Black girls (and Latino and Asian American girls) from the most strictly gender-coded types of play. An exception here is Mattel, which markets Black and Hispanic product lines extensively. As Susan Willis has observed, "[Such dolls] sum up for me the crucial question of whether it is possible to give egalitarian expression to cultural diversity in a society where the white middle class is the norm against which all else is judged. . . . whether it is possible for Afro-American culture to find expression in a mass cultural form." [12]

48. *The African American girl observing the white girls' play with a blond doll.*

49. *Subtle details of placement on the television screen mark African American children as different: the white boy dominates the image in terms of visual composition and body language.*

Judging from the commercials on Saturday morning television, the answer is no. The role of the princess is clearly reserved for the white girl and the white doll. On the other hand, African American and white girls on Mattel commercials are frequently portrayed as close, intimate friends—embodiments of interracial friendship as a utopian ideal. There is far more integration and interracial friendship on children's commercials than there is on most prime-time television or, for that matter, in most of the classics of children's literature.

Children of Color

From an adult point of view it is obvious that the role on children's commercials that has the greatest status in terms of future economic power—the genius—is strictly cast with white males. It is important to consider the impact of positive stereotypes as well as negative stereotypes. Sociologist T. E. Perkins has argued persuasively that the learning of stereotypes involves both what one can and cannot be:

> Insofar as socialisation is to a large extent concerned with learning to aspire towards social values and to recognise the desirability of those values, there is a contradiction in the socialisation of groups who "may" not, in fact, aspire to those values. Girls, blacks and to a lesser extent the working class, must also be taught that they themselves "do not have" these desirable attributes and that they "*should not*" aspire to them. They must aim for values which have a relatively low status. . . . This contradiction is of course aggravated by an "egalitarian" ideology.[13]

Handing the roles of leader, instigator, or prodigy to white males communicates something to girls and children of color about behaviors *not* to be expected from them. Here again, however, commercials are contradictory. Television commercials simultaneously exclude children of color from certain roles adults might value *and* associate them with qualities considered enviable by children. Black children are often used to define the product as "cool," modern, up to the minute. They are set up as more lively, more cool, more fashionable, more with-it than whites. Thus their presence verifies the product's fashionability. This also means that we are most likely to see Blacks in ads for the trendiest products. It is one of the contradictory and compensatory aspects of stereotyping that Blacks are presented as enviable for their greater vivacity and looseness. But in making these the qualities of Blacks exclusively, the representation is ambiguous, suggesting by default that these qualities—though perhaps more fun—are not to be valued in the long run.

Black children are routinely granted a privileged relation to sports and music in commercials. By the late 1980s, Black children appear in nearly all ads for sports shoes (even infant Nikes), thus emphasizing their presumably "inborn" athletic ability. A television commercial for Apple Jacks cereal uses a rap soundtrack and a basketball game to envision the "teamwork" of whites and Blacks playing together. One of the Black boys makes the final slam dunk of the cereal box at the end: the only starring role repeatedly offered to Black boys. In a commercial for Pocket Rockers top-forty singles available on miniature cassettes, a Black girl is given center stage, flanked by her white playmates as they dance down the street. Achievement in sports and in music is obviously a proud and valuable aspect of Black culture. But in advertising these achievements are distorted because they appear not as aspects of culture but as innate, natural talents. Music and sports are the only arenas for achievement and ambition allowed Black children.

As I have said, McDonald's commercials portray the largest number of children of color, but the leads are still reserved for the white children. In "Report Card," a variety of children are seen at school as they first open their report cards. The children react with a range of emotions—joy, excitement, fainting, grief. But the single Black boy is seen opening the card and rapidly closing it, in a quick shot in which his reaction is open to a variety of readings (shock? relief?). The kids head off to McDonald's to recuperate. The Black boy joins them at the table, but he is seen only from the back in an over-the-shoulder shot. In "Big Dreams," a group of children discuss over their burgers what they want to be when they grow up. A girl says, giggling, "I want to be a lawyer, or maybe a fashion designer." A song describes three of the dreams in flashback/fantasies—to be a dancer, rock-'n'-roller, rodeo rider. When we cut back to the scene at the table, two Black girls are briefly shown, on the edges of the frame, slightly out of focus. This imitation documentary style (hand-held camera, imperfect framing, loss of focus) is frequently used to pan quickly past children of color. It is a way of signaling their presence while "accidentally" passing them over. They are not given speaking parts. The range of possibilities discussed by the kids, from aerospace engineer to electrocardiogram technologist, is the province of the white kids.

McDonald's has also hired the Burrell Agency in Chicago to produce commercials depicting family life. The Burrell Agency specializes in commercials with specific cultural appeal to Blacks and has been a leading critic of the advertising industry for its tendency to cast African American actors merely in commercials whose settings and themes are those of middle class white America. When I began researching this project in 1988, I was hard put to find any African American children on television commercials aside from their secondary roles on children's television. This was somewhat understandable in the Pacific Northwest, but when I taped local programs in Durham, North Carolina, or in Chicago or from the cable station Black Entertainment Television, I found, to my surprise, that Black children were nearly absent there, too.

When the Burrell Agency provided me with a sample reel of ten commercials with children produced over the past decade, McDonald's commercials predominated. These commercials were strikingly different from the commercials shown on Saturday morning produced by the Leo Burnett Company. In one example, "Joey," a tired mother picks up her three-year-old from a day-care center. They get on the bus together, where Joey is full of energy while his mother appears so weary from her working day that she dozes off. The bus stops at McDonald's where father meets them and the family enjoys a happy, lively meal, ending in Joey falling

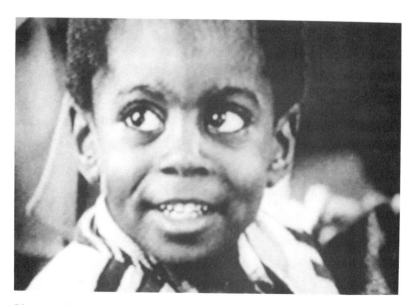

50. Burrell commercials: "Joey" looks up at his devoted, loving mother.

asleep on his father's shoulder. A singer soars in the background: "You can't be together until your work is through . . . He's only three. So treasure this moment—you know they won't last, time is flying, children grow up fast, take a little break today at Mc-Donald's." In "First Glasses," a Black girl of about eight is the center of the story. First we see her being fitted with glasses at the optometrist's office; brother is teasing her about wearing glasses. Father, mother, brother, and she head into McDonald's, where the woman behind the cash register is an attractive teenager, who wears glasses herself, and tells her "nice glasses." At the table, eating a burger and fries, she successfully rebukes her brother's teasing. "How many fries am I holding up?" the brother teases her; "None," she says jokingly as she swipes them out of his hand and eats them. In "Special Delivery," a young girl sings the "narration" about the family's busy morning routine. Dad leaves for work early, and the mother and daughter hurriedly get ready for work and school. Mother and daughter drive through McDonald's for breakfast and then make a special delivery to the father, a mail carrier working his route. "Daddy," yells the girl as she gets out of the car; she then runs to her father with his breakfast and receives a big hug.

In these commercials African American children are surrounded by devoted, loving parents, but the hardships of working parents are

51. In "First Glasses," a rare starring role for a Black girl.

also acknowledged. As a Burrell executive, Sarah Burroughs, has explained: "My mother worked, her mother worked, I grew up assuming that I would work." [14] These commercials hint at a different kind of family life in a "different culture when children understand maturely the kinds of burdens the parents, especially the mother carries." [15] The Burrell commercials provide celebratory, utopian, unabashedly sentimental pictures of family life. They offer more to African American children than most television programs—with the exception of some situation comedies. Unfortunately, these commercials are primarily targeted at parents and broadcast during select local and national programming. Burrell's ads are not seen on network Saturday morning programming.

Major national advertisers have also begun to address the Latino market through Spanish-language commercials for the cable station Univision. Mendoza-Dillon, a Los Angeles–based advertising agency, also provided me with a sample reel of commercials for diapers, medicines, and soap that featured Hispanic children— usually girls—in more significant roles. McDonald's has produced a string of Spanish-language versions of its Saturday morning Happy Meal ads. Mattel has begun producing commercials featuring its Hispanic Barbies that were to appear on the Spanish-language cable network Univision. [16] Some critics have bemoaned target mar-

52. *Warm affection between African American fathers and children.*

keting as further exploitation of an already economically disadvantaged group. But there are two sides to target marketing: yes, it may make these children want to buy, but it also supports them with images they recognize on the screen and decenters the dominance of all those blue-eyed blondes they see so much of when they watch Saturday morning TV. Commercials targeted at Black and Hispanic children, where Spanish is spoken as well as English, where recognizable parents and children in urban settings are celebrated, where children of color hold the spotlight, are gift horses many parents would be prepared to accept.

Children's commercials are not bad because they are goofy or unrealistic or silly—much of children's literature shares this predilection for the fantastic and the comedic—and children shouldn't be shamed for liking them. Children's commercials are bad when, through casual accidents of casting, composition, and plot line, they reproduce a worldview in which white males are the eternal heroes, the stars of the show. They reproduce race and gender hierarchies while they speak to democratic, utopian themes. To successfully teach children about the ways that commercials work, they need to be discussed not only in terms of "selling intent" but also in terms of the repertoire of visual and aural signs that help to form children's common vocabulary. Any media education program should concern itself not only with the discriminatory but with the utopian aspects of television commercials as well.

Children's commercials do more than teach children to consume things. They also introduce children to the consumption of media. Children's commercials mirror the genre and formula types typical of American popular culture. They bind children together as an audience defined in opposition to adults—by encouraging a social identity based on age, by ridiculing and inverting the values of adult culture. At the same time, they segment the children's audiences in the same ways that the U.S. film and television industries historically have segmented adults—most importantly and blatantly by gender, more subtly by race and ethnicity. Paradoxically, commercials strive to create in children the sense of separateness—but they do so in the same aesthetic language as that of adult popular culture genres and, in a sense, establish the taste for and the familiarity with these codes to be called upon in other media experiences, such as movies, recorded music, and television programs.

In the next two chapters I turn to children's animated series of the

1980s, which were accused of being little more than commercials themselves and faulted for promoting gender segregation. This gender segregation had different consequences for boys and for girls. I argue that some benefits accrued when girls were no longer forced to share the stage with boys on children's programs. Boys' and girls' animated series share with commercials a tendency to borrow freely from established popular culture genres—with mixed results.

5

TOY-BASED VIDEOS FOR GIRLS

MY LITTLE PONY

When in doubt, use boys.
—CY SCHNEIDER, *Children's Television*

Television producers, like most children's authors, cartoonists, and moviemakers, have favored male characters in action-packed adventures for boys. Male characters predominate because conventional wisdom has it that boys will not watch girls on television but girls will watch programs for boys. Until recently, little girls were not thought to constitute a large enough market to justify the cost of the programming. In the 1980s, with the rise of home video recorders and rental tapes, animated series were specifically designed for girls for the first time. The shows *Strawberry Shortcake, The Care Bears, Rainbow Brite* (1983–1987), and *My Little Pony* (1984–1986) were denigrated as the trashiest, most saccharine, most despicable products of the children's television industry. Yet these series were the first animated shows that did not require girls to cross over and identify with males. I want to take a close look in this chapter at *My Little Pony*— a limited, toy-based series of videos unmistakably coded as feminine—as representative of children's animated series and their appeal on the basis of gender.

The Boys' World of Children's Fiction

The preference for male characters in children's media has its origins in popular children's books from the nineteenth century, though the marketing of children's books to the middle class began in the eighteenth century, with strongly moralistic books that were intended for boys and girls alike. As Elizabeth Segel has explained, "Neither the Puritan aim of saving the child's soul nor the characteristic Georgian aim of developing good character seemed to require the distinction between girl-child and boy-child." Instead, children's books of the late eighteenth and early nineteenth century "clearly taught obedience, submission to authority and selflessness as the cardinal virtues of both girls and boys." In the 1850s a division between adventure stories featuring male characters and domestic chronicles first appears.

> Before the boys' book appeared on the scene, fiction for children typically had been domestic in setting, heavily didactic, and morally or spiritually uplifting, and this kind of earnest family story remained the staple of younger children's fiction. The boys' book was, above all, an escape from domesticity and from the female domination of the domestic world. . . . The liberation of nineteenth-century boys into the book worlds of sailors and pirates, forests and battles, left their sisters behind in the world of childhood—that is, the world of home and family.[1]

The differentiation between boys' and girls' books coincided with the nineteenth-century expansion of the book market and the attempt to expand sales through segmentation.[2] Pulp fiction in the form of romances for girls developed later than boys' action stories. The rise of girls' popular romances coincided with the growth of the middle-class "cult of domesticity" and the notion of separate worlds for male and female. In fiction—as in ideology—boys belonged in a public world of work and adventure, girls in a domestic world of personal relationships. According to Segel, from the outset of a gendered distinction in popular children's literature, boys shied away from girls' books, while "girls were avid readers of boys books from the start."[3]

Decades later, Walt Disney set the standard for gender representation in children's motion picture productions. In adapting fairy tales and literary sources, he handed out a few starring roles to young women: Cinderella, Sleeping Beauty, Snow White, and, more recently, Ariel in *The Little Mermaid* and Belle in *Beauty and the Beast*. In each case, however, the heroine was innocent and selfless, and the story placed her in a situation of enforced passivity whether through physical confinement, muteness, or death. (Belle was supposed to be a different kind of heroine—feisty and bookish—but her narrative function closely resembled her predecessors.) Any deviance from these characteristics immediately marks a female character as villainous in Disney's universe. Disney's best-known animated film characters—and the most fanciful—were always male: the Dwarfs, Jiminy Cricket, Bambi, Dumbo, Peter Pan. All of the popular cartoon characters, at Disney and at Warners and Hanna-Barbera, were males: Mickey Mouse, Donald Duck, Tom and Jerry, Daffy Duck, Elmer Fudd and Bugs Bunny, Coyote and Road Runner, Tweety and Sylvester. In many of the cartoons, two male characters are locked in a sadistic game of entrapment and punishment. On the relatively rare occasions when female companions were used—Minnie Mouse, Daisy Duck, Petunia Pig—they were given human breasts, heavily made-up faces, short skirts, and high heels. Sybil DelGaudio has characterized the gendered roles of the cartoons this way:

> the female as comic foil for the male is superseded by all-male rivalries in which comic incongruity is created by means other than sex differences . . . the cartoon seems to be a favorite place for the depiction of the pursuit/capture plot structure. When female characters enter the picture, they automatically take their places in line with the pursued, while the means of pursuit is changed to seduction and the end is clearly sexual.[4]

The striking difference between the female characters in the toy-based series of the 1980s involving licensed characters and in the cartoons of the classic period is that the heroines for the first time are not pursued but pursuing—the initiators and actors on a quest. Strawberry Shortcake, My Little Pony, and Rainbow Brite were not token female members of a male gang; and they are not drawn in the sexualized caricature of adult women repeated since Betty Boop.

One of the axioms of motion picture and television production (and of publishing) is that the female audience will take an interest in stories about male adventurers (the Western, the detective story, science fiction, action-adventure) but the male audience will not take an interest in stories about female adventurers (the romance, the domestic melodrama, the family saga). Thus, female characters were rare on the science fiction children's shows produced in the 1950s, and the heroes were adult men such as *Captain Video and His Video Rangers* (1949–1955), *Commando Cody, Sky Marshal of the Universe* (1955), and *Tom Corbett—Space Cadet* (1950–

1955).[5] These live-action shows were forerunners of the science fiction and superhero cartoon series produced in the 1960s and 1970s. *The Adventures of Johnny Quest* (a very successful show, intermittently aired between 1964 and 1980) was based on the characters Dr. Benton Quest, anthropologist, his blond son Johnny, and his son's Asian Indian companion, Hadji. *The Fantastic Four* (1966–1970) included one female, Sue Richards, on its team of superheroes. Sports and music series with a more comical bent featured a cast of male protagonists; among these were *The Monkees* (1966–1972), *The Harlem Globetrotters* (1970–1973), and *The Jackson Five* (1971–1973). *Fat Albert and the Cosby Kids* (1969–1977)—one of the longest-running and most critically acclaimed children's television series for its depiction of African American children—counted not a single girl among its gang of seven living in the inner city. *Fat Albert* attempted to deal realistically with childhood problems and feelings—and its positive messages emphasizing self-esteem were later borrowed by shows like *My Little Pony* and *The Care Bears*.

Girls fared somewhat better in children's shows based on family situation comedies. Equal numbers of boys and girls enabled the battle-of-the-sexes theme to flourish on shows such as *The Flintstones* (1960–1966), *The Jetsons* (1962–1963), and *The Brady Kids* (1972–1974). Only as teenagers, however, were girls given primary roles—as though it was beyond the writers' ability to create story lines that included girls without some element of heterosexual flirtation. Thus animated shows followed the conventions of *Archie* comics, with their long-standing rivalry between Betty and Veronica, even though the Saturday morning television audience was in large part made up of young, preadolescent girls. Judy Jetson loved to dance and chase her rock idol. Pebbles, born in 1963, was given a love interest in Bamm-Bamm Rubble, the boy next door, while still a toddler. When she was given her own show, *Pebbles and Bamm-Bamm* (1971–1976), the screenwriters accelerated her development so as to make her an adolescent.

Throughout the 1970s, teenage girls appeared as tokens on shows like *Hot Wheels*. Two popular series starred teen girls, notably *Josie and the Pussycats* (1970–1976), featuring the sweet redhead Josie, the brainy Black girl Valerie, and the scatterbrained blond Melody; and *Samantha the Teenage Witch*, based on an *Archie* character. *Josie* was a landmark for its establishment of the comedy adventure—or "let's get out of here"—format involving teenagers menaced by supernatural foes. *Scooby-Doo*—probably the most successful series of this type—originally featured two teenage girls—Daphne, the pretty one, and Velma, the smart one—to complement the beatnik Shaggy and the straight-laced Fred.

Designers of children's commercials and promotional campaigns have also preferred male characters. The roster of mascots is entirely male: Captain Crunch (cereal); Tony the Tiger (Frosted Flakes); the elves Snap, Crackle, and Pop (Rice Krispies); Sugar Bear (Super Golden Crisp); Ronald McDonald; Geoffrey Giraffe (Toys "R" Us). Conventional wisdom in the advertising business has it that a female trademark for a children's product will immediately turn away every boy in the audience; their belief is repeatedly proven to them by market research. Even in the world of educational programming for preschoolers, where combating sexism was explicitly placed on the agenda in the 1970s, we find ourselves in a man's world. Adult women all but disappeared in the 1960s as hosts and puppeteers—Shari Lewis with Lamb Chop, Romper Room, and Fran of Kukla, Fran, and Ollie—only Mister Rogers and Captain Kangaroo remained.[6]

Big Bird and Bert and Ernie dominate *Sesame Street*. All of the beloved monsters are male: Snuffalupagus, Honkers, Grover, Cookie Monster. The two females in residence on *Sesame Street*, Betty Lou and Prairie Dawn, are human-looking muppets rather than more fanciful creatures and tend to be strictly bound to realistic, rather than fantastic, actions and story lines, as though the celebrated creativity of *Sesame Street*'s writers and puppeteers dried up when confronted with female heroines.[7] Miss Piggy from the Muppet shows and films is an exception to this, but she is a figure bound to incite feelings of confusion and ambivalence in little girls, combining as Piggy does a flamboyant willingness to break the norms of girlish behavior with an obsessive pursuit of her romantic interest, Kermit, and an avid pursuit of beauty with a ridiculous, porcine appearance.[8]

The Controversy over Toy-based Programs

The girls' cartoons *Strawberry Shortcake, The Care Bears, My Little Pony*, and *Rainbow Brite* were produced in the 1980s during a boom in licensed characters in the toy industry. A firm called Those Characters from Cleveland, established in the late 1970s to create popular characters for the toy industry and its many licensees, chose as its first task the job of reaching—in some ways creating—the young girls' market, using interviews, focus groups, and storyboards of character designs to determine what girls found most appealing. Before the 1980s, Barbie and Mary Poppins had been the only successful girls' licenses. This effort was made because the market for girls' toys was underdeveloped and seen as a potential income producer. Innovations in girls' toys are relatively rare: season after season, toymakers limit their new toy lines to baby dolls that mimic human babies in different or more realistic ways (in 1990, all the major manufacturers planned dolls that soil their diapers). Perhaps this is because the industry's executives are overwhelmingly male. Whatever the reason, toy store owners consider the girls' market harder to buy for than the boys' market. For a brief period, the heyday of licensed characters portrayed on videos, there were many new toys for girls: Rainbow Brite and her friends the Color Kids (Canary Yellow, Patty O' Green, Buddy Blue—a token male character); the Care Bears, each a different color and different emotion;[9] Strawberry Shortcake and her girlfriends in lime, lemon, orange, and blueberry, and She-Ra, Princess of Power (twin sister of He-Man); and a lengthy procession of My Little Ponies.[10] Significantly, the critic Tom Engelhardt labeled the process of first designing characters using the tools of market research and then producing a cartoon the "Strawberry Shortcake Strategy," suggesting the special link between licensed characters in the eighties and the girls' market. To a large extent these toy-based cartoons resulted from the discovery and exploitation of a marketing niche of girls aged three to seven, produced by the overwhelmingly male orientation of classic cartoons, comic books, and toys.

Many critics found these characters especially offensive because they were developed specifically for marketing purposes. Manufacturers wondered aloud why what they were doing was considered substantially different from what Disney had done since the 1930s in licensing the likenesses of cartoon characters for use by manufacturers of watches, clothes, cereal boxes, toys, and other items. But the toy-based shows offended cherished notions of creative integrity. Engelhardt charged, "[F]or the first time on such a massive scale, a 'character' has been born free of its specific structure in a myth, fairy tale, story, or even cartoon, and instead embedded from the beginning in a consortium of busy manufacturers whose goals are purely and simply to profit by multiplying the image itself in any way that conceivably will make money."[11] ACT led the protest against these programs and filed suit with the FCC to get them banned from television.

Some of the most virulent attacks on the licensed character shows were in fact diatribes against their "feminine" appeal. One of the reasons they seemed so dopey, so contrived, so schmaltzy was that they borrowed from popular women's genres—the romance, the soap opera, the family melodrama. Engelhardt complained that "a group of bossy, demanding, doll-like creatures dominate the relentlessly 'happy' realm of girls' TV." These remarks reveal a lack of familiarity with the stories, which actually concentrate to a large extent on unhappiness, suffering, and feelings of worthlessness. One reason these programs appeared so artificial to critics such as Engelhardt was that a willed, intentional act—the act of targeting the female consumer—was required to revise the dominant conventions of the twentieth-century children's story so as to center on female protagonists and the conventional concerns and play of little girls. Engelhardt noted with irritation that in the absence of the adventure plots and special effects typical of boys' cartoons there is an emphasis on prosocial, pop psychology values:

> An endless stream of these happy little beings with their magical unicorns in their syrupy cloud-cuckoo lands have paraded across the screen demanding that they be snuggled, cuddled, nuzzled, loved, and adored, generally enticing children to lay bare their emotions so that they can be examined and made healthy.[12]

Girls' cartoons, like women's soap operas, were about emotional life. Engelhardt argued that the proliferation of characters on these shows leads to "personality fragmentation," and he worried about the effect on the audience in a tone that recalls concerns for the mental health of the soap opera viewer:[13]

> If we all have trouble with caring or hugging, if intervention is called for, and if you also have to sell lots of licensed characters, then you have to present the managing (or healing) process as a highly complicated one that needs lots of cooperation by lots of highly specialized dolls, so specialized that instead of being complex individual personalities, they are no more than carefully labeled fragments of a personality: Tenderheart Bear, Share Bear, Cheer Bear, Grumpy Bear.[14]

But personality fragmentation is not an invention of Those Characters from Cleveland. It could be found in early Disney films, such as *The Three Little Pigs*, which was praised by critics for its original "character differentiation." The single adjectives used to designate the Seven Dwarfs of Snow White (Grumpy, Happy, Sleepy, etc.) are probably the first examples of this trick in animation. But Disney's work was enthusiastically embraced by critics, probably in large part because of his painstaking attention to animation.[15] (Today, Disney's work is the standard for the genre.)

The difference between Disney's animation and today's television programs is above all that of style. The limited-animation techniques used to produce children's television series were pioneered by Hanna-Barbera in the late 1950s. The television series were made for a fraction of the cost and in a fraction of the time spent on film cartoons. Characters stand in one place more of the time, and the same background drawings are repeatedly used, now stored in memory with computer animation. Discussing the cartoons based on licensed characters, communications scholar Stephen Kline complains:

> The cartoon creature who acts, thinks, and feels just as humans, but is simplified in form and personality provides a perfect vehicle for children's characterizations. The drawings appear infantalized. Characters' features and expressions are reduced to the simplest and most easily recognized by the young. Animators emphasize those features and expressions that children most quickly and easily identify with. Indeed, the characters rarely learn anything in these programs—their nature is inherent and fixed by their species-specific and immutable characteristics.[16]

Kline's criticism concerns simplification and fixed character types: he wants characters that change and grow, the individualistic, well-rounded characters of the nineteenth-century realist novel. But between the lines in these critiques one also hears a denigration of the emotional and psychological, an irritation with the actionlessness of these shows. These are precisely the same grounds on which adult women's genres have been denigrated. Engelhardt and Kline note with dismay that these cartoons submerge the child in a fantasy world unknown to the parents; they complain that they are too specific to the child's gender and age group; they ghettoize the child's viewing. But if the narrative situations and plots are as simple as Kline and Engelhardt claim, shouldn't a parent be able to catch on quickly? I read in these passages a father's irritation at the daughter's immersion in a program and a fictional world just for girls. The licensed character shows were not essentially different from other animated programs for children that had been around since the 1960s: what was new about them was that it was girls—and very young girls at that—who were being approached as a separate audience.

My Little Pony: Toys and Videos

My Little Pony toys are popular with girls as young as two years of age and as old as eight. In 1990, most children had heard of them, seen other children with the toys, watched the programs, seen commercials for the toys, discussed them with playmates at preschool or day care by the age of three. This will not last forever; the license is already past the peak of its popularity. But in 1990, I had never met a girl between the ages of three and six who did not either already have a pony or want one.[17] Many girls collect ten, twenty, thirty ponies. According to Hasbro, 150 million ponies were sold during the 1980s.

According to Sydney Ladensohn Stern and Ted Schoenhaus, My Little Pony was the result of some "blue sky" research with little girls. "Hasbro asked the little girls, 'what do you see when you go to bed and close your eyes?' and the answer was often 'Horses.'"[18] In 1982, Hasbro was surprised when half a million brown plastic ponies sold without any advertising. The next year they changed the ponies from brown to "fantasy colors" and sold $25 million worth of them. Sales increased with advertising to $85 million in 1984 and $100 million in 1985, and with the production of the *My Little Pony* television shows and movie. Individual examples of My Little Pony are differentiated from one another based on body color, hair color, and decoration. The ponies are kitschy, anthropomorphized creatures with brightly colored, flowing manes and tails, and large blue eyes adorned with eye shadow, eyeliner, and thick lashes. Their manes and tails are made of rooted synthetic hair and can be combed, unlike those of the many molded horses that preceded them. The eyes are especially prominent because no other features are painted on the rubber body of the pony. There are two small indentations for nostrils, two rounded ears on top, and a curling, smiling line of a mouth, but except for the eyes, ponies are a solid color of molded rubber. The poses vary slightly, but the ponies always stand very solidly on four broad-based hooves caught in stride. My Little Ponies are available in a range of pastels and in more intense colors such as bright turquoise, hot pink, and deep

53. Horses in "fantasy colors": packaging for Sparkle Ponies.

purple. The palette of colors is based on the exclusion of brown and black (the colors of real animals) and of primary red, blue, and green (the colors of boys' clothes and boys' toys). Each pony has a different name and a different decoration painted on the haunch that stands as a totem for its name (butterflies, stars, flowers). All ponies are made in China; all come with a brush; all cost between four and ten dollars. They are sold at Kmart, Target, Toys "R" Us, Costco: never at upscale toy stores or stores that specialize in educational goods.

My Little Ponies appeal to girls as collectors, cultivating an appreciation of small differences in color and design from object to object. The toys themselves are low-tech. The principle for line extensions is based almost entirely on cosmetic changes, on distinc-

54. A child's My Little Pony collection: small differences in color and design.

tions of appearance and name. As with consumer goods targeted at adult women, such as clothing and home furnishings, the shopper is encouraged to buy many different products in the same category. Color or other design features (style) are the realm of diversification among objects that are essentially similar.[19] Like all fashions, conformity and individuality are involved here: choosing one's favorite pony means exercising individual taste while acquiring a toy that will look like all other ponies. This principle applies to most toys available to girls: there are relatively few successful brands or models (Barbie, Cabbage Patch), compared with boys' toys, but there are hundreds of different styles within each brand.

Ponies live in an idyllic outdoor world of flowers, birds, butterflies, bunnies, and fun. The name on the package is written across a rainbow. The packaging emphasizes that Ponyland is a world of miracles and magic, of helpful, laughing, playing ponies. Every package includes a cheerful story about the pony that emphasizes its visually dazzling qualities and its physical agility:

> "Rise and Shine," Sunspot called to the sleeping ponies, but they only yawned and snuggled deeper into their beds. "I know how to wake them!" she thought, flying into the air. She flew up to her friend, Mr. Sun, and whispered in his ear. Smiling happily, she sent sunbeams into the ponies' bedroom windows. The sunbeams filled each room and sprinkled glittering flecks of sunshine on the ponies. They awoke with smiling faces, and cheerfully tossed some of the bright flecks on Sunspot as she skipped into their bedrooms.[20]

Being ponies, rather than baby dolls to be taken care of, these toys allow for a certain kind of freedom: fantasies of galloping, flying, swimming. They are not, however, for riding. Play involves being a pony yourself, not owning one as a pet. The ponies exist outside the world of mommies, grocery stores, automobiles, schools, shopping malls. All of the ponies, like the groups of children who play with them, are girls, with the exception of the rare appearance of a baby brother. Boyfriends and the attraction of the opposite sex, which figure so prominently in other toys for girls, have no place here. Neither the human characters from the animated series nor the villains are available for purchase.

The success of My Little Pony spawned many imitations. Mattel worked vigorously to launch a competitor. Its Little Pretty line of kittens and puppies bore a strong resemblance to the ponies. Little Pretties were sold in sets: for example, the Little Pretty Polished Paws Kitty set included Catra, Peekablue Kitty, Bow Kitty, Happy Feet Kitty, and Dixie Kitty. Mattel, whose fortune was made with Barbie, tried to combine Barbie's glamour and interest in the opposite sex with the animal motif. (The kitties are female, the puppies male.) One package reads:

> "I'm a Polished Paws Kitty and I love to look pretty" sang Catra, as she pounced on a leaf. Just then her puppy pal Dixie ran up: "Quick, we're going to have our pictures taken for the newspaper!" Catra quickly polished her paws her favorite shade of red, then purring proudly pussyfooted it to the photographer.[21]

The Little Pretty line has met with only limited success. One reason was that parents and children were resisting the obsessions with clothing and boys that characterize Barbie and her many imitations. My Little Pony has proven singular in the longevity of its success as a girls' license. I believe this was due to the relative innocence of the concept and the depth of little girls' identification with the utopian world of the ponies. Many middle-class parents are offended by the kitschiness of the ponies' design, which mirrors low-culture taste, but at least they aren't Barbie.

My Little Pony and *My Little Pony, The Movie* were never part of the Saturday morning network schedule—they were one-shot specials and limited syndication offerings—but they live on long past their original release dates (1985–1986) as rentals at the home video store.[22] *My Little Pony* is the kind of tape that girls pick out from the shelves at the video rental store; they recognize from the pink boxes and from the flowers, animals, and rainbows that this is for them. In educated middle-class families, the girls' enthusiasm for *My Little Pony* (and their satisfaction in correctly identifying the videos targeted at them) is met with parental disdain for kitsch and disapproval of sex-stereotyped entertainment. Some parents recommend substitute tapes, such as educational shows, fairy tale adaptations, or videos with more realistic settings and a mixture of male and female characters—in short, the public television–style fare favored by the college-educated middle class. Parents want more from children's videos than mere entertainment and try to inculcate this lesson through discussions at the video store. Such attempts to get children to emulate the respectable norms of television consumption meet with limited success, since young children tend to be more interested in real or imagined peer-group affiliations than in adult approval.

Parents and children recognize that, in Bourdieu's formulation, "taste classifies," but they have different systems of evaluation at stake. When middle-class parents complain of their children's bad taste in videos—judging children's selections as escapist, repetitive, trivial (out for fun rather than redeemed by a loftier educational goal, such as learning letters and numbers or zoological information)—they repeat the familiar strategy of dismissing the consumption of lower, inferior groups as merely hedonistic. Rarely do middle-class parents explicitly recognize that the conflict stems from the fact that mass-market children's toys and videos lean toward working-class aesthetics, gender representations, and popular genres. The parental position, which encourages more ambitious motivations for consumption than mere enjoyment, has been well described by Bourdieu, who argues that it "implies an affirmation of the superiority of those who can be satisfied with the sublimated, refined, disinterested, gratuitous, distinguished pleasures forever closed to the profane."[23] One of my local video stores (staffed almost entirely by college graduates in film studies) stopped carrying *Rainbow Brite* in 1990 because it received too many complaints from parents—"The children loved it but the parents hated it!" the manager told me.

My Little Pony plays its childlike and female orientation totally straight: no attempt is made to appeal to a broader audience—and this, I argue, is the reason for its success. Something was gained and lost when marketers and video producers began exploiting little girls as a separate market. Little girls found themselves in a ghetto-ized culture that no self-respecting boy would take an interest in; but for once girls were not required to cross over, to take on an ambiguous identification with a group of male characters.

In the following section, I offer a plot synopsis of three *My Little Pony* videos, focusing on their borrowing from women's popular culture genres, their range of character types, and their psychological themes. Doing this has taught me above all that children's cartoons have complicated narratives. It was surprisingly difficult to summarize these videos, given the many twists and turns of plot that occur within half an hour. There is an important lesson in this: adults tend to think children's videos are simple and closed to any but a single interpretation, because adults rarely watch children's videos in their entirety. By describing each video at length, I hope to demonstrate both their complexity and their openness to a variety of interpretations. As with most television, children watch these with mixed levels of attention, focusing in on what they consider the good spots, often letting their attention waver—perhaps while they play with their miniature plastic replicas of the characters on the screen.

In "Mish Mash Melee," Windwhistler, Dizzy, and two other ponies experience an adventure that takes them to the brink of ecological disaster and back again. The episode takes place in the "mystificent" forest of the Delldroves, gnomelike male creatures who replenish their land by polishing stones and hammering acorns in an underground factory. As Windwhistler notes, "They are an orderly and well-balanced society, and they do all this work without any glory or reward." While in the factory, the ponies accidentally upset a barrel marked "Balance." Colored drops called Frazzits escape, causing the Delldroves to smash the acorns and pulverize the stones and the ponies to act out of character. The ponies celebrate the fun of "being somebody else" with a musical number, but they realize that balance must be restored. Dizzy, who is usually scatter-brained, organizes a scheme that returns the Frazzits to the barrel for good. The Delldroves gather to thank the ponies, and Wind-whistler credits Dizzy with saving the day. When Dizzy, scatter-brained again, says, "I did?" the group shares a good laugh, and the screen goes to black.

This episode employs a number of narrative conventions from science fiction and fantastic literature that are frequently used in the plots of contemporary children's cartoons: the escape of a contaminating substance (the Frazzits); the existence of a parallel or lost world (the Delldroves); the placing of familiar characters in altered states induced by changes in body chemistry or sometimes by the substitution of a mechanical double (the ponies' altered personalities when the Frazzits are released). In "Mish Mash Melee," the altered-state device from science fiction provides the motivation for the cartoon's obligatory musical number. All of the girls' cartoons include musical numbers in which the characters express their true feelings of the moment. In boys' cartoons, none of the characters burst into song unless it is motivated in the story or clearly set off from the rest of the story as a music-video interlude.

The ecological themes in "Mish Mash Melee" are common to a variety of boys' and girls' cartoons produced in the 1980s: *Rainbow Brite, He-Man, Ghostbusters, Thundercats, The Care Bears.* (In 1990 the theme became the mainstay of Ted Turner's *Captain Planet* series.) Animators render pollution and toxic waste as colorful enemies that allow considerable artistic freedom in their visualization. The vaguely environmentalist themes that emerge in the cartoons are usually inoffensive to parents, prosocial and relatively nonviolent. Pollution can be seen as a contemporary interpretation of the images of blight and infertility that have typically motivated the hero's quest in the romance.[24] Often the cartoons portray the terrible effects of pollution, which temporarily transforms the cartoon's setting into a wasteland: Ponyland is frozen or stripped of color;[25] Rainbowland is turned brown; a ruined, smoking Manhattan under a sort of postnuclear holocaust sky appears repeatedly in *Ghostbusters.*

In girls' cartoons, the threat of toxicity and the turning of a homeland into a wasteland often motivates a group to act together as a team, replacing the traditional figure of the lone hero setting off on a quest. Thus, a set of cute, tiny girls (or furry female creatures) proves to be capable of nothing short of saving the world. In girls' cartoons, redemption often takes the form of a cleanup rather than a direct battle with a villain using weapons. In *Rainbow Brite, Strawberry Shortcake, The Care Bears, Fraggle Rock,* and *My Little Pony,* there is a vision of work behind the scenes that typically represents natural forces in the form of the industrial factory. The color in Rainbowland, for example, comes from "Star Sprinkles" that are produced by midget mascots called Sprites; working in an underground operation that is a cross between a factory and a bakery with a furnace and conveyor belt, the Sprites press out stars with cookie cutters. In "Mish Mash Melee," we find a typical attribution of natural processes (weathering of stones or sprouting of trees) to industrial techniques and the assembly line. Underlying the forest floor is a factory. In *Fraggle Rock*, a society of miniature workers, called Doozers, exists parallel to the Fraggles. Doozers do nothing but build. These representations serve both to relegate all natural processes to industrial ones and to form an image of a perfect society of workers: the Delldroves work all day without glory or reward. Although the workers are represented as very tiny and nonhuman, they essentially represent adulthood.

The girls' programs take cognizance of work behind the scenes, the work that adults do, and sometimes express an admiration for the discipline, order, and hard work that constantly occur. This workers-behind-the-scenes motif is exclusive to girls' cartoons. On boys' shows magic, bravery, weaponry, and combat produce the results; no imagination is wasted on the boring, sacrificial, repetitive work that adults might do. (And the main characters are themselves often already adults, as in *Thundercats, Ghostbusters,* and *He-Man*, or nearly so, as in *Teenage Mutant Ninja Turtles.*) In the magical settings of the girls' cartoons, a less exciting, more mundane picture of adult work and responsibility is never far out of sight.

In "Baby, It's Cold Outside," the ponies again save the world, but this time by teaching a wise lesson about compassion and emotional warmth. Evil King Charlatan of the North Pole, a penguin, wants to take over the world by freezing it with his new machine. His first victim is Sunny, a little duck who is also his son's best friend. Back in Ponyland, Galaxy has noticed that the rivers and even the ever-present rainbow are freezing and sends Surprise to find Megan, the human heroine of the series, a blond, blue-eyed girl of about eight. Surprise sings a song of determination and courage ("We're not gonna freeze, no sir!") and then travels with the other ponies and Megan to the North Pole. There they find themselves trapped in a maze, chased by a gorilla, captured, and imprisoned. After applying various kinds of problem solving (can they tunnel out? bend the bars?), they escape and join forces with Prince Edward and the frozen Sunny. The group finally reaches King Charlatan, who reacts with such rage that he freezes his own son. Megan sings her argument with the king as she boldly points her finger at him: "How can you be so cold?" During the song, we see flashbacks of King Charlatan as a good father, giving the infant Edward a bottle, cradling him and playing with him. The king is moved to tears, which melt the ice around his son, and the ponies blast the evil machine with a magic ray. Megan and the ponies smile approvingly at the scene of paternal love and walk off into the sunset.

Both boys' and girls' animated series of the 1980s routinely associate villainy with technology, thus borrowing a strain of technophobia from science fiction novels. Male and female heroes use different means to wrest the technologically based power from the villains. In boys' cartoons, evil uses of technology—typically, the desire to take over the world and subordinate all others—are pitted against good uses of technology by the heroes. The audience hopes that the good guys' guns, lasers, swords, or ninja weapons—combined with cleverness—will be sufficient to put down the bad guys. In girls' cartoons, direct conflicts employing weapons or evil machines are avoided. In "Baby, It's Cold Outside," Megan tries to talk King Charlatan out of his evil, while his power is turned against himself. Megan and the ponies encounter mazes, traps, and physical barriers on their journey to confront the villain. Overcoming obstacles and extricating oneself from a trap provide the suspense, rather than direct, hand-to-hand or weapon-to-weapon battles. Once the villain is encountered, the heroines must shame him into admitting error and showing remorse. In *My Little Pony* the villains resemble those of the classic quest-romance, as described by Northrop Frye: "The antagonists of the quest are often sinister figures, giants, ogres, witches and magicians, that clearly have a parental origin." [26] The end results in the girls' cartoons are rehabilitation, reform, and reintegration into a community rather than, as in the boy's cartoons, zapping away the villain forever or locking it in a "ghost trap" or "containment chamber" as in *Ghostbusters*.

In *My Little Pony*, as in *The Care Bears* and *Rainbow Brite*, threat is founded on feeling. Typically, emotional coldness is the real evil: King Charlatan's icy stare propels the machine that could take over the world. Feelings rule the world. All of the childlike heroines, whether as teams or as individuals such as Megan and Rainbow Brite, possess the acumen of psychotherapists and the bravery of saints. They demonstrate that most courses of action can be changed through increased self-knowledge, through understanding a deed's consequences, through remembering someone you love. Emotional insight turns out to be the most powerful force in the world, and all the heroines possess it to a superior degree and in abundant quantities. The villains are usually male (even in the case of an evil queen, her henchmen are always male); the healers are female. Often the villains are incorrigible, infantile figures, like the *Rainbow Brite* villains Murky, a short, balding, middle-aged man, and his companion Lurky, a big, brown blob of a creature; or the bald Professor Coldheart of *The Care Bears.* All men are babies in this world order, and hostility and aggression can be cured by a combination of firmness and kindness.

Absent in *My Little Pony* is one of the central figures of girls' fiction: the rebellious, headstrong, egocentric preadolescent who eventually gets her comeuppance. Like Madeleine or Pollyanna, these girls end up, like many adult women in melodramatic fiction, bedridden from illness or accident. A number of series designed for a mixed audience of boys and girls, of the kind stamped with the approval of the National Education Association and shown on PBS, feature such a female as a permanent character in a predominantly male cast: Miss Piggy of *The Muppets* and Baby Piggy of *Muppet Babies* are examples of this type, as are Red of *Fraggle Rock* and Whazzat of *Zoobilee Zoo.* These female characters enjoy more latitude in their behavior than does a figure like Megan—they get to be tomboys or to be unapologetically narcissistic or selfish—but in the end there is usually punishment and remorse and an explicit moral lesson about the dangers of selfishness. On *My Little Pony*, there are only mature big sisters who already know how to act like wise, sympathetic mothers. They are ever prepared to deal with the feelings of all, to ferret out sorrow or inadequacy or coldness. There is a kind of power in Megan's position when she stands up to the penguin father and lectures him about his coldness. Though she does not break many rules of femininity, she is allowed the privilege of being always right. Unlike the more rebellious heroines who are eventually chastised for their selfishness and immaturity and lack of consideration, the ponies and their friends always possess moral rectitude. The girls are always on the side of the angels.

In "The Glass Princess," the threat to Ponyland is tied to one pony's sense of inadequacy and self-doubt. The forty-five–minute episode, planned as an hour-long special for television, opens with Shady repeatedly failing exercise drills for the pony olympics: "Everyone thinks I'm useless, and they're probably mad at me for messing things up." Meanwhile, Princess Porcina, a vain middle-aged pig who lives in a messy castle, discovers that her magic cloak is wearing thin. The cloak allows her to turn all things into glass so she can admire her own image everywhere. Her henchmen, the Raptorians, capture a group of ponies, whose hair they plan to

55. The vain Princess Porcina giving orders to the pony Galaxy.

56. The grooming conveyor belt: hair care as torture.

weave into a new cloak. They tie the ponies on a conveyor belt and move them through an operation that resembles a carwash: shower heads, dryer, mechanical arms with towels, curlers, powder, combs, brushes, and makeup. Once Porcina has the new cloak in hand, she unthinkingly turns Ponyland into glass at the request of the Raptorians, who have their own evil designs for world conquest. Back in Ponyland, Megan learns of the kidnapping and begins to organize a rescue mission, while Shady blames herself for all the trouble ("If only I hadn't been so oversensitive, maybe I could have helped."). It is Shady, though, who hatches the plan that saves the day. When the characters finally confront each other, Porcina sees the error and, instead of turning the ponies to glass, turns the Raptorians into ice ("Don't worry, they never felt it. They never felt anything, not about you or me."). Porcina becomes a groomer for the Bushwoolies, a group of diminutive forest creatures who live in Ponyland and occasionally help the ponies. Megan praises Shady: "Your bravery and good thinking came through when we needed it most."

Shady's feelings of inadequacy form the backdrop for the formidable complications of plot in "The Glass Princess," as they do in several other episodes and in *My Little Pony, The Movie*. Shady's often repetitive recitation of her own worthlessness provides the story's only breaks from the action. Many girls' cartoons focus on a character's wounded or resentful feelings, and often these feelings function as a catalyst in the plot by leaving a character sufficiently vulnerable and isolated that she is easily taken advantage of by the villain. Males such as Murky and Lurky in *Rainbow Brite* and the

57. The Raptorians aggressively combing pony manes.

58. An interspecies democracy of peers. The rescuers: Megan as the leader, surrounded by ponies and Bushwoolies.

Raptorians in *My Little Pony* prey on the female feelings of inadequacy. One of the most common character flaws in girls' cartoons is being too sensitive and self-critical. While there is always a cheery ending, characters often suffer from an underlying depression. But Shady is also ambitious in a way; she wants to stand out from the crowd, to make a unique contribution, to gain some credit and recognition. Porcina has obviously gone too far in this direction; her narcissistic ambition has left her ridiculous and vulnerable.

Shady's voice is especially grating to adults: a high-pitched, singsong, nasal whine. Early in the episode, Maureen, Megan's younger sister, comforts Shady as she sings, "All wrong, all wrong, all my plans always go all wrong . . . I'm a klutz and I don't belong." Each of the ponies has one personality attribute that is primary: Shady's is feeling insecure and inadequate. She is unable to distinguish herself with a special talent; she is inept at sports; she inadvertently does the wrong thing; she causes trouble for her friends. If Shady represents a masochistic response to the problem of being a little girl, she at least represents an acknowledgment of that identity as problematic. The drama of the girls' cartoons regularly revolves around feelings of worthlessness, a narrative motivation unheard of—perhaps logically impossible—in the boys' cartoons.

59. Maureen comforting Shady, who feels "all wrong." Shady's feelings of inadequacy are taken seriously in the story.

Why is there this difference from boys' cartoons? Valerie Walkerdine has analyzed the precarious position of girls in a world where the official word as handed down by liberal teachers is that gender is unimportant. To succeed in the classroom, girls must present themselves as active learners; but our culture symbolizes activity as male, passivity as female. There may be an irreconcilable conflict between identifying with the female, and with the mother, and identifying with the part of the good student. Walkerdine argues that the failure to acknowledge the conflicts inherent in the role of the little girl, and these split identifications, can be especially harmful:

> Our education system in its most liberal form treats girls "as if" they were boys. Equal opportunities and much work on sex-role stereotyping deny difference in a most punitive and harmful way. . . . A denial of the reality of difference means that the girl must bear the burden of her anxiety herself. It is literally not spoken. She is told that she can be successful and yet the painful recognition that is likely to result from the fear of loss of one or the other (her femininity, her success, or both) is a failure to be either, producing neurotic anxiety, depression or worse. . . . In a sense, then, rather than perpetuating the denial operating in the

spurious circulation of needs, fulfillment and happiness, a recognition of struggle, conflict, difficulty and pain might actually serve to aid such girls.[27]

Shady's feeling "all wrong" seems to represent the very struggle Walkerdine suggests: Shady feels inadequate, and then she feels ashamed for feeling dejected. Male peers are not around to compete with; traditional femininity is validated. Megan's skills and achievements are those of the good mother. But the ponies, unlike the girls, are allowed to feel negative, sad, listless, and insecure.

Most obviously, girls' cartoons present an unambiguous, segregated world of the feminine. Segregation by gender (within the audience and among the characters), the display of traditional feminine behaviors, and the use of kitschy aesthetic codes (pink and furry) in the girls' cartoons have offended many television critics and child educators, whose position is usually implicitly informed by a liberal feminist political agenda and middle-class norms for cultural consumption. Adults prefer their children's consumption to be rational and politically correct and associate certain political beliefs (equality of the sexes) with the selection of clothing, toys, books, and videos that gravitate toward "gender-neutral" styles: primary colors, coeducational groups of characters (boys and girls together), and more abstract decorative motifs, such as those based on alphabets, numbers, or geometric shapes. My Little Pony violates these adult-oriented and upper middle-class taste codes and offers instead representations that historically belong to "low culture": flamboyant colors and hairstyles; wide-eyed, babyish animal figures; and a baroque flair for decorative detail. Thus some adults perceive their child's interest in My Little Pony as a consumption error, driven by peer-group identification but inappropriate to their familial class membership. Parents are disturbed by children's lack of individuality, their herd instinct for loving My Little Pony and other mass-culture fads (while often failing to recognize the large measure of conformity that generally governs adults' seemingly more individualistic and "unique" selections among "higher-class" consumer goods). Children's taste for My Little Pony embarrasses educated middle-class parents because it represents an emulation of working-class aesthetics and a blatant marking of gender difference that seems incompatible with liberal feminist ideals.

In *Feminist Politics and Human Nature*, Allison Jaggar has argued that rationality and individualism are the cornerstones of political rights in liberal political philosophy, so liberal feminism must assert the female capacity for both of these. Liberal feminists minimize gender differences. Liberal feminism looks forward to a future in which psychological differences between men and women, boys and girls will be much less pronounced and education, once it is truly providing equal opportunities, will further enhance the female capacity for the development of reason. But female gender socialization, as well as the work women are expected to do as adults, poses special problems for the liberal conception of individualism and rationality. As Jaggar explains:

> The instrumentalist strand within the liberal conception of rationality equates rational behavior with the efficient maximization of individual utility. To be rational in this sense it is necessary, although not sufficient, for an individual to be egoistic. As we saw earlier, liberal theorists assume that all individuals tend toward egoism, even though they may be capable of a greater or lesser degree of limited altruism. While this model may provide a plausible approximation for the behavior of contemporary males, it is obvious immediately that it is much less appropriate to the behavior of women, who often find their own fulfillment in serving others.[28]

Megan and Maureen encourage the ponies to voice their emotions, so they can be cured of the negative ones. It is easy to see this aspect of the plot as simply parroting a therapeutic, self-help strategy made popular through television talk shows, talk radio, self-help groups, and popular advice literature, as Stephen Kline has done. But rather than reinforcing the need for individual solutions to problems, *My Little Pony* emphasizes the importance of the loyal community of females. "I tried to be so helpful," sings Shady. Maureen assures her: "Shady, it's not your fault." The self-deprecating pony makes herself or others vulnerable to the more powerful forces of evil, but in the world of *My Little Pony* there is safety in numbers. Shady's sulking might cause some ponies to be captured, but another group will come to their rescue. As Tania Modleski has said about the seemingly powerless heroines of the romance, "victims endure." In the end, the group rallies around to affirm the importance of each member. Like the members of a good family, Megan, Maureen, and the ponies learn to respect individual differences and to be vigilantly attentive to one another's feelings.

The commitment to and sense of belonging in a group surpass the individual's needs. This is the moral of the story.

"The Glass Princess" expresses a deep ambivalence toward those aspects of girls' socialization having to do with physical appearance. The most traumatic moment in the cartoon is when the ponies are tied down to have their hair washed and curled, a routine familiar to little girls in many different cultures. Porcina verbally directs this torturous exercise, but it is the sinister Raptorians who carry out the dirty work and seem to relish the ponies' distress. Hair care is such a traumatic and difficult aspect of gender socialization that a host of consumer products have been developed and marketed that promise to make it a happier experience for parents and children: no-tears shampoo; headbands and neck rests to help keep soap out of eyes; cream rinses to take the pain out of combing wet hair. Feminists have seen hair grooming as the first lesson in submission for the sake of appearance. It is a long and troubled one, especially for African American girls. The success of the My Little Pony toys may largely be due to the fact that they double as bath toys. Girls' play with ponies often involves doing to the ponies what mothers' have done to them, washing hair, combing and brushing it, fixing it with ribbons and barrettes.[29]

Girls' animated series in the 1980s borrowed from popular genres for adult women. In *My Little Pony*, the ethos of the soap opera—that feelings are all important—is combined with some conventions of the paperback romance, which, as Tania Modleski and Janice Radway have argued in their powerful work on the subject, are worthy of serious consideration by critics interested in the possibilities for producing popular feminist narratives. Like the soap opera, there is an emphasis on understanding the often mysterious codes of feelings. Unlike the soap opera, the characters never appear in the domestic sphere. In *My Little Pony*, Megan is transported away from her real home to straighten out the world. Adventure comes with her departure from her home (when the ponies come to pick her up, she is usually already out in the yard of her house). Megan's position is similar to that of the sympathetic heroines of soap opera: the mothers who worry over all their children's (read ponies') competing desires.[30] In the animated series, there is a somewhat more affirmative order, a greater effectivity of female action than on soap opera. The axioms of popular psychology *work* here: revelations change evildoers instantaneously, and males can be quickly set right.

These cartoons dramatize the thrill of vulnerability found in the paperback romance, minus the romantic love. The ponies often find themselves wandering through a maze, similar to the heroine's search through the mansion in the gothic romance. (Feminist critics have argued that the house represents the mother's body.[31]) The good characters on girls' cartoons resemble the heroine of the romance: modest, unassuming, average, flawed. In the end the heroine in the romance is loved for just who she is: so on the girls' cartoon the individuals in the group are accepted no matter what their feelings, no matter what mistakes they have made.

Tania Modleski has argued that a utopian strain exists in the traditional women's genres of popular culture, the soap opera, gothic novel, and romance. A utopian element also exists in the girls' animated series. The animals live in a happy playful world of love and friendship. When in danger, a coterie of friends always arrives to back them up; the word is more powerful than the sword. The viewer can shift between identifications with the humans Megan or Maureen, or with the ponies themselves, and thereby acquire a long list of magical physical abilities, such as flying or disappearing. These are the pleasures to be gained by an identification with the universe of the girls' series.

The criticism of the toy-based shows as a practice made it harder to notice what was most unusual about many of the shows: that they were reaching out to the audience of little girls, and that this necessitated changing and adapting the conventions of the cartoon in significant ways. Of course, not all of the toy-based shows catered to the audience of girls in the same way or to the same extent. *The Smurfs*, for example, counted a lone female called Smurfette among its dozens of characters, and *The Smurfs* television series relied on standard male-adventure plots. *The Pound Puppies* used roughly equal numbers of male and female dogs and mixed melodrama and detective fiction in its stories about locating dog owners or lost puppies. But marketing for girls brought about some interesting innovations in many of the animated television series: however crassly commercial the toy tie-in, shows like *My Little Pony* and *Rainbow Brite* created fictional worlds in which females were dominant. It was hardly feminist, and it starred blond, blue-eyed girls, but it offered much more than the literary and media fare in which girls are nearly always required to identify with boys and men. In that respect, *My Little Pony* achieved something rarely accomplished in educational public television—the television fare most palatable to the intellectual middle class. Parents should understand that for the little girl at the video or toy store to choose *My Little Pony*, then, is to make a quite rational choice among the limited offerings of children's consumer culture. The choice is not made out of identification with an insipid and powerless femininity but out of identification with the limited sources of power and fantasy that are available in the commercial culture of femininity.

6

ACTION TV FOR BOYS

SLIMER AND THE REAL GHOSTBUSTERS

> They don't trust humans, they don't want anything to do with people or cities. They're vicious, fearless, and very mean.
> —EGON IN *Slimer and the Real Ghostbusters*

In 1991, *Slimer and the Real Ghostbusters* began its fifth year on Saturday morning network television. Like *Teenage Mutant Ninja Turtles*, it can be seen every day of the week in syndication on cable stations such as the Fox network. Kenner introduced Ghostbusters figures in 1986, and they enjoyed three years at the top of the best-selling toys list (before being replaced by Teenage Mutant Ninja Turtles). The vice president of licensing for Kenner products described the development process this way:

> The Real Ghostbusters line gave kids power over ghosts, helping them alleviate their fears. In time, and in direct correlation to the success of the line, the concept was elevated to levels that weren't immediately apparent in initial stages. . . . The popularity of the TV animation has been a major factor in the appeal of the product among three- to five-year olds, as is true for many other top properties in the industry. This was particularly important with a property such as Ghostbusters, which, in its original incarnation as a feature film, appealed to an older audience.[1]

In its transformation from popular adult film to children's cartoon, *Ghostbusters* drew on conventions of the male action team developed in Hollywood war films and on Saturday morning television series such as *The Fantastic Four*; on the mix of comedy and ghost-chasing detective work established on *Scooby-Doo*; and on the fascination with technology and science familiar from 1950s science fiction films and from children's series such as *Johnny Quest*.

Like the movie, Ghostbusters toys mix humor with action-adventure. Toy industry experts currently believe humor is the wave of the future in boys' toys. There is a blatantly parodic, tongue-in-cheek aspect to Teenage Mutant Ninja Turtles, Toxic Crusaders, and Barnyard Commandoes. The conventions of action-adventure genres are obviously both available as play fantasies *and* being lampooned by Ninja Turtles, who use pizza cutters as weapons and revere a Japanese rat as their master.[2] In comparison with the Ghostbusters, a character such as G.I. Joe seems stuck in another era and an older tradition of realist play. Ghostbusters action figures—like Turtles, Barnyard Commandoes, Garbage Pail Kids, and Toxic Crusaders—are themselves caricatured figures, replicas of the cartoon, not the movie version. Action figures and weapons are the standard ingredients of boys' play, but Ghostbusters added the element of "grossness" now common to boys' toys. For example, one Ghostbusters toy called Fearsome Flush is a toilet in which a red tongue and teeth pop out of the seat while a hideous face pops out of the tank. In stark contrast to the predictable niceness of girls' toys, nasty surprises lurk everywhere in the Ghostbusters toys: they are ugly, transformable, "gross," rude, completely outside conventional civility and politeness. For example, Granny Gross Ghost is a little old woman whose abdomen opens up to reveal a huge gaping mouth. In this way, some of the Ghostbusters merchandise seems calculated to attract little boys by repulsing mothers—a marketing strategy that is obviously limited for age groups in which mothers generally make the purchases for young boys.

The animated series includes most of the characters from the movie, with Peter Venckmann (the part originated by Bill Murray) and Egon Spengler (Harold Ramis's role) in the "starring" roles; two other Ghostbusters, Ray Stantz and Winston Zeddmore, and the secretary Janine Melnitz play the supporting parts. The children's cartoon omits the Sigourney Weaver character and expands the role of Slimer, a green, flying ghost about the size of a dog, who is a mascot permanently in residence at Ghostbusters headquarters. Slimer is amorphous, sentimental, supremely infantile, and obsessed with food. In his voice (high pitched and slurred) and androgynous appearance he resembles many of the animated blobs who inhabit the girls' cartoons: the Sprites in *Rainbow Brite*, the Bushwoolies

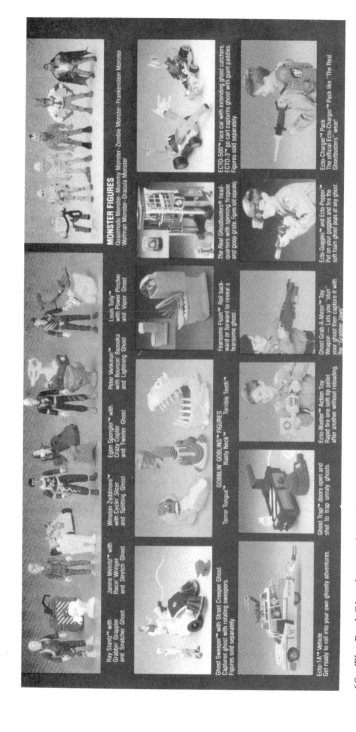

60. *The Real Ghostbusters line of toys: nasty surprises lurk everywhere.*

61. Slimer is amorphous, infantile, and obsessed with food.

in *My Little Pony.* Unlike them, Slimer is a single character rather than one among a legion of such creatures. He plays baby brother to the Ghostbusters and is so important to the plots that he gets top billing and the starring part in the third of the three segments (about fifteen minutes each) that make up an hour's broadcast.

In the cartoons devoted to Slimer, he is teamed with Janine, as the adult figure, and her pet cat, Slimer's nemesis. These segments follow classic formulas of chase and combat, in the tradition of Tweety and Sylvester, Tom and Jerry, Porky Pig, and Bugs Bunny. They are short on plot and long on chaos. Slimer's stories are pitched to a younger audience than the Ghostbusters' segments and offer a chance to unwind after the scary bits of the Ghostbusters' stories. The plots on *Slimer and the Real Ghostbusters* are less intricate than those of *My Little Pony*: there are fewer characters, and repetitive displays of chase and combat are emphasized rather than repeated twists and turns of fate that must be understood in a specific temporal order. In addition to differences in forms of narrative organization, boys' and girls' cartoons use different generic codes: *Ghostbusters* relies on horror, science fiction, slapstick; *My Little Pony* on romance and melodrama.

In the opening of "Kitty Cornered," a cat riding on a witch's broomstick falls out of the sky and lands on a pizza, which is delivered to Slimer at Ghostbusters headquarters. Slimer, who had not ordered the pizza, is delighted and becomes very attached to the cat. Soon the Ghostbusters surmise that the cat is a "familiar" that can focus the witch's magical powers. "Attuned only to supernatural beings," the cat is now granting all of Slimer's wishes (and had, in fact, read his unspoken wish for the pizza). Egon warns, "No more wishes, Slimer; having unlimited wishes could prove entirely dangerous," and tries to separate the two at bedtime. But the cat escapes and settles in to sleep on Slimer's stomach. When Slimer dreams of "chow time," the refrigerator fills with animated food that attacks Ray. When he dreams about a toy cat to replace a broken one, a huge "Transmogrifier" appears and demands to play. A dream about Christmas produces a tree with presents under it and an aggressive Santa three stories tall. Just then, the witch arrives to reclaim her familiar. She gets into an argument with Santa and, with a thick Bronx accent, orders him away. As she and the familiar depart, Slimer whispers one final wish in the cat's ear. When the Ghostbusters return to the kitchen, they find a sandwich as big as the room awaiting Slimer for his midnight snack.

As in the classic ghost story, feelings are taken out of the realm of personal interactions and projected onto the supernatural. When Slimer's desires assume ghostly form, they become unpredictable, often menacing, and typically need the Ghostbusters' technological control. In "Kitty Cornered," the familiar seems harmless (a sweet feline pet), but there is a sinister aspect to her creations: the demanding food, the domineering toy, the slightly seedy Santa. In other episodes hauntings result from past injury, from historical wrongs left unavenged: a wicked capitalist returns to reclaim the fortune he has buried so as to evade taxes; the victims of a train wreck haunt the subway; a witch executed during the Salem witchcraft trials wreaks havoc in a girls' school. What goes around comes around, and the Ghostbusters often must do some historical research to discover the injustice of the past that is producing ghosts in the present.

Slimer is a supernatural being with decidedly human desires: unlimited orality and greediness for consumer goods. There is a lot of trouble when Slimer gets everything he wants. Supernatural forces regularly "possess" the products of consumer culture, which Slimer desires, and these things take over the (domesticated) space of headquarters, wreaking havoc and destruction. In *My Little Pony* and in *Rainbow Brite*, everything takes place outdoors, in a magical pastoral scene. Commodity culture does not exist in that universe: absent are food, toys, cars, even houses. In contrast, *Ghostbusters* takes place in a world filled with commodities that prove to be haunted. This is one of the recurring themes on the series—the monstrousness lurking behind everyday consumer goods. Products take on a power of their own and threaten to take over the humans. Hideous growths that turn into ghosts may arrive in the pizza delivered to the door; ghosts invade the new compact disk player, and the machine begins ejecting disks so rapidly that they become a kind of lethal Frisbee. Ghosts take over the supermarket and begin throwing food down the aisles. The coin-operated kiddie ride outside the grocery store grows to an enormous size and walks off its stand. When Slimer wins the lottery, the money itself turns out to be dirty and possessed. So each of the gifts he buys for the Ghostbusters turns out to be haunted as well: a new suit of clothes attacks Peter, and the new Cadillac for Winston turns into an incinerating death trap.

Slimer represents the pleasure *and* the fear of regression on two levels: in his relationship to consumer goods *and* in his ego development. Slimer delights in consumer goods while he discovers their unreliability as sources of satisfaction. *Ghostbusters* offers a split identification between Slimer, who wants it all—what the Freudians would call unlimited orality—and the Ghostbusters, who try to contain the demons and thwart Slimer's desires. The stories make room for a great deal of ambivalence. It would be fun to have your dreams come true (as in "Kitty Cornered"), but that is only possible through identification with a younger self, a self vulnerable to parental force feeding, to nasty scares from toys and Santas. In this and other respects, *Ghostbusters* seems to beg a Freudian interpretation of the story as a battle between the id (Slimer, the baby) and the superego (the adult Ghostbusters). In contrast to this, Megan, her little sister Maureen, and the ponies are unerringly selfless, committed to the group, ready for sacrifice and bravery. (There is no battle of superego and id in the girls' cartoon: the superego has already won.) They are already grown-up: regression of the Slimer variety is no longer an option. Occasionally, Megan's little brother Danny appears in the story lines, a wild little boy who is naughty enough to require Megan's constant surveillance and correction. In these animated series, regression to the pleasure principle is permitted only to males never to females.

"Camping It Up" follows the Ghostbusters on a vacation camping trip. Ray (the father figure in this episode) takes them on an adventure-filled drive to the campground. When they arrive, Janine assembles them for a group photograph. Unknown to them, Big Foot, a huge apelike creature, lurks in the trees. As the Ghostbusters set up camp, they tease each other good-naturedly about what each one packed: Peter's TV, Egon's special gadgetry. Around the camp-fire that night, the Ghostbusters discover Big Foot hiding behind a tree, eavesdropping on Ray's ghost stories. They chase and catch Big Foot and then welcome him into the group when Egon assures them that he is harmless. Janine feeds him and cares for him like a child. Soon Egon notices that "strong PKE readings" are coming from Big Foot. After a lightning storm, he announces that Big Foot must be returned to his home on the other side of a waterfall to restore environmental balance, and with one of his gadgets he in-flates a raft that takes them there. The falls are the "door between our world and another," and the Ghostbusters walk to the heavenly and unreal-looking "other side," where Big Foot says a sentimental farewell to his little friend Slimer. Packing up at the campsite, Peter grabs Egon's tent and loads it into the car, Ecto I. He accidentally drops Egon's remote control, which inflates the tent and blows everything up. "Maybe we should hang around here a few more days," Peter jokes sheepishly.

62. Big Foot gives Slimer a fright.

In this type of episode, *Ghostbusters* employs the convention—familiar from a broad range of action-adventure films—of the expert crew. In the movies, groups of four or five men on a mission, each with a distinct personality, ethnic origin, and technical ability, have worked as pilots, astronauts, spies, crime fighters, SWAT teams, ship's crews. The Ghostbusters are re-creations of familiar types: the egghead/scientist/leader (Egon); the cutup/the clown (Peter); the regular joe/klutz (Ray); the exotic tough guy, differentiated primarily by his racial or ethnic difference from the whites in the group (Winston); and the nerd (Louis Tully), occasionally appearing as a comic mascot whose fear serves to highlight the bravery of the others.

While there has always been an element of childishness about these teams, underscored by the constant teasing and prankish play, *Ghostbusters* pushes this much further. The Ghostbusters are children thinly disguised as adults. In "Camping It Up" and many other episodes, the characters are presented as a family, moving in and out of the roles of parent and child. In "Camping It Up," Ray Stantz plays the comical, klutzy father in the beginning scenes, then Egon steps in as the intelligent, prepared father. While Egon Spengler usually plays a mature figure, he too is given to a childlike obsession

63. *The expert crew posing for Janine's snapshot: the scientist/leader, the cutup, the regular joe, and the Black tough guy.*

with his scientific gadgets. *Teenage Mutant Ninja Turtles* handles the contradictions about maturity by positioning its characters as adolescents whose actions vacillate between those of children and adults, and leaving to Splinter, the Ninja Master-Rat, all character-istics of adult restraint. In the *Ninja Turtle* theme song, the descrip-tions of the four turtles follow the same formula for the team of guys as that of *Ghostbusters*, arranging the turtles on a sliding scale of maturity and knowledge: "Splinter taught them to be Ninja teens/ Donatello leads, Leonardo knows machines/Raphael is cool but crude/ Michelangelo is a party dude." In this respect, the male ad-venture teams are quite the opposite of Megan and the ponies, who are children on the outside but adults on the inside: childlike in appearance but eminently adult in their emotional maturity and dedication to problem solving.

Winston Zeddmore, the only Black Ghostbuster, plays a some-what marginal role. Unlike the other men, he seems trapped in adulthood, unable to join in with the kinds of joking and horseplay Peter does; lacking the hobbyist paraphernalia of Egon. Winston's job often seems to be just a step up from that of chauffeur: he is often doing mechanical work on the car, Ecto I. In "Camping It Up," where the trip bears every resemblance to a family vacation, Winston is not in the family in the same way that the other charac-ters are. He still talks about his role as a job, as in his exasperated comment when he takes Slimer into the forest to relieve himself, "Man, the things I have to do in this job!" (This kind of remark is very commonly heard from Winston.) In the world of Ghostbusters there is a lot of joking among intimates, teasing about the foibles of those close to you—but only the white males are inside the circle of camaraderie.

Janine is crucial as a maternal figure.[3] In "Camping It Up," she plays the mother explicitly: snapping photos for the family album, taking in Big Foot like a lost child and feeding him. She is always peripheral to the main action, however, relegated to babysitting Sli-mer, providing food, taking messages. There is no possibility of a sexual relationship with Janine, because she is so maternal and be-cause her lower social position trivializes her and marks her as an unsuitable partner for a hero. A similar taboo is respected in *Teen-age Mutant Ninja Turtles* by making the lone female character, the reporter April, a member of a different species, as well as about a decade older than the others. Janine is drawn differently from epi-sode to episode, but something always establishes her as off-limits

64. *Janine in a maternal role, examining her "family" snapshots.*

65. *Janine's "overdone" appearance marks her off-limits as a romantic partner for the Ghostbusters.*

to the Ghostbusters, a figure of comic relief, whether it is her Bronx accent, her glasses, her tendency to overdress in garish fashions, or her incessant work on her nails. Vivian Sobchack has identified this as a recurring strategy in science fiction films: "[W]omen are sexually defused and made safe and unthreatening by costume, occupation, social position, and attitude."[4] Successful boys' cartoons with more attractive female characters establish that the woman is off-limits to the males because she is a twin sister (the She-Ra/He-Man relationship) or a member of another species entirely (Cheetara of *Thundercats*).

As Ghostbusters stories go, "Camping It Up" is not very scary. In the hundreds of episodes that have been produced, there are different levels of horror and fear, pitched at different age groups of children. In "Camping It Up," the threat is explainable and containable without combat or conflict of any kind. Like the problem with the Frazzits in "Mish Mash Melee," a cosmic disturbance must be brought right by getting something back in place. In this episode the solution, to send Big Foot back through the hole he entered through, seems to be a birth metaphor in reverse. In more violent episodes, the Ghostbusters achieve their success by getting things back in boxes, forcing the monsters into the ghost trap. They accomplish this by shooting the antagonist with a stream of electricity from their guns: the phallic imagery of a group of guys shooting a stream from their hips is pretty unmistakable. Sobchack suggests that science fiction films typically portray the control of reproduction through technology. With all the jokes about the irksome younger sibling Slimer, *Ghostbusters* also offers the fantasy of reversing the birth of a younger sibling, getting the little monster back in the box, as it were.

"Mrs. Rogers's Neighborhood" highlights some of the contrasts between *Ghostbusters* and *My Little Pony*. In this episode, the Ghostbusters are bored because business has been slow. The phone rings, but it is only Janine's sister calling with a recipe. The next call, however, dispatches them to an ornate house with stone lions at the door. Peter comments on the "cute kitties," but once he turns his back, they become fierce monsters. A small old woman holding a bird cage opens the door and tells them the house is haunted. The guys laugh. She says she's afraid of the ghosts, so Ray takes her to headquarters to wait with Janine. Janine orders Slimer to watch the bird while she gets milk and cookies, and when she returns, she dismisses his warning that the bird is actually a monster. The old woman asks for a tour of headquarters. When they reach the ghost containment chamber, Janine turns her back and the old woman becomes a hideous hunchbacked monster thirty-five feet tall. Once Janine mentions that she doesn't have the access code, the monster shrinks back to normal. Meanwhile, as the Ghostbusters wander throughout the house, they joke about the old woman's fears but soon discover ghosts everywhere: in picture frames, lamps, closets, ceilings. The Ghostbusters battle the ghosts until they run out of energy from their proton packs and are sucked through a hole into a hellish netherworld. After lots of pyrotechnics, they restore their failed equipment and contain the ghosts. Suddenly they realize— unlike Janine, who remains blithely ignorant—that the old woman must also be a ghost, and they hurry back to headquarters. After another heated battle, in which the old woman takes the shape of a multiplying series of demons, the Ghostbusters zap her and all her demons into a ghost trap. The episode ends with some jovial remarks about what a quiet day it has been.

Many episodes of *Ghostbusters* begin with a mundane scene of the everyday. Like the classic ghost story, the plot can be divided into two sections: the Recognition, the time until the hero "perceives himself unquestionably in the presence of a supernatural being"; and the Release, everything that occurs until the heroes escape from the ghostly beings.[5] Most of the suspense in *Ghostbusters* derives from various delays in the recognition. The Ghostbusters pose as skeptical, wisecracking adults, and they do not like to give in to the fear that they are being haunted until they have to. Often their technical gadgetry—a high PKE reading or one of Egon's scientific explanations—is needed to confirm their suspicions. (The series contains many jokes on scientism, and science is usually put at the service of confirming the supernatural.) Despite their vast experience in ghostbusting, they continually fall for appearances, especially appearances that are feminine, innocent, feeble. The little old grandmother is a hideous monster and her quiet home a seething hell that threatens engulfment. The episode's title plays on the popular television show for younger children, marked by Mister Rogers's indefatigable sweetness and attempts to cultivate a feeling of security in small children. In this world, as in Disney's films and cartoons, the very young and the very old and the female are likely to be evil: kindness or feebleness is usually a veneer. (If the ponies ever visited here, their pastel colors, high voices, and generosity would be a dead giveaway that they were really ghosts.) The tame, familiar scenes of middle-class suburbia can turn out to be as horribly haunted as the alleys of New York City.

The lifeblood of *Ghostbusters*'s animation is a rapid procession of hideous monsters. Villainy is not personalized or individualized here; rather, a multitude of threatening ghosts appear and constantly transform themselves from one grotesque form to another. Typical of *Ghostbusters* is Egon's characterization of a group of invading trolls in the episode "Troll Bridge": "They don't trust humans, they don't want anything to do with people or cities. They're vicious, fearless, and very mean." On many episodes, there are extended battles with legions of horrifying figures. This allows for considerable freedom in the animation—and the artists freely borrow from the masters of expressionism. For example, there is a strong influence of the German cartoonist Georg Grosz, famous for satirizing the decadent bourgeoisie. At other times, science fiction comics provide the models for a series of mutant monsters.

Humor is the only virtue, and it is needed as a defense against emotion, a way to disguise fear. Slimer, when he gets too excited or affectionate, leaves a sticky, gooey liquid all over the person he comes in contact with. The Ghostbusters call this "getting slimed," and it is the source of much humor on the show. Slime is a bodily fluid associated with emotional vulnerability, and it is embarrassing and uncomfortable if you let it get on you. Being associated with a younger, more infantile self—being associated with slime (read: feces, urine, vomit, saliva)—and being associated with emotions are all things to be avoided, all equally humiliating. One of the innovations of *Ghostbusters* was to emphasize the ironic posture of the rather fallible hero. By contrast, there is little humor in the animated series for girls; the heroines are incapable of making wisecracks and represent a better version of ourselves.[6]

The ghosts in *Ghostbusters* represent impersonal terrors: the thing to do is blast the monster away immediately, negotiating only slows things down. In *My Little Pony*, the word is more powerful than the proton pack. In *Ghostbusters*, only the right combination of weaponry and cunning can succeed. Girls' cartoons tell moral tales about personal relationships. If there is any moral to the boys' cartoons, it is that one must constantly be on guard, especially against the familiar, the weak, the everyday, the domestic—and often, the feminine. The morality of the world is in doubt: meaning, such as it is, is derived from male camaraderie, from getting the job done.

66. *The thing to do is blast the ghosts away immediately; talking only slows things down. The Ghostbusters firing their proton packs.*

The scheme below summarizes the structuring differences between girls' and boys' animated series, and *Ghostbusters* and *My Little Pony* in particular.

Ghostbusters	*My Little Pony*
adult men	girls
the hero as equal	the heroine as our better self
hierarchical group	interspecies democracy of peers
emotions masked	emotions valued as truth
regression to younger self (Slimer)	repression of childish self
playful attitude towards work	putting play aside to save others
boastfulness	insecurity
fear as an enjoyable thrill	overcoming fear
blast the enemy away	persuade the enemy to change
violent conflict	moral persuasion
technology	nature
contemporary urban setting	timeless pastoral setting
comedy and horror film	the musical and the romance
dystopia	utopia

Gendered Genres

Since the early 1970s, feminist film and television critics have explored the notion that popular genres are gendered and employ a mode of address that speaks to an audience in the terms of a normative—if also contradictory and conflictual—identification as male or female. To argue that many popular culture genres are "gendered" is not to say that, empirically speaking, the audiences who watch or enjoy each genre consist only of men and boys or women and girls. The soap opera has been seen as a women's genre that stresses utopian values of community while measuring out suffering to its virtuous heroines in large doses, yet many men are avid fans. Critics have viewed detective fiction (in print and on film and television) as quintessentially male with its unsentimental, independent hero devoted to discerning facts and meting out punishment, yet women make up the audience for these in large numbers. Certainly children cross gender lines frequently in their preferences for television material, although we can predict that this will more often take the form—as it has done throughout motion picture history— of female audiences attending to masculine genres than vice versa.

To describe popular genres as gendered is not to propose that a natural relationship exists between gender and narrative preferences. Boys are not born with a love of action, violence, and adventure; girls are not born with an interest in personal relationships and promoting the happiness of others. These interests may develop as a result of gender socialization at home and at school, of exposure to and comprehension of a social environment in which many kinds of employment and many chores in the home are assigned exclusively to mothers or fathers. No biological predilection is assumed in the entertainment choices individuals make; rather, stories and conventions tend to group audiences in a process that involves social learning in institutions such as the family and the school. The film and television industries' attempts to specify and dictate audience groups through distribution, exhibition, advertising, and marketing build on these social structures and ideologies. Genres and their gendered address are historically specific and capable of change. The cartoons that I have discussed, for example, combine generic conventions—science fiction with melodrama; ghost stories with slapstick comedy—in ways unfamiliar to adults of the previous generation.

No fan of popular culture is entirely free in the choices she or he makes. This is especially true of television because it is a domestic appliance, and so what gets watched on television is usually something that must be negotiated with others in the household. Children struggle with parents over permission for what and when to watch, and with siblings with whom they may have to share television viewing time. The choice of television shows and videos is also influenced by friends and schoolmates: to watch a certain show is to acquire familiarity, even expertise, which may be demonstrated in conversation on the playground. The choice of what to watch is not solely a matter of individual taste and personal idiosyncrasy: social conformity enters in when children recognize the differences between television programs that peers consider to be normal and acceptable and those considered so by adults. A boy with an older sister may watch a lot more *My Little Pony* videos than a boy without sisters, but he will probably choose not to discuss his enjoyment of these shows with groups of other boys. Similarly a girl, especially a younger sister, may have less power in the family's negotiation over what to watch or which videos to rent, and she may acquire her knowledge of television culture primarily through an older brother's selections. She may then be better able to enter into conversation and play with boys at school but will be at a distinct disadvantage among girls who have first choice over television viewing at home.

Feminist film critics in the 1970s adopted a psychoanalytic model to examine Hollywood film narratives. Film critics such as Laura Mulvey, Claire Johnston, and Pam Cook described films as complicated semiotic texts that created a position for the spectator, forcing certain (characteristically masculine) identifications and ways of viewing and rendering untenable the situation of the female viewer.[7] According to these critics, Hollywood narratives relentlessly focused on Oedipal scenarios, in which women were either presented as fetishes for the visual pleasure of the audience or punished for their lack of the phallus: in short, Hollywood was seen as a relentless purveyor of patriarchal ideology. Children's television bears similar marks of Oedipal obsession and the denial of female subjectivity, and Mulvey's work has influenced my analysis. *Ghostbusters* seems guilty of this when it banishes Janine from the plot or presents the maternal Mrs. Rogers as a monster. Psychoanalytic film criticism has demonstrated the awkward position of female moviegoers—and I would add here girl viewers of Saturday morning television, who necessarily spend a lot of time watching stories dominated by males and tainted by misogyny. As Laura Mulvey wrote in her widely quoted remarks about Hollywood films, this means that "for women (from childhood onwards) trans-sex identification is a *habit* that very easily becomes *second Nature*. However, this Nature does not sit easily and shifts restlessly in its borrowed transvestite clothes." [8]

But the psychoanalytic model has been revised throughout the 1980s after being rightly criticized as overly deterministic on the one hand and universalist on the other. Increasingly, feminist critics have deemed a psychoanalytic model inadequate to explain the experience of real spectators in the movie theater or real people watching television in the living room. [9] One of the best alternatives to the psychoanalytic model is Christine Gledhill's notion of "pleasurable negotiation." [10] Gledhill conceives of the relationship between a moviegoer and a film (or a viewer and a television program) as a give-and-take process, in which a struggle takes place between different frames of reference (those of the producer and the consumer, for example), different experiences (often informed by gender, race, and class), and different motivations. Gledhill allows for unforeseen uses of media texts and commodities—and I would include here toys. For media criticism, the implications of such a model are several. The meaning of a film or television program is not set once and for all. Critics cannot predict the reaction of audiences looking at the film. Media is not "swallowed whole": viewers often are selective and partial in their media preferences. In interpretation, they may vacillate between meanings based on knowledge of the genre or program type and those based on knowledge of "reality." Gledhill does not believe that "anything goes" in the ways viewers understand a film, but she argues that neither can feminist critics determine the ideological effect of a film, whether reactionary or progressive, radical or conservative.

The meaning of a film or television program changes over time and is influenced by interventions such as the interpretations produced by critics and the associations and contexts produced by advertising and—in the case of children's media, especially—the marketing of a wide range of consumer goods based on fictional characters and plots. My critical readings of *My Little Pony* and *Ghostbusters* have revealed extensive borrowing from adult gendered genres, such as soap opera, romance, science fiction, and horror. Children learn a great deal about the conventions of these adult genres from watching "children's" television, which imparts to them a lot of information about popular culture and about dominant ideologies of gender. The girls' cartoons are filled with many "prosocial" messages routinely delivered to children, such as the importance of cooperation, kindness, and acknowledging the feelings of others. The boys' cartoons, despite their violence, also convey many deep-rooted cultural principles, such as the notion that the strong (usually men) have an obligation to protect the weak, that the use of force can be justified, that people need to learn to check their emotions, and, perhaps above all, that male bonding is fun.

The ultimate effect of these cartoons on children, psychological, ideological, or otherwise, however, cannot be ascertained from critical study of the programs alone but depends instead on negotiations between individual children and the cartoons, an aspect that needs more empirical investigation. Although the dynamics of gender representation in these series are sometimes depressingly rigid, children still enjoy considerable latitude in their viewing and in their play with this type of television material. Even *Ghostbusters* allows children to shift from the adult male heroes to the infantile Slimer to the monsters in the closet. Girls are more likely than boys to develop creative abilities for "pleasurable negotiations" because they are most likely to be well versed in the conventions of *both* boys' and girls' television series.

Television Play

Many parents are disturbed by the monsters and demons on *Ghostbusters* and object to the incessant replaying of the heroes' battles with frightening, evil figures. I think that these objections must be understood as motivated by contemporary American views of childhood, which favor Piaget over Freud: an orderly, rational cognitive development, as opposed to the irrational, magical thinking of the unconscious. As Bruno Bettelheim wrote, "[W]e want our children to believe that, inherently, all men are good. But children know that *they* are not always good; and often, even when they are, they would prefer not to be. This contradicts what they are told by their parents and therefore makes the child a monster in his own eyes." [11] As in fairy tales, television's starkly drawn contrasts between hero and villain make them satisfyingly transparent to the child, who can identify, as Bettelheim suggests, with both the evil and the good as dual aspects of his or her personality. The monsters in *Ghostbusters* speak to the fear of devourment that Bettelheim noted in so many fairy tales—and the reassurance provided by the victory over the monsters at the stories' end.

Erik Erikson played a major role in elevating play in the eyes of parents, teachers, and psychologists. As a psychoanalyst, Erikson refuted the trivial associations with play by proposing that children's play was the stuff of weighty psychic drama.[12] He proposed that play could itself be used as a kind of text for psychoanalytic interpretation of the unconscious in children and that play could be used as a therapy, with positive, healing effects from the reenactment of psychic conflicts. (His theories were often used to bolster the experts' advice to parents to buy lots of toys.) He described the play age as a point in the life cycle when children had mastered the numinous (mutuality of recognition), the judicious (discrimination of good and bad), and the dramatic (dramatic elaboration).[13] In Erikson's formulation, play with toys is explicitly linked to the ability to create "a coherent plot with conflict in turns and some form of resolution."[14]

Commercial television programs—toy-based or not—enhance this ability in young children, and the fact that they do so helps to explain the popularity with children of toys based on cartoon characters. For Erikson, dramatic play has an explicitly therapeutic basis,[15] offering

> a micro-reality in which [the child] can use toys (put at his disposal by those who sanction his play) in order to relive, correct, and re-create past experiences, and anticipate future roles and events with the spontaneity and repetitiveness which characterize all creative ritualization. The play themes of this age, however, often prove to be dominated by the usurpation and ambitious impersonation of victorious self-images and the killing off of weak and evil "others"; and we nominate for the principal inner estrangement which finds expression, aggravation, or resolution in childhood play the *sense of guilt*. Thus, the playing child, in initiating a toy scene, often can be seen to play out the question of what range of activity is open to him and what direction will engulf him in guilt.[16]

I quote Erikson at some length because this passage vitiates a common criticism of children's commercial television and the toy industry: namely, its division of the fictional world into good and evil characters. (Villains of any sort are rarely available for sale in the educational toy store.) Licensed character toys are predominantly used for just the kinds of play Erikson describes here: creative ritualization, victorious self-images; killing off weak and evil others. "Toy-based cartoons" like *My Little Pony* and *Ghostbus-*

ters, She-Ra and *He-Man* were criticized by ACT precisely for reducing the world to a series of stark contrasts of good and evil. The formulaic, generic nature of these toys and videos, however, makes them especially adaptable for the kinds of play that Erikson suggests, and therefore they are especially attractive to preschool age children. In fact, they probably encourage this kind of play more than abstract toys such as wooden blocks do. Because they are mass-media goods, these kinds of toys actually facilitate group, cooperative play, by encouraging children to make up stories with shared codes and narratives. Yet play with action figures and character dolls and play that makes references to television characters and situations are excluded from the category "creative" by educators interested in manifestations of individuated personality and intellectual achievement in children.

Television play is often social, shared, collaborative—and very creative. *Ghostbusters* is typical of Saturday morning television in its references to other television shows and its introduction of characters from other stories—Big Foot, Santa Claus. Marsha Kinder has argued that this "intertextual" quality of children's television "helps to facilitate not only the comprehension and recall of stories, but also the development of more complex schemata of what stories are like, with their highly complex patchwork of similarities and differences in plots, characters, iconography, mise-en-scene, and modes of image production."[17] Vivian Gussin Paley's journal-style observations of children in nursery school and kindergarten offer hundreds of examples of the kinds of stories children make up together using unexpected combinations of toy and television characters. For example, Paley recorded the following story told by a five-year-old kindergartner—a mixture of *Star Wars*, Grimm's fairy tales, and Saturday morning cartoons:

> One day Princess Leia and Cinderella had a tea party. After that they went for a walk and met Scooby Doo. They said, "Hi, Scooby. Are you looking for a clue?" He said, "Yes, I'm after a mystery. A ghost is somewhere. That's why I'm walking this way." "Do you want to come to a party?" said Cinderella. "Who's having a party?" "It's all yours, Scooby. It's your birthday." So they all went to the party.[18]

My point here is that a psychological rationale for condemning mass-market toys as inhibiting fantasy has in fact functioned as a sort of smokescreen for elitism, which often takes the form of despising television and popular genres on the basis of a largely baseless fear that they mentally impoverish children. In an empirical study of first and second graders' play, Patricia Marks Greenfield and others looked for deficiencies in "transcendent imagination" caused by television/toy tie ins. The authors concluded that "television, particularly when combined with thematically related toys, functions as a cultural tool that aids the imaginative development of younger children" and suggested that "it is probably more accurate to say that television and program-related toys change the *source* of imagination, rather than its creativity or quantity."[19] In another study of preschoolers' play at a day-care facility, games that included television characters were participated in by children who did not even watch the shows, and the scenarios children created often deviated wildly from any version of the TV show's plot structure adults would recognize.[20] The fear that children's creativity and individuality are under assault from exposure to *Ghostbusters* and *My Little Pony* owes more to the antitelevision bias of many intellectuals and child experts than it does to the observation of children's play.

Even the strict gender coding of toys does not necessarily predestine them for stereotypical uses in play. As Susan Willis comments, "Barbie can slide down avalanches just as He-Man can become the inhabitant of a two-storey Victorian doll's house. I have observed such situations and day care teachers can describe thousands more where play disrupts gender roles."[21] To facilitate such play, I would like to see more female characters given more to do in all children's television programs, and more children of color developed as fullfledged characters. In fact, the best that could happen to children's television would be for boys' series to borrow some of the emphasis on communication and feeling so typical of *My Little Pony* and for girls' series to stir up more play interest in things like computers and technology. Girls' heroines could stand to gain a sense of humor and might express a bit more anger on television. Boys' heroes could lessen their reliance on guns and gadgets—and try talking their way to victory instead.

7

TOYS "R" US

MARKETING TO CHILDREN AND PARENTS

> Every girl says Barbie is her favorite, most imply that their mothers disapprove, and the teachers tell me privately that they wish Barbie dolls were left at home.
> —Vivian Gussin Paley

Toys incite in parents strong feelings that are a tangle of nostalgia and generational and class values. Attitudes toward toys are social and strongly tied to educational background and cultural capital. Many parents believe that what is given to children in terms of material culture is an important communication about the future. Grant McCracken has argued that consumer goods—and, I would add, especially toys—express and negotiate generational conflicts. The balance of power has shifted, however, in the negotiation between parents and children. Mass media targeted at children have shortened the period of exclusively parental influence over children. A distinctive, peer-oriented consumer culture now intervenes in the relationship of parents and children, and that intervention begins for many children as early as two years of age.

What is often at stake in parent and child conflict over toy purchases is not the difference between advertised and unadvertised toys but rather the difference between mass-marketed promotional toys targeted at children, such as My Little Pony and Ghostbusters, and niche-marketed "educational" or classic toys targeted at middle-class, college-educated parents, such as Playmobil dolls and theme sets. With the growth of commercial television in the 1950s, the market for toys began to be divided both in a business sense and in the sense of cultural distinctions between consumers of different

class backgrounds. The divisions were between nonlicensed and licensed toys, between toys advertised to parents and toys advertised
to children, between toys that refer to film and television characters
and toys that do not. When protesting the commercialization of
childhood and the rapid growth of the toy industry, intellectuals tend
to exclude the categories of "quality" toys and "creative"
play—that is, the kinds of goods and services targeted at their own
children. They fail to recognize that these categories are linked to
intellectual and professional aspirations that some parents have for
some children. Rather than embodying an absolute ideal of healthy
play, educational toys merely constitute the "high-end" segment of
the toy market. Too often childhood experts write as though the
advertising and marketing of children's consumer goods is something that only happens in the mass market, that only involves the
goods for sale at Toys "R" Us. They do not recognize promotional
techniques when they themselves are targeted.

The growth of the toy industry has horrified many parents, teachers, and social critics, who have voiced this horror frequently in
newspapers and magazines.[1] Since the 1950s, marketers have tried
to sell the products of a commercialized peer culture—whose values
may conflict with those of parents—to younger and younger groups
of children. Parents may lose their children to a peer-influenced culture of toys and videos—ones unfamiliar to them from their own
childhood—at an earlier age.[2] The fact that toys have become a
billion-dollar industry driven by aggressive marketing techniques
that bypass parents and go directly to the kids is widely recognized
and often deeply resented by journalists, educators, and parents.
The toy industry's marketing practices fly in the face of both the
cherished cultural image of children existing outside the economic
sphere and the value placed on parental authority over children and
control of children's leisure.

Behind My Little Pony and Ghostbusters toys stand developments
and strategies now institutionalized in the U.S. toy industry today:
deseasonalization, the encouragement of toy buying at times other
than the Christmas season; character licensing, the use of popular
fictional characters for a fee or a share of the profits as the design or
decoration on toys; consumer research, in the form of test marketing; and line extensions, new characters and accessories added to
successful toys. Each of these can be readily observed in the retailing practices and physical space of the giant of the retailing industry, Toys "R" Us, where licensed toys are found in the greatest

abundance for the cheapest price of all toy stores. Toys "R" Us and the mass-marketed nationally advertised goods (known in the toy industry as promotional toys) that fill its shelves offer one version of toy culture. Educational and so-called classic toys—often explicitly identified by their difference from promotional toys—sold in smaller, posh toy stores in the United States and Western Europe offer quite another. These two types of toy stores offer different rewards and penalties, pleasures and dissonances, and typify trends and forms of economic and cultural stratification embodied in marketing practices today.

Mass-Market Toys

In the past forty years the toy industry has changed in much the same way that other U.S. manufacturing industries have changed. Today, because of mergers and acquisitions in the 1980s, more toys are manufactured by a smaller number of larger corporations than ever before. Some acquisitions involved food industry giants already heavily dependent on the children's market: Quaker Oats purchased Fisher-Price toys; General Mills acquired Kenner. (Both companies were later spun off.) Some large-scale mergers have occurred, such as that of Coleco (purchaser of Appalachian Artworks, the makers of Cabbage Patch Dolls) and Tyco Toys.

Toy manufacturing has also been affected by the consolidation of ownership in the retail sector. Toys "R" Us, a discount store chain devoted to toys and infants' and children's goods, steadily grew throughout the sixties, seventies, and eighties. It now determines the course of the entire industry, having succeeded early in the internationalization of toy retailing and established a strong foothold overseas prior to the unification of the European market in 1992. Many department stores ceased to sell toys, unable to compete with the prices of the discount chain; many individually owned and operated toy stores also went out of business. One of Toys "R" Us's major competitors, the East Coast chain Child World, went bankrupt in the early 1990s.

Toy manufacture has increasingly moved to Asia, especially China. The trade journal *Playthings* reported that in 1989, 55 percent of all dolls and 40 percent of all other toys imported into the United States were made in China.[3] Toy making often involves painstaking work, especially sewing and hand painting, and U.S. workers are less willing to do this kind of work for long hours and low pay. In many respects the toy industry has paralleled changes in the clothing industry: factories moved abroad, while design and market research remained in the United States. (The same is true in animation: scripts are produced in the United States, but the frame-by-frame work of animation is often done in Korea.) A division of labor—mental versus manual—exists between the U.S. corporations and the Asian factories. The toy industry is now so reliant on China for cheap labor that in 1990 the Toy Manufacturers of America urged everyone in the business to write to Congress protesting the end of China's most-favored-nation status, a charge that would subject imported toys and dolls to a duty as high as 70 percent of the purchase price.[4] Provincial Chinese workers, many of them young enough to be only children themselves, work long, tedious hours under unsafe conditions. This exploitation, however, has created a profitable turn of events: in 1989, the Standard and Poor index placed toys number one on a ranking of the top one hundred U.S. companies.

Television advertising to children also altered the way toys are made and sold. In their analysis of the toy industry, Sydney Ladensohn Stern and Ted Schoenhaus argue that when the power of advertising to children was recognized, toys were designed specifically in terms of their potential for demonstration on television and their photogenic qualities. Battery-operated dolls and vehicles that could perform for the camera were favored. Designers selected colors on the basis of their photogenic qualities. Toys advertised on television, called "promotional toys" in the industry, delivered higher profits to the manufacturers, lower ones to the retailers (who compete fiercely on the heavily advertised products with discount prices), and a lot of business to the advertising agencies. Too often, however, the role of television advertising in the growth of the toy industry is overestimated, while other factors are ignored. Along with the growth in television advertising, many other techniques for marketing to children have been developed since the 1950s, including the deseasonalization of consumer demand, line extensions, licensed characters, and sophisticated merchandising techniques and test marketing common to other retail industries.

The toy industry has responded to the problem of market saturation by increasing the number of times per year each consumer makes a purchase. Thus, the industry has quite self-consciously pushed for the deseasonalization of buying, so that toy purchases (either impulsive or planned) become a weekly or monthly occurrence rather than a twice-a-year event occurring at Christmas and birthdays. The toy industry has multiplied holiday buying seasons so that they occur throughout the year. This tactic has characterized many other branches of the retail industry (that target women consumers), especially greeting cards, home furnishings and decorating, gifts, and clothing. Retailers and manufacturers established a secular calendar of special events (and special seasonal gifts and games, costumes, equipment, and greeting cards) that are reinforced in most preschool and elementary school curricula: Christmas, Valentine's Day, St. Patrick's Day, Easter, Summer/Outdoor, Back to School, Halloween. Advertising on television has of course provided children with a steady flow of new product information throughout the year. Supermarkets and "superstores" (palaces of one-stop shopping such as Kmart, Shopko, Target, Fred Meyers, Wal-Mart) offer in-store displays and promotional specials celebrating these retailing "holidays," and these stores also sell toys. For many mothers, the purchase of an inexpensive promotional toy to distract and please a child while she accomplishes the household shopping is a small enough price to pay. Discount chains often offer toys such as My Little Pony, Ghostbusters, Teenage Mutant Ninja Turtles, Barbie, or plush animals in the $5 range as "loss leaders." New versions or sets of these toys are placed in stores and advertised on television every two to three months. These items, also known as "traffic builders," are sold at cost to attract mothers in the hope that they will then shop for other items throughout the store.

As I mentioned earlier, young children pose special problems for marketers in terms of product awareness. They cannot read, so they are not accessible through direct mail solicitations, billboards, or magazines. Exposure to television commercials is limited both by parents and by the availability of broadcast and cable programming for children. Toy designers have landed on character licensing as one solution to this dilemma, by making a product instantly familiar to a child. Licensing offers manufacturers the possibility of inspiring recognition at the point of purchase, in the store, even if the child did not know about the product before. Today, licensing is an industry of its own with separate trade shows, agents, and marketing specialists. Toy manufacturers make up about 15 percent of the business in licensing, which includes not only fictional characters but also tradenames, corporate logos, the names and images of real-life stars, television programs, and sports teams and organizations. Licensing agents believe that the imprint of a recognizable character can magically raise a product above the clutter of competition.

Manufacturers pay a fee to use the graphics, design, and name of the character for a product. For example, toymakers might sell a doll of the movie character Beetlejuice, while other manufacturers might use a picture of Beetlejuice on a bedsheet, a lunchbox, or a pair of pajamas. Proponents of licensing optimistically state the benefits of using long-lived characters: "[M]illions of dollars have been spent over many years to build an image. It's more cost efficient to translate that image to your product than to not have a license and start at ground zero to build an image."[5]

Licensed characters are a means of positioning a product in advance for a target audience. Matching the character with the right target market is the job of special "licensing consultants," one of whom complained: "Sometimes you see the darndest combination in the market. Be sensitive to the licensed character's demographics and be sure those demographics suit your needs and that you're both going after the same audience."[6] In the business of contemporary licensing, each character has his or her own demographics: gender, age, and sometimes social class. Trade publications distinguish between "high-end" licenses and "mass-market" licenses; manufacturers seek to match their products and price tags with the income and the taste of the group attracted by a given character or theme.

Licensing has existed since the early twentieth century: Buster Brown and Teddy Bear were early examples; Charlie Chaplin and Shirley Temple were popular in the twenties and thirties. Toys, as well as characters from cartoons, films, or television programs, have had a healthy life on lunchboxes, clothing, school supplies, and home decorations (especially for children's rooms).[7] Licensing is a kind of branding, a form of promotion and advertising. These are not new features of retail merchandising. Disney built a financial empire on the careful handling of character licenses from his cartoons and films. Because many of his early films were adapted from nineteenth-century European children's literature, Disney enjoyed a number of advantages: he did not pay for the rights to use the original story and characters, the characters were in some cases already known through fairy tales, and the stories enjoyed the cultural prestige associated with the nineteenth-century illustrated children's book.[8] Widespread critical acclaim for the 1991 release *Beauty and the Beast* attests to the continuing success of this strategy.

Disney's licenses are the longest-lived and the most successful in the toy industry. The Disney organization devotes considerable time and money to the project of igniting interest in its characters among successive generations of children and parents. The Disney Channel is a perfect publicity outlet in this regard. The Disney theme parks promote its licenses extensively through theme rides and costumed characters who wander through the park to greet children, pause for photo opportunities, and perform live dance numbers throughout the day. Old and new licenses feed off each other: during the wait to visit Mickey Mouse in his dressing room at Walt Disney World, "guests" are treated to promotional trailers for Disney rereleases, such as *101 Dalmatians* and *Peter Pan*, and for new programs produced by the Disney subsidiary Buena Vista Television, such as *Tale Spin* and *Gummi Bears*.

Marketing professionals warn of numerous pitfalls in toy licensing. Licensed products can fail because of overexposure, parental objections to graphics or other associations with the character, a short "shelf life" for popular characters (often no more than ninety days to six months), a bad product mix (i.e., an inappropriate character for the kind of toy offered), and, finally, because of the fickleness of children as a market and rapid changes in their tastes. Teenage Mutant Ninja Turtles were a rare and unanticipated success of the late 1980s. When the creators of the comic book offered the license for sale, all the major toy manufacturers turned them down because of lost faith in such licenses. (Subsequently, Teenage Mutant Ninja Turtles made a fortune for Playmates, hitherto a small, struggling company.)

Licensing has been institutionalized as a secondary industry to the toy and entertainment businesses. Today, children's movie characters are licensed for a vast array of products designed for preschool-age children, including premiums with fast food (McDonald's Happy Meals) and soundtracks and videos. In her case study of Batman, Eileen Meehan demonstrates that licensing (and its potential profits) is crucial to the health of film production companies and that licensing potential can dictate the selection of creative properties. Similarly, toy industry stocks tend to decline when Wall Street analysts detect the "maturing" of a popular license. In 1991 Kenner suffered from the perception that both Ghostbusters and Beetlejuice had nearly come to the end of their life span—typically four years. Although the toy industry has distanced itself from direct engagement in television series production, it still relies heavily on licensing. The trade journal *Toy and Hobby World*, for example, rates the fall lineup of Saturday morning network television shows specifically for the licensing potential, or lack thereof, of each program.

The ambitions of toy licensees are global in scope. Because toys produced by U.S. companies are now marketed vigorously in Europe, both My Little Pony and Ghostbusters became part of an international consumer culture. Marks and Spencer, the renowned British department store, was selling My Little Pony underwear in 1990, and neighborhood video stores in England offered an array of Pony titles. In Germany, Toys "R" Us sells Meine Kleine Pony and in France Mon Petite Poney. My Little Pony was voted by retailers in Spain the best girls' toy of 1989. Similarly, Ghostbusters as a movie, animated videos, toys, and clothing are available widely in Europe, where they have done exceedingly well. Some minor changes are occasionally made to suit the local taste: Slimer's name has been changed to Green Ghost on some products in England, presumably to surmount parental objections to the grossness of the original concept. Kenner, expecting a decline in Ghostbusters sales as they entered their fourth year on the U.S. market in 1990, nevertheless reported great "sales momentum" for Ghostbusters in Canada and Europe.

The toy industry increasingly uses sophisticated test-marketing methods to aid in the design, display, and packaging of toys. Computerized inventory control (available with large chain stores such as Toys "R" Us as well as B. Dalton Bookseller, Tower Records, Blockbuster Video) and test marketing provide the major manufacturers with children to provide information about shifts in styles and preferences. Like most market research, toy testing seems to exist somewhere in the space between ethnography and anecdote. The largest toy manufacturers engage in extensive testing of their toys with play groups. At initial stages of product design, market researchers provide toy designers with exact lists of children's preferences, tastes, and current interests. Manufacturers build prototypes of new toys, to be used in laboratory play groups of children whose level of interest and attention span are carefully recorded by observers. This kind of product testing is especially true in the preschool market: Fisher-Price weighs the results of these tests very seriously and redesigns its toys accordingly. Little Tykes tests its products at an on-site day-care center for employees, whose children are observed by designers as they play with the toys. The children at the center are in a mixed age situation so that their play will resemble an at-home family situation. Little Tykes's manager of research and child development explained this aspect of their market research: "Our system is unique, because we can see the long term experience. Whenever you give a child a new toy, there's always going to be some excitement for a few hours. But we get to see what happens after two or three hours, or when there are other toys in the environment, when the child is tired or frustrated, or in a group situation." [9]

Despite these innovations, manufacturers have a great deal of apprehension about the success of products: toy production and sale is a high-risk industry. From the manufacturers' point of view children are exceptionally fickle consumers. While everyone agrees that television advertising is effective, market researchers report that children are frightfully prone to changing their minds about a purchase and that they are easily distractable once inside the toy store, no matter how often they have seen a toy's commercial on television. Superstitions of various kinds abound about ways to predict the success of toys and cycles of popularity among children, but many decisions seem to be based in large part on the reactions of the executives' own children to prototypes. Each year there are huge losses, and the major manufacturers, some of them staggering under the weight of debts incurred through mergers and takeovers, often stake the survival of the whole business on the success of one toy, as Coleco did with the reintroduction of Cabbage Patch in 1989.

In the 1930s and 1940s, toy manufacturers relied on demonstrators to display the toy in department stores, and most toys were packaged in cardboard boxes. Parents, rather than children, were presumed to be determining what would be bought. Today packaging and displays have become more elaborate. Toy manufacturers focus on the problem of making the toy visible on the floor-to-ceiling shelves of the toy supermarket, Toys "R" Us. The attraction of dynamic graphic design, the importance of the feeling that the toy is virtually within grasp (made possible by plastic bubble packaging that does not hide the toy behind cardboard), and the insignificance to children of the words printed on a package are a few of the research findings that have recently influenced package design.

The toy industry has increased its efforts to attract shoppers visually. Mattel packages Barbie and her costumes and accessories in fuchsia cardboard, creating a "wall of pink" easy to spot aisles away. When Mattel introduced a new Disney line of preschool toys, its salespeople insisted that store managers allocate a separate space within each store and erect elaborate displays for the products. Each toy in the line was packaged in bright red cardboard, recognizable at some distance as the Disney toys. Industry analysts now attribute Mattel's enormous and speedy success in entering the preschool market to these strategies. Fisher-Price uses the same red-and-blue design on all of its boxes and carefully weighs a decision whether to use a "try-me" box that allows the child to operate some feature of the toy while it is still in the package. The company balances the opportunity to excite the child about the toy while it is still on the store's shelf with parental concern about how sanitary the toy is, a concern its researchers have picked up from focus groups with mothers.

These advances in packaging are not environmentally friendly. Lego is currently trying to "depackage" its building toys to avoid waste. Ted Turner, in selling the license for Captain Planet toys (based on a television show featuring an environmental superhero) insisted that the packaging must use recycled paper, despite the fact, as a *Toy and Hobby World* writer remarked, "that the action figure itself will probably last through the next few millennia." [10] Children's television series, echoing the classroom curriculum, have repeatedly emphasized environmental themes, helping to create a generation of children often vocal and adamant about recycling and the avoidance of waste. Toy production, however, typically involves huge amounts of waste and toxic chemicals. [11] In the future this conflict promises to pose an interesting problem for the toy industry's market researchers.

The mass-market toy industry, like all fashion industries, is under constant pressure to increase sales volume. Creating line extensions of successful toys solves the problem more simply and reliably than creating new toys. The industry would, of course, prefer to produce many blockbusters each year. But a runaway success like Teenage Mutant Ninja Turtles happens only every few years. Every year, the major manufacturers precariously balance old successes with new launches, most of which fail. As security against the failure of the new toys introduced each year—that is, the failure of a new blockbuster to materialize—toy manufacturers make do with small-scale innovations on proven product lines and categories.

Mattel's Barbie is the line extension success par excellence. (Playmobil's success is based on line extensions, too, but the company calls them by the lofty title "interactive play system.") Barbie has miraculously exceeded the logical limits of consumer demand. In 1989 Barbie had been so widely disseminated that Mattel claimed that 90 percent of girls in the United States owned a Barbie by the age of three. New generations of parents come along to buy their children Barbies as they themselves once had them, and Barbie's outfits and accessories change with real-life fashion trends (and become outmoded just as fast). New versions of Barbie appear throughout the marketing year and appear in special seasonally limited editions from Holiday Barbie sold at Christmas (which toy stores reported as 1990's top-selling item) to Wet-n-Wild Barbie and Animal-Lovin' Barbie in summer.

Being "into Barbie," as the girls on Mattel's television commercials proudly exclaim, means being into a rather adult style of consumption. The accessories that make up the Barbie line extensions—and those for many other popular toys—often mirror, in miniature, objects of adult consumption such as cars, home furnishings, and clothing. The child's desire to participate in the adult version of these expanding cycles may explain part of the Barbie phenomenon. Everyday accessories such as furniture and cars have been popular every year, as well as Barbie's more elaborate sets like the ice cream parlor and television studio (for Barbie to play newscaster).

Just as television relies on the series and the motion picture industry increasingly relies on the sequel, the toy industry surrounds its successful characters each year with new companions, adversaries, locations, and older or younger versions of the original toys. Children add on to already familiar toys by purchasing new characters (resembling television's guest stars) and new sets and locations for their dramatic play. Girls' mass-market line extensions involve the addition of siblings or peers, rather than adversaries, and the expansion of domestic space. For example, Mattel introduced Magic Nursery Babies in 1990, (the "magic" being that the doll had to be brought home and a special packet immersed in water before discerning the doll's sex). In 1990, Magic Nursery Toddlers, Magic Nursery Newborns, and Magic Nursery Pets followed. My Little Pony introduces as many as ten new lines of ponies a year with names such as Tropical ponies, Flutter ponies, Bride ponies, and Carousel ponies. Within each new category, five or six different ponies are sold separately, as with the Sparkle pony set: Twinkler, Starhopper, Sunspot, Sky Rocket, Stardancer, Napper.

The line extensions for boys' action figures involve an infinitely expandable array of villains and monsters—each sold separately, on a bubble card. Boys' action figures and My Little Ponies are encased in plastic and attached to a card roughly eight inches by eleven inches, which hangs from a rack. This bubble packaging maximizes the use of retail space and makes the entire line visible to the child at once. For boys, successful toys such as Ghostbusters or Ninja Turtles or Masters of the Universe offer a couple of dozen characters in the cast: heroes, comic relief types, and villains and monsters. Additionally, weapons, vehicles, fortresses, hideouts, and headquarters may be purchased. For example, the Real Ghostbusters line includes the sets and props used in the cartoon: the firehouse, cars, gadgetry, and a series of gross ghosts who transform themselves into repulsive ghoulish faces—stomachs open up to reveal fangs, heads disappear, clothes peel back to reveal skeletons.

The line extensions of mass-market toys are a paradigm for consumer goods in general: they are at the same time always the same and always different (and for the moment, new). Children especially seem to enjoy the repeatability of the experience of purchasing toys; each time they visit Toys "R" Us, they can count on finding new versions of their favorite product lines. On the other hand, when line extensions die out, the consumer, looking for a new item of a different brand, may miss the comfort and security of selecting from a known line. Line extensions create a ready-made set of desires once a single item in the line is purchased and favored.

This phenomenon is not unique to children's consumer habits, although it is today a crucial element in their cycle of demand. Grant McCracken argues:

> It appears to be the case that consumer goods do not communicate well when they exist in isolation or in heterogeneous groups. The meaning of a good is best (and sometimes only) communicated when this good is surrounded by a complement of goods that carry the same significance. Within this complement, there is sufficient redundancy to allow the observer to identify the meaning of the good. In other words, the symbolic properties of material culture are such that things must mean together if they are to mean at all. . . . It is the cultural, meaningful aspects of goods that help to give them their secret harmonies.[12]

Children are not very different from adults in their desire to acquire matching goods. They vacillate between collage, creating new combinations of consumer goods, and loyalty, being quite rigid about purchasing and combining only certain brands.

Children's demands for certain kinds of goods over others, their obsessions with particular kinds and classes of goods, cannot be adequately explained by resorting to hedonism as an explanation for consumption behavior. Children's desire for promotional toys signals a mastery of the principles of consumer culture, that is, the accurate perception by the child of a system of meaningful social categories embodied in commodities and sets of commodities. The significance of these social meanings is often hidden from adults, who, as I have indicated, may be puzzled or offended by the toys most prized by children. Mass-market toys offend parents because they represent an alternative system of meanings, an inversion and confusion of adult culture. At an early age, children may exhibit an exceptional knowledge about toy categories and invest with enormous import things held in contempt by their parents. Parents frequently complain that children always want to get the same thing, never anything new; parents cannot understand the difference between one version of My Little Pony, for example, and the next and are baffled by the value the child places on the toy.

The mass-market toy industry is most often attacked for encouraging a separation of the sexes in play and for fostering violent play through "war toys," issues I address at the end of the chapter. The rarer but, to my mind, more serious and legitimate criticisms concern the toy industry's exploitation of young workers in Asia (under circumstances that are difficult to gather information about) and its contribution to environmental troubles through pollution and packaging waste (made obvious in the amount of garbage created each time a mass-market toy is unwrapped). A Malaysian friend told me that at the Mattel plant at home young female workers engage in collective fits of screaming provoked by their long silent hours at low pay. Because my study concerns the culture of childhood in the United States, I have not explored these issues here; but I would like to suggest that these might well be legitimate cause for future consumer boycotts of specific toys or manufacturers.

Toys "R" Us

Toys "R" Us forever changed the way mass-market toys are sold in the United States, and ultimately perhaps in Asia and Europe as well. Charles Lazarus opened the first Toys "R" Us store in 1957. Thirty years later Lazarus was the highest-paid executive in the United States, and there were 358 Toys "R" Us stores in the United States and 52 abroad. For the fiscal year ending in January 1990, the company reported sales of $4.8 billion and net earnings of $321 million. Market analysts predict that the chain will account for a 50 percent share of national retail toy sales by the end of the 1990s.

Toys "R" Us now sets the course for the entire industry. Many department stores ceased selling toys in the 1970s, unable to compete with the prices of Toys "R" Us; many individually owned and operated toy stores went out of business. Toys "R" Us wields a powerful influence on toy manufacturers as well as retailers. The way that Toys "R" Us operates its stores is typical of practices throughout the retail industries. Buying for each of the U.S. stores is centralized in New Jersey. Individual store managers merely unload the trucks that arrive at their loading docks; which toys and how many they will receive are determined at headquarters. Thus, Toys "R" Us's buyers have the ability to make or break each new mass-market toy displayed at the annual toy fair. National inventory control at Toys "R" Us carefully monitors the rate of toy sales. Losers and winners are quickly spotted, as are demographic trends in toy popularity. This information can be relayed back to the manufacturer, influencing decisions to alter television advertising campaigns or cancel or step up production. Toys "R" Us is able to offer slimmer profit margins on the most popular toys, and it is intensely resented for this by smaller toy sellers. (One of the few chains that competes successfully—Kay-Bee Toys—specializes in discontinued merchandise at drastic reductions.)

The idea behind Toys "R" Us was simple. The store is self-service. No personnel are available for counsel or personal service. A customer's interaction with the store's personnel is limited to the cashier at the door. The locations for the stores were carefully selected as so-called stand-alones, that is, they are not part of a mall. A trip to Toys "R" Us must be a separate stop on a shopper's itinerary. Customers drive to the store's parking lot, enter the store to make their often unwieldy purchases, and return directly to their cars (often pushing a grocery cart full of toys). Locations in shopping malls were avoided because parents would then have to carry the goods around with them, and this might limit their purchasing enthusiasm. Because shoppers cannot reach Toys "R" Us on foot, children cannot usually get to the store without their parents. In addition to toys, the store carries disposable diapers, infant formulas, and equipment such as strollers, cribs, and high chairs at discount prices. Securing the first-time mother's loyalty to the store when her child is only a newborn was a secret to the chain's success. Recently, Toys "R" Us has opened clothing stores, located adjacent to the toy stores, called Kids "R" Us.

Managers in New Jersey plan the stores' layout and send out in-

67. *Toys "R" Us ads depict many ethnic minorities and emphasize prices,
and aim at securing the first-time mother's loyalty.*

structions to each of the branches about where things should go in
the store and how they should be set up. Stores are arranged similarly, whether in Birmingham, England, or San Diego, California.
The major difference is between a right-hand or a left-hand store,
referring to the side of the entrance. The structures themselves

resemble unfinished warehouses, with white linoleum floors, bright fluorescent lights, and unfinished ceilings. The organization of each Toys "R" Us store and the divisions made between kinds of goods reflect the primary categories/divisions used by toy manufacturers. If one were to walk up and down each aisle, zigzagging until reaching the cashier area, these are the sections one would find, and this is the order in which they would be found:

> Seasonal goods (such as party favors, Christmas decorations and wrapping paper, Halloween costumes and candy,Easter baskets, summer pool supplies)
> School supplies, games, and computer/video software
> Sports, trucks, cars, and action figures
> Dolls, arts and crafts, play food
> Preschool toys, diapers, cribs, high chairs, strollers, playpens
> Indoor/outdoor playsets, pools, and sandboxes; cashiers

The store's layout reveals a few prominent themes and conspicuous "clusters." Its aisles are a spatial representation of the rules and boundaries of childhood socialization, marking what types of play are appropriate for different children, based on cost (income), gender, and age. There is a distinction between mental and physical forms of play, and this distinction is reinforced by the prices of the toys. Educational toys and high-tech toys (the most expensive ones available in the store) are encountered before dolls and action figures; computers and electronics are given the privilege of the first encounter. Toys "R" Us's physical layout stages a negotiation between parents and children about social aspirations, about values, and about the realities of spending money.

Toy aisles are carefully divided by age groups: infant (newborn to eighteen months of age), preschool (eighteen months to five years) and so on. They are also divided by gender: action figures, weapons, and cars and trucks; and dolls and ponies—most of which are marked for children three and up. Many of the national top sellers are inexpensive. In 1991 a toy like Hot Wheels cars sold for only a dollar each; action figures went for five to seven dollars; tiny dolls and multicolored ponies sold for five to nine dollars. In a right-hand store, boys' toys are encountered before girls' toys—so that girls must pass the boys' toys before reaching their own sections, but boys can completely avoid the girls' aisles, which are clustered

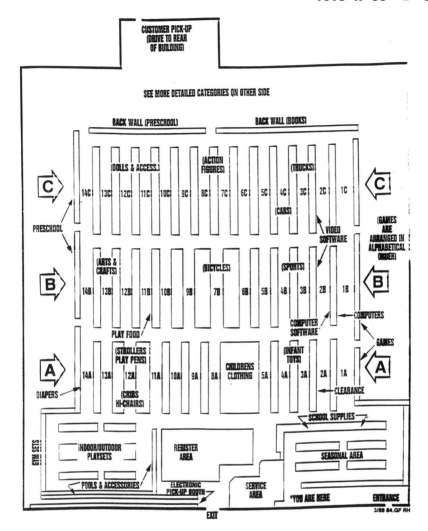

68. A typical floor plan for Toys "R" Us: the boys' and girls' toys are segregated.

in the far corner of the store. The aisles are made distinct by the striking color coding of the packaging: the trucks and cars aisles are full of metallic tones and dark and primary colors; the dolls and accessories aisles are a riot of pink and purple. Children learn to recognize Barbie's "wall of pink" by the age of three (girls in order to seek it out, boys to avoid it). Parents and children must walk through most of the store before finding the discounted diapers and baby formula, thus maximizing the chance for an impulse purchase.

Adjacent to the cash register area are the outdoor playsets where (despite signs claiming these are for display purposes only and the store is not responsible for injury) children play freely, rambunctiously with play houses, slides, and toy cars; parents often have to drag the children away in tears to leave the store.

The girls' sections are adjacent to the preschool toys and the infant goods, which are typically packaged in a supposedly gender-neutral—that is, inoffensive to boys—color, primary red and blue. The arts and crafts section—with paints, modeling clay, and sewing projects—is located near the dolls section, in a spatial metaphor that seems to suggest that arts and crafts are to girls' toys as sports are to boys' toys. The busiest aisles are those for toys most heavily advertised on television and most strongly gender typed in their design and packaging.

Since the Toys "R" Us store is not located in a mall, it becomes a world apart, a world devoted to the (commercial) subculture of child rearing and its material artifacts. Toys "R" Us is a store where you must spend a good deal of time, a fact necessitated by the sheer physical space of the store (around 15,000 square feet). Parents spend that time with others who are also parents or grandparents. A certain freedom comes with this separateness. Mothers exchange knowing smiles when children have tantrums, eye each other's selections, and give spontaneous tips to one another on toy selection. New babies are complimented by strangers. Toys "R" Us is one of the best public arenas outside church or the mall for parents to show off their new babies.

The scarcity of employees enhances the feeling of being part of a consumer subculture. No salespeople hover waiting to help. Children may run and shout and cry and rip packages and drop merchandise, and it almost seems that no one is watching. For many mothers, Toys "R" Us is a place where children can be brought to kill time, to play on indoor equipment when the weather is too bad to go to a park. It is an experience in which parent and child are at once "in public" and yet more anonymous than they would be at a neighborhood store or playground. Parents and children come "just to look" as a form of entertainment in itself. Children find a great sense of drama in making purchases, often before the eyes of a long line of waiting families. If Toys "R" Us is itself the entertainment, the cash registers are the place where the dramatic climax is reached.

In most locations, large numbers of African American and Hispanic families shop at Toys "R" Us; and the assortment of dolls for sale—one indicator of the racial and ethnic makeup of a toy store's clientele—is multiracial. Although parents from a wide range of income brackets shop at Toys "R" Us, the clientele skews toward the middle and working class. But one often sees parents in the store who have plenty of money to spend. In some locations the lot is filled with late-year minivans, jeeps, and Volvos, and totals at the checkout counter routinely exceed two hundred dollars. I know many middle-class mothers who refuse to shop at Toys "R" Us. These women often have postgraduate education and object to the gender stereotypes and war toys for sale. I also know churchgoing mothers who see the store as promoting material rather than spiritual values and who find some of the merchandise offensive. Some mothers refuse to shop at Toys "R" Us simply because they have had too many quarrels with their children there. I suspect that as both income and education rise, the percentages of Toys "R" Us's clientele probably dwindle, but I suspect that education is a more direct corollary than income.

A visit to Toys "R" Us can involve a great deal of dissonance and frustration. At any moment in the store, one can witness multiple scenes of parents battling for control of their children's consumer desires. Teaching children the limits of a household budget is one of the most difficult tasks for parents, since children are confronted with so much mass marketing of toys and food and with their peers' ownership of them. Toys "R" Us provides myriad opportunities for conflict between parent and child and is thus a place where parents can hardly avoid giving children a few lessons (often very explicitly) in right and wrong ways to make purchases. A lot of crying takes place in the store, as children request toys so temptingly packaged in "window" boxes and bubble cards as to appear within grasp. I've overheard a lot of working-class parents sternly lecturing their children on wasteful spending; on the finality of "no"; on the fact that it is one sibling's turn and not another's. Other parents just feel cheated: "Remember when we bought you X and you never played with it?" they scold. "It won't happen this time. *This* is what I really want," the child pleads. Working-class parents eye the mountains of merchandise they cannot afford and try to get out of the store with a birthday celebration within their means.

Some working-class parents' fears about spoiling children and their attempts to teach frugality, saving, and self-restraint are directly at odds with the modern conception of childhood as a sacred, Edenic period and toys as the key to the development of the indi-

vidual child. Toys "R" Us strains modern child-rearing philosophies to the breaking point. Covert forms of control, such as positive reinforcement, joint decision making, and "talking feelings
out," are preferred by child experts and many middle-class parents,
yet these strategies often fail in the face of children's keen desire for
promotional toys.

Affordability is one issue; aesthetics is a tougher one. The heart
of the middle-class objection to advertising on children's television
may be its tendency to develop in middle-class and upper middle-
class children a taste for toys that their parents deem garish, kitschy,
and "inappropriate." For this reason, many parents refuse to go to
Toys "R" Us. At the store private conflicts become (extremely)
public, easily overheard. Little girls whose mothers are feminists
demand Barbies and My Little Ponies; the sons of ex-hippies beg
for G.I. Joes and Robocops. Sometimes this play involves middle-
class children with occupational fantasies deemed unsuitable by
their parents. Boys imagine life as a soldier or a truck driver; girls
imagine life as a hairdresser or housewife. Yet play with these toys
may involve more drama than play with the abstract construction
sets and educational puzzles favored by the middle class. Thus,
class difference is enacted, practiced, compared in the aisles of the
store and in the kinds of toys that parents choose for their children.
As every family stands in the checkout line, the consumption patterns of wealthier families are very conspicuous; the scale of the
birthday party being planned is obvious from the numbers of toys
and party favors.

Toys "R" Us, like the toy industry itself, has taken the heat from
parents and consumer groups who are angry because the job of
controlling children's consumer desires is so difficult. What these
protests usually address, however, is not the problem of children
wanting toys parents cannot afford but of children wanting toys that
parents do not want them to have. Consumer protection groups such
as ACT rarely make explicit the middle-class values embodied in
their protest. To some adults, the physical environment of Toys "R"
Us is intolerable: the noise, the smell of plastic, the crowded aisles,
and the massive displays of merchandise revolt them, and they find
much of the merchandise—especially the promotional toys—tacky
and offensive. This same group of parents tends to have a great deal
of disposable income and a proclivity for indulging children with
gifts. For parents who can afford to spend more money on toys,
there are alternatives to Toys "R" Us. These toy stores were set up

with upper middle class parents in mind, and they stress the educational, "creative," or noncommercial value of toys.

Educational Toys and Yuppie Parents

As with other areas of consumer culture such as travel and bookselling, the more familiar marketing techniques targeted at the educated middle classes are never attacked with the strong sense of moral outrage extended to television mass marketing. Toy industry critics normally exempt educational toy marketing from the attacks leveled at promotional toys. In the late 1980s, upscale toy marketing with a strong educational emphasis began to flourish. A niche was discovered that consisted of affluent, educated parents intending to spend lots of money on "quality toys" for their children. Alternatives to Toys "R" Us, these specialty toy stores feature names like the Early Learning Centre, Imaginarium, Teacher's Pet, Alphabet Soup, Old World Toys, and Creative Kids. Most of these are independently owned and operated, but they are much more selective about their inventory than the old family business toy store. Some chains have made an effort to capture this market as well. Waldenkids, a toy store developed by Waldenbooks (a subsidiary of the discount giant Kmart) to target higher-income consumers, built stores only in the most exclusive shopping malls. These stores cater to parents willing to pay a higher markup for European-made toys. A retail analyst described Waldenkids's target market as "parents whose kids are taking ballet lessons at age four. They all want their kids to go to Harvard." [13] The business press calls them "yupscale" stores.

Whether independently owned or a subsidiary of a larger retail company, the stores uniformly feature track lighting, soft music, carpeting, and hands-on displays of toys. The soothing, comfortable physical space of these stores contrasts starkly with Toys "R" Us's harsh, bright lights, its uncarpeted floors, its enormous size and crowds. In the upscale toy store, design helps to disguise the fact that this is a place that sells things, and instead it fosters an association with the schoolroom. Toys are routinely taken out of their boxes and displayed at children's height. Young visitors are encouraged to play freely with the toys, a sales strategy that is reported to be very successful. Salespeople are middle-class, educated—even trained in early childhood development—and readily available with advice on gift selection. Complimentary gift wrapping is usually included in the stores' roster of services. (Like many other upscale stores, there is an attempt to imitate the roster of services associated with department stores at the turn of the century.)

Imaginarium, one of the toy retail industry's biggest success stories, is a company with twenty-four stores in California that has recently expanded to the East Coast. Imaginarium calls its clerks "toyologists" and claims that they are trained to get children playing as soon as they walk in the store (through a special kids-only entrance). The store offers special presentations, such as puppet shows, face painting, musical performances, and mime, and encourages parents and children to hang around playing or reading books together. Seventy-five percent of Imaginarium's products are imports ("Yuppie parents seem to like the imported items," reports one toy store owner. "They gravitate toward the boxes labeled in a foreign language." [14]). No mass-market toys and no violent toys are allowed. According to Jana Machin, the vice president of merchandising for Imaginarium, "no sexist delineations like girls' and boys' toys are allowed inside the walls of Imaginarium." [15] The industry trade journal *Playthings* gave Imaginarium an award for its "Imagine France" month-long promotion, which included a drawing to win a trip to Paris, decorations and informative signs, on French culture throughout the store, 250 French toys and books, a Babar boutique, and a "Babar à la mode" exhibit of seven Parisian scenes with Babar toys dressed in designer fashions. Employees were dressed in Imagine France T-shirts and French berets and were given a special training session on "fun facts" about French toy companies. [16]

In his book *Distinction*, Bourdieu recommends that any study of the toy market should determine "the meaning and function which the different classes consciously or unconsciously confer on toys according to their own schemes of perception and appreciation and, more precisely, according to their educational strategies." [17] Bourdieu argues that the extent to which toys are linked to an educational function will depend on the degree to which the family's social position depends on cultural rather than financial capital, as with teachers and their families. Bourdieu hypothesizes that the "logic of competition between firms of different types" will be decided by "different categories of clients." Wooden toys have enjoyed a revival because of the "taste for natural material and simple shapes" among the intellectual factions. The boom in educational toys is helped by the increasing competition for educational credentials. Bourdieu also links the emphasis on what he calls the "strictly unverifiable" educational value of toys with the supportive role of teachers, psychologists, charity groups, all those "with a stake in a definition of childhood capable of producing a market for goods and services aimed at children" and "who present their own lifestyle as an example to others and elevate the inclinations of their own ethos into a universal ethic." [18] The homes of intellectuals—and I would add here nursery schools—serve as a kind of "unsolicited advertising" for toys. These people tend to be those parents who do not allow or strictly limit television viewing; who forbid the purchase of licensed character toys; who ban Barbies as sexist and G.I. Joe as violent; who refuse to shop at Toys "R" Us.

The toys for sale at Toys "R" Us often make claims for their educational value, too. As I demonstrated in Chapter Two, claims to educational value have been a constant in toy advertising since the 1920s. The learning aids at Toys "R" Us, however, tend to promise education through mere contact with the object. In these kinds of educational toys, the object promises to replace the parent or the teacher. The emphasis is on memorization and rote learning, such as computers that drill a child on "basics" like arithmetic or spelling. The learning aids section at Toys "R" Us offers new technologies—gadgets—to give the child an edge over others at school (and to make up for any deficiencies the parents might feel in their own skills). Here we have a clear example of commodities offering the utopian promise of dissolving class differences, of leveling the playing field for the next generation. It is a "false" promise in one way because, as Bourdieu argues, nothing can replace the kind of early learning that takes place through daily exposure in the home to the bourgeois lifestyle. The kinds of learning aids for sale at Toys "R" Us do nothing to foster the kind of behavior that teachers consider "creative."

The toys for sale at Toys "R" Us usually violate the aesthetic codes of European toy manufacturers. For example, simple blocks are adorned with television characters, made of plastic, and manufactured in China rather than France or Germany. Upscale toy stores (and manufacturers) provide products that are decorated in primary colors (Ambi toys) and are made of natural materials (wooden trains, cotton or wool dolls). Even when they are made of plastic—as many of them inevitably are—their packaging emphasizes precision artisanship and painstaking design. Specialty stores are more likely to sell abacuses than the calculators available at Toys "R" Us. "Quality toys" are modestly packaged in primary colors;

noticeably missing are the shocking pinks and purples signaling the girls' mass-market toys. Upscale toys are more abstract in design (Lego). They figure scenes set in the past (Playmobil's Victorian dollhouse; medieval castle; cowboy and Indian sets); even baby dolls for sale are often replicas of styles fifty or one hundred years old. Toys are likely to come in sets that cost over fifty dollars to get started and can be expanded into the hundreds and hundreds of dollars.

One of Mattel's most successful experiments of the last few years has involved toys that change colors when they come in contact with hot and cold water (everything from dolls' hair, makeup and clothes to miniature cars and airplanes). These are the kinds of toys that are strong sellers at Toys "R" Us. But none of this kind of gimmickry is for sale at the upscale toy store: no fancy technology, no quick changes, no transformations (unless it's in a science kit). The toys, like the image they encourage of their owners' lives, are solid, well built, constant. They are not seasonal to the same extent as mass-market toys: the stores offer no closeouts, no discontinued lines, no remainders. Models tend to remain the same from year to year.

When the toys available in such shops feature licensed characters, they are characters made famous in books, not on television. The favorite licenses are those of classic European children's books such as Babar or Beatrix Potter's animals or Madeleine. Book displays occupy a large percentage of the store's space, and weekly story-telling times (usually on Saturday morning) are routinely offered in specialty stores. (Thus the toy store with its more exclusive clientele seeks to replace the public library as the place to go for children's storytelling.) Toys "R" Us sells books, too, but only those that are relatively cheap: no fifteen-dollar picture books for sale, only paperbacks.

Above all, the toys found in educational stores are not advertised on television. If advertised at all, these toys are advertised in magazines for parents or for teachers. The ads for these kinds of toys routinely connect the toy with the child's future career aspirations: as a doctor, an executive, an artist, a professor. The advertising campaigns designed to appeal to parents are remarkably uniform in their emphasis on individuality, creativity, and the presentation of play as children's work. Market researchers report that "older, wiser and richer" parents are concerned about the cost of education, workplace competition, and future earning capacity, and this fuels the demand for educational toys.[19] The price tags on the toys, the genteel school-like atmosphere, and the lack of objects recognizable from television mark these stores as comfortable havens of the professional middle classes. This is a shopping experience in which everyone in the store tends to be of similar age and socioeconomic background and everyone may participate in the same self-congratulatory feel of being dedicated to fostering her or his child's mental development. Most of the shoppers are white, as are the faces of the dolls—usually European-made.

Playmobil's line of toys typifies the aesthetic of this market: abstraction rather than detail; minimalism rather than decoration; creativity over mechanics. The Playmobil line is a staple offering of upscale toy stores. Playmobil offers new lines each season (knights with castles, animals and circus performers, Inuit with igloos, Native Americans with tepees, cavalrymen with forts, summer vacationers and their water sports, doctors and nurses at hospital). Each year Playmobil releases a free catalog that depicts the dolls staged in elaborate dramatic scenes; such care is taken with the photography and lighting that each picture resembles a movie still. The hands of each figure grasp and hold, and all the pieces are interchangeable, at 3½-inch scale. Playmobil only sells its toys to specialty stores and department stores, so no price cutting goes on. "We're not in Kmart and Toys "R" Us and we have no plans to be in the future," proclaimed president Alan Hess in *Toy and Hobby World*. Playmobil often refers to the fact that its founding company is the German manufacturer Geobra Brandstaetter, 114 years old. The toys have repeatedly won prizes such as the *Parents' Choice* award, given by an association of educators and parents who provide a listing of quality books, toys, videos, and computer games each year.

In 1990, Playmobil introduced a new line of toys packaged in pink tones. The packaging and the specific appeal to girls were something of a concession to the mass market. The color coding, a pale, lavender shade, echoed the packaging of mass-market toys but did not exceed the boundaries of good taste. At the top of the line was a Victorian dollhouse, retailing for $185. Small independent toy stores across the country reported the dollhouse to be one of their best sellers throughout the year. The catalog for the Victorian dollhouse introduces the character Vicki, "a little girl from a good-home who lived during the turn of the century. . . . Vicki's family belonged to 'high society,' because after all her father was the

69. Playmobil's Victorian dollhouse: a different class of fantasy compared to Barbie.

Chancellor of Commerce. Naturally, you can understand that Vicki should be raised by a governess." [20] The same brochure offers Vicki's diary—a first-person account of her trials and tribulations at her new London home, from her dealings with the French governess to her friendship with the cook—thus placing the story line somewhere between a child's *Upstairs, Downstairs* and the nineteenth-century women's novel. The advertising is thus embedded in a tonier kind of narrative than children's television commercials: "Suddenly the carriage stopped in front of a huge house. 'That one?' I asked; my father nodded. I was speechless. At first I thought it was a castle. 'How elegant and fascinating,' my mother said. 'I can't take my eyes off it.' "[21]

A comparison between Playmobil and Barbie dolls reveals some of the ideological differences embodied in the two kinds of toys. Although Playmobil clearly offers different sets to boys and girls, the toys are interchangeable and are not identified with one gender or the other in a television advertising campaign. The packaging is more discretely gender coded than mass-market toys. Girls' sets emphasize maternal fantasies rather than heterosexual romance, offering mother and child duos whether in a contemporary or a Victorian setting, boxed in lavender. Boys' sets emphasize action (police and ambulance teams) and adventure (cavalry and knight sets) and are boxed in blue. Unlike mass-market toys, which tend to be segregated by gender, all Playmobil sets include male and female figures, as well as different generations of dolls, and emphasize either some accurate rendering of the historical past or professional worklike settings. All of Playmobil's goods benefit in the American mind from the classy association with European settings.

By contrast, Barbie is exclusively for girls, thoroughly American, and thoroughly focused on leisure consumption activities—definitively, of course, changing clothes. Barbie comes with lots of furniture sets and vehicles for other leisure activities, but the class associations are quite different from Playmobil's: beauty parlors, mobile homes, Corvettes, bedroom sets.

Catalog Sales

Parents can avoid toy stores altogether by ordering toys from mail order companies, whose catalog toy sales have multiplied rapidly over the past decade. Marketing analysts attribute the surprising recent growth of catalog sales in an otherwise sluggish retail environment to the constraints on women's time. (Catalog sales have increased in many retail categories, including home furnishings and clothing.) Toys in catalogs usually duplicate much of the merchandise available in upscale toy stores. Mass-market toys are never available through the mail. In part this may be due to the lack of consumer demand, since the kinds of mothers who can afford to order toys through the mail are the kinds who do not want to buy Barbies and Ninja Turtles. Another factor is that the mail order companies' standard markup is so much higher than Toys R Us that promotional toys would be uncompetitively priced.

Some licensed toys do appear in some catalogs, just as they are sold at the specialty stores—typically, Disney licenses (My Little Mermaid), Sesame Street, Thomas the Tank Engine. Videotapes are routinely sold, although catalog copy explicitly claims their difference from commercial children's television. The catalog for Music for Little People, which advertises itself with the lofty claim that it believes in "the innocence of children and the sacredness and magic of life," sells tapes under the heading "videos worth watching." "Television in its present state leaves much to be desired. But those crafty little TVs always find a way to grab your kids' attention . . . we have chosen the best in educational and interactive alternatives."[22] The selection is entirely based on literary adaptations or documentaries. The pages selling Thomas the Tank Engine claim: "These fascinating tales about toy steam engines with very human personalities and problems are wonderfully narrated by Ringo Starr. Colorful live-action animation opens windows to the make-believe world of childhood games. . . . Now, you can also get the videos with a colorful metal toy train car!"[23] Here the deal on offer—see the television show, buy the toy—is no different from My Little Pony; but because the pitch is made to adults and the cultural associations—PBS, the Beatles, the magical world of make-believe—are more acceptable to middle-class adults, this type of marketing is rarely singled out for criticism.

Mail order catalogs share with the upscale toy stores an emphasis on "personal service"—the courteous voice to greet you on the other end of the phone, the owners mentioned by name and pictured with their children in an open, rather personal "letter" to the customers. ("The past 10 years have brought tremendous change, for me personally, and for the world . . ." reads a letter from one company president.) Catalog copy emphasizes the care that went into the selection of available items and the criteria of quality and educational value. Often the catalogs explicitly dedicate themselves to the mission of early childhood education. The text often includes advice or information about developmental stages; product claims emphasize how many of the child's different abilities the toy will challenge. Several children's catalogs refer to themselves as digests and are laid out so that they increasingly resemble magazines.

The "naturalness" of the toys' materials is emphasized—"100%

wool," "100% cotton," "natural wood," especially on the most expensive items. The fetish for materials parallels the vast expansion of the market for 100 percent cotton–children's clothing now offered in many specialized catalogs and expensive children's clothing stores. Plastics and polyester—the synthetic materials that fill Toys "R" Us and Kmart—are the devalued terms, and parents are urged to surround children exclusively with "natural" materials.

Mail order catalogs sometimes position themselves in terms of an alternative, "green," hippie aesthetic rather than a yuppie aesthetic, although there is much slippage between the two. The HearthSong catalog features materials used in Waldorf schools and emphasizes traditional games, crafts, cooking, handwork, and natural materials—wood, beeswax, wool, cotton. Enjoying a resurgence of popularity in the United States, especially in California and the Northwest, Waldorf schools were founded in Germany in the 1920s by philosopher Rudolf Steiner and emphasize a holistic approach to curriculum, dramatic play, handwork and crafts, and historical recreation.[24]

Waldorf parents are urged to strictly monitor children's consumption of television, movies, or mass-market toys. HearthSong's open letter states: "With a love of children, a reverence for life, and a desire to support you in your task of parenting, we offer you our service and our products—toys you'll feel good about giving"—thus implicitly damning the vast numbers of toys parents feel bad about giving. HearthSong's copy makes exalted claims for the durability of toys and their links with cultural traditions: "For more than 200 years people have been curious about . . ."; "Northern Europeans have been making and enjoying . . . for centuries"; "invented in 1834"; "first published in 1882"; "for nearly a century . . ."; "used traditionally in Central America." Such claims of a distinguished ancestry starkly contrast with the emphasis on newness in children's television commercials. (Of course Barbies could claim to be descendants of eighteenth-century European fashion dolls, and action figures were preceded by centuries of toy soldiers: both specialty and mass-market toys usually belong to types of toys that have been around for centuries. But young children are unlikely to be impressed by such a pitch.) The offerings at HearthSong are legitimated—and their high cost justified—by their association with history and cultural tradition. We worry a great deal about children being duped by toy advertising, but parents can also be persuaded to pay exorbitant prices for toys whose added value derives from rather dubious claims for a link to an older, folkloric tradition currently in fashion among some segments of the educated middle class.

More numerous than alternative companies such as HearthSong are toy merchants such as Troll Learn & Play, Childcraft, and Toys to Grow On. The Early Learning Centre states in its policy: "A constructive approach to childhood means we avoid toys which blatantly express violence or which rely on fashion and TV fads. So we can assure all caring parents that our products are there to stimulate development, imagination, creativity and confidence—without compromise." [25] The values and overall look of these catalogs are very similar to those of *Parents* magazine and toy ads for parents. Interspersed throughout the catalog are set-off columns of parental advice:

> "Pretend play forms a safe basis for children to make sense of the exciting world around them. Safe, because in a child's imagination any role, situation, character or job can be explored freely. Even anxieties can be dealt with once a child discovers how to act through the problem of finding a happy solution. Dressing up, copying parents and forming scenes are all special pleasures of childhood, invaluable for the future and a delight to watch today." [26]

The toys for sale intended for dramatic play include toy phones, doctors' kits, face paints, baby dolls, tool kits, cars, roadways, and tea sets—and Playmobil. There is nothing misleading about these claims, except that they are narrowly applied to "realistic," adult-oriented play with careers or domestic scenes. The same principle, however, makes sense for cheaper licensed, mass-market dolls and action figures and play involving television characters, fantastic scenarios, villains and monsters.

The new zip code system and the practice of selling mailing and subscription lists have boosted catalog sales. A subscriber to one parenting magazine is likely to be deluged with other offers for books and magazines. After a relative orders a toy for a child's birthday from one mail order toy company, the mailbox will be filled with other companies' toy catalogs. Mail order marketing with its emphasis on magazine subscriptions and residential location successfully lumps consumers by income bracket and taste culture. For a higher price than parents would have to pay for similar items at

Toys "R" Us, parents can avoid public skirmishes with children over toy selection. The parent selects the items and makes a phone call, and the goods appear at the door—thus circumventing the child's attempt to participate more directly in the selection of toys.

Opting Out

Today, children's consumption is often the focus of an anxiety that was previously centered on the consumer habits of working-class men and women of all classes. As Daniel Horowitz concludes in his study of nineteenth- and twentieth-century discussions of consumption, "corruption, decadence, self-control, [and] higher aspirations have remained the central terms of the discourse." [27] Mass-market toys are often portrayed as depraved and their purchase and ownership a sign of decadence. Educational and quality toys are usually exempt from this critique because they represent the imposition of adult control over the child's desires and an aspiration to higher things. Upscale toy stores and catalogs stress the uniqueness of their product mix, thus appealing to an adult's sense of individuality and value in things that are rare. Promotional toys, sold by the thousands at Toys "R" Us, derive their value for children from the fact that the toy will be exactly the same as someone else's.

When childhood experts discuss toys, they usually ignore the social nature of toy play and purchase. The possibility of social communications among children through toys is never considered or valued by these adults. But it is this potential for social communication within a community (whether peers, neighbors, parent groups, or co-workers) that the makers of mass-market toys are best at exploiting. Promotional toys serve to strengthen peer-group identification at an early age. Toys that are based on or developed alongside television programs group children as a market, but they also identify children with each other ("hey, she has a My Little Pony just like I have one") in powerful ways, frequently instigating conversation and even friendship.

While mass marketing of toys has facilitated interaction among very young children, it has deeply disturbed many parents—especially intellectuals. [28] Unlike teenagers, who may earn some of their own spending money (in minimum-wage jobs) and consume their subcultures outside the home in malls and movie theaters, when young children become fans of a certain toy, their mothers are called upon to buy the toys, rent the videos, or take them to the movie. The toys are played with at home, left around the living room, a constant reminder of the taste clash between parents and children.

Some women worry that if they provide children with mass-market toys like G.I. Joe and Barbie, others will judge them as bad mothers, guilty of promoting sexism or violence. The tension between what many middle-class mothers perceive as a duty to resist some aspects of commercial culture and their desire to express affection through gifts is an unhappy and ultimately unresolvable one. It understandably causes a lot of frustration and anger. Many mothers resist mass-market toys for years or months at a time and later cave in to their child's requests for several months at a time. Well-to-do parents vacillate between spending money on toys they select and approve of from the upscale stores and going to Toys "R" Us and letting the child pick anything he or she wants.

Some parents refuse to buy children's clothing with licensed characters on it because they object to children displaying the signs of commercialism on their bodies. Sometimes the restriction of mass-market goods is based on a sincere protest against consumerism. But a less idealistic rationale can also underlie such behavior. By opting out of the most common and popular forms of fashion, parents effectively mark their children off from others as "more" individual, a strategy recognized by Georg Simmel at the beginning of the century. Simmel commented that a departure from fashion "may result from a desire not to make common cause with the mass, a desire that has at its basis not independence of the mass, to be sure, but yet an inherently sovereign position with respect to the latter." [29]

What I wish to challenge here is the notion that total resistance to the commercialization of childhood by buying only "quality" toys is possible. Instead, this route consists of participation in an *alternative* market that is in many ways equally manipulative and "over-commercialized." That alternative is more elite and its advertising and retailing more "refined" in that it continually lays claim to higher aspirations. But it is a market nonetheless.

When it comes to dolls and character toys, gender distinctions are equally present in the educational toy store, if less conspicuous. Female characters are usually located in domestic settings: the baby dolls, the Playmobil Victorian dollhouses. Although the preteen Ginny or the Madame Alexander dolls favored by upscale toy sellers are younger and less voluptuous than Barbie, their accessories primarily consist of clothes changes. Having girls play with girl dolls whom they care for and whose clothes they change probably has the same effect—and that may be nil—on their potential as feminists whether the doll is a $16 Magic Nursery Baby or a $120 European baby doll, a Madame Alexander version of Scarlett O'Hara or a Hawaiian Fun Barbie.

The Playmobil and Lego sets are filled with male characters in action-adventure settings. The tiny cannons, spears, or guns—although justified by their historical setting—are as plentiful in many Playmobil sets as they are in the bubble packs of G.I. Joes or Ninja Turtles. One only has to look back at toy commercials from the 1950s to be convinced that the emphasis on shooting guns, firing missiles, and fighting has been standard practice in the design of boys' toys—to be advertised on television—for nearly forty years. Thus there is nothing disingenuous about the toy industry's puzzled response to critics: we're doing nothing different so why all the fuss now? As any parent or teacher who has tried to enforce a "no weapons" policy at home or at school can attest, little boys are phenomenally creative in turning found objects into guns when no toy guns are provided. The passion little boys feel for acting out aggressive fantasy scenarios is understandably disturbing to any pacifist baby boomer, but to lay all the blame on toy manufacturers is to avoid confronting the difficult and troubling question of the sources of this aggression within our children. As with gender differences, if we look more closely at what is normally considered acceptable in different social worlds, we find that upper middle-class boys' aggressive play is merely chaneled into forms—often legitimated by some link with another culture or historical setting—more acceptable to parents than Ghostbusters and Ninja Turtles. Thus the educated middle class generally prefers Playmobil pirates to G.I. Joes, karate belts to cowboy pistol holsters, archery sets to machine guns.

The distinctions that I have outlined here between mass marketing of toys and upscale marketing are signs of a much broader set of differences in what marketers would call "lifestyle," what Marxists call "class." These differences are reflected in the pronouncements of market researchers *and* continually reproduced in advertising, product design, and store layout and decoration. Class differences are not only portrayed in words and images about children, they are lived in the objects that surround children at home, at school, at friends' houses—and at the places they go to shop.

The fear that children's creativity and individuality are somehow under assault from exposure to promotional toys is probably unfounded. That fear stems more from the aspirations of middle-class parents than from any observation of children's behavior. Hodge and Tripp and Paley have recorded remarkable examples of children's complex understandings of narrative, genre, and social difference as embodied in television characters (many of them also made into toys). *Some* toys found in upscale stores and favored by teachers tend to be more abstract than representational, and exposure to these materials gives some kids a leg up over others when it comes to what will be required of them at school. But often the differences between promotional and "quality" toys have more to do with aesthetics and the taste codes associated with different classes than they do with any observable differences in how creative children can be with the toys.

The promotional, mass-market toys sold in Toys "R" Us and most available to and popular with working-class children are the toys most likely to be excluded from the culture of the classroom. So-called quality toys, the materials that conscientious, affluent parents will have provided for kids when they have taken expert advice to heart (and had the time to follow through on it by providing recommended toys), will be precisely the kinds of things the child will encounter in preschool and kindergarten. The familiarity of the school materials—including toys—will be just one of the many advantages that will bear on the child's future success in the classroom. Promotional toys, on the other hand, are likely to meet a cool reception by teachers. No Barbies or Ninja Turtles will be among the toys supplied by the school, and some evidence suggests that many children will rapidly learn not to talk about their favorite toys with teachers, or about what they have seen on TV.[30] In describing her observations at a kindergarten, Vivian Gussin Paley noted, "Every girl says Barbie is her favorite, most imply that their mothers disapprove, and the teachers tell me privately that they wish Barbie dolls were left at home."[31] Teachers of young children usually frown at the garish gender coding of toys. They are repulsed by the violence or grossness of many of the children's favorites and may ban them from the weekly "show-and-tell" or "sharing" time. When teachers attempt to censor popular toys, they may inadvertently contribute to a situation in which the children most in need of comfort, security, and involvement in school are the ones most disadvantaged.

CONCLUSION

arents and children negotiate all kinds of deals over television and toys. One mother refuses to allow Barbie in her house but buys Barbie's preteen sister Skipper for her daughter. Another mother permits Teenage Mutant Ninja Turtles at home but bans G.I. Joes. A child may succeed in persuading his mother to buy him a Terminator action figure but fail in persuading her to rent the video. Girls' makeup sets are banned when face painting is allowed. Water pistols are accepted when toy rifles are ruled out. Playmobil pirate sets are purchased willingly and multiply by a mother who refuses to buy more than one Batman action figure—and does that begrudgingly. One mother celebrates a child's participation in fandom, decorating a room with sheets, comforters, and curtains of My Little Mermaid or Ninja Turtles. She finds the toys and paraphernalia cute and appealing and feels that toy buying is a pleasurable means to relive an improved-upon version of her own childhood. Another mother may eliminate television from the household entirely and restrict her children's access to popular television characters to secondhand knowledge from the playground or visits to friends' houses. Often a mother restricts her children's viewing in the first few years to *Sesame Street* and *Mister Rogers*, but as the child grows older, she finds herself fighting more and more with her child over access to commercial shows. The battle lines between public versus commercial television, educational videos and literary adaptations versus toy-based animated series, this video versus that one, or one more hour of viewing versus one less are redrawn continually in parents' and children's daily lives. Tight budgets and frayed nerves mean that all parents must set some limits on their children's consumption, and these limits will depend on a complex interplay of factors including income, cultural capital, workload—both inside and outside the home—and beliefs about the nature of childhood.

As the mother of two small children, I am embroiled in these negotiations daily. While I wish to challenge some adult assumptions about toys and commercial television, I do not mean to trivialize the concerns that parents have about them or diminish the difficulty of setting limits on children's consumption. I have adopted a more permissive policy with regard to toy purchase and TV viewing than most of my friends, but I do so on a comfortable income and in the knowledge that my own job as a university professor serves as a safety net for my children. My children enjoy the advantages of easy access to high culture as well as popular culture. Even so, my Ph.D. and my professional specialization have not eliminated anxiety over the effects of toys and television on my children. As many women commented in response to a survey in *Working Mother* magazine about children and television, merely being asked about my children's consumption patterns is enough to prompt feelings of guilt and uncertainty.[1]

For mothers and for preschool teachers, babysitters and day-care workers—the vast majority of whom are female—decisions about children and consumer culture are very difficult and carry potentially serious consequences. Women bear the brunt of enforcing discipline and receiving blame when children's behavior is disruptive. Women are the ones who scrape together the money, who stretch the household budget to buy the pleaded-for birthday gift, who scour clearance shelves and garage sales for toys they can afford and clothes their children will like. Women are the ones who get the blame if the child appears spoiled to relatives and friends and husbands. Women are the ones children nag and the ones who try to provide alternative entertainment—sometimes searching everywhere for alternatives that are more acceptable to adults—when children are denied the toys or television shows they want. Women are the ones who have to rearrange their schedules to do their grocery shopping alone if arguments over buying become too intense and too embarrassing. When boys kick and fight in the manner of the latest cartoon hero, it is usually a woman on the job seeing that no one gets hurt.

Given all the problems consumer culture causes for mothers, why have I advocated its acceptance as a fact of contemporary life? Because I believe that the condemnation of commercial television and cheap, mass-produced toys has itself placed an unreasonable and somewhat unnecessary burden on mothers and has actually served to disadvantage children whose parents do not have the money and the time to acquire the approved alternatives. By way of conclusion, let me spell out some of the gains and losses involved in a young child's engagement with commercial television and mass-market toys, while suggesting that critics strive to be easier on mothers, tougher on "educational" toys and videos and classic children's books, and more sensitive to the school needs of working-class children.

Most adults interested in the project of a nonsexist education bemoan children's consumer culture for promoting aggression in boys and vanity in girls. One reason some women who care for children are harshly critical of television is that they want to discourage aggression in boys, and they perceive television as causing boys' aggression. Scapegoating television for boys' violent behavior is an understandable and satisfying response, because television may seem easier to control than the many other factors that loom too large to tackle, including innate aggression, violence at home and in the community, and a culture and industry of guns. But I do want to suggest that television often gives form to aggressive behavior some of which would manifest itself in other, "old-fashioned" ways anyway. The problem of aggressive behavior in boys predates television. The mission of all those who care for young children must include fostering an understanding of the differences between symbolic and real aggression, and the empathetic imagination of the victims of violence. Popular children's series are rarely straightforward promoters of violence. The truth is that children's television—as critic Louis Menand describes all of mass culture—is "a very unreliable postal service. Some messages that get sent are never received, and many messages are received that were never sent." [2] Adults need to take a second look at boys' animated series and recognize their complexity and the ways they offer a hybrid of messages about consumer culture, violence, environmentalism, and technology.

On the other hand, some girls' shows that appear to be noxiously feminine may provide a reasonably fertile ground for imagination compared with the long history of male heroes in children's stories in books and on the screen. When parents interested in combating sexism openly deride their daughters' toys as silly and kitschy, they may unwittingly compound the very feelings of female inferiority that they hope to oppose. The strict delineation of gender roles is perpetuated by the toy and television industries' conventional wisdom—and those industries can be faulted for declining to make much in the way of innovations in the toy styles and gendered stories that have been around for centuries. But we must also consider the toy manufacturers' response that they are merely catering to what their market research tells them children want. Many parents see toys and television programs as out of line with the modern world, as purveyors of outdated ideologies of gender. They are baffled by the appeal of rigid gender categories to young children. But I think that the appeal to children of gender stereotypes conveys an important message for adults: things have not changed as much as we might wish to believe. Children still live in a world where mothers and not fathers take primary responsibility for raising children and where nearly all of their paid caretakers are women. In their everyday lives children are exposed to the gender-based segregation of occupations everywhere they go: the nurse and the office receptionist are still likely to be women, the doctor a man; the grocery checkout clerk a woman, the store manager a man. At home most parents—no matter how committed to feminism—are more likely to praise their daughters for being polite and sensitive to the feelings of others and attractive, and their boys for being assertive and inquisitive and athletic. It is less than candid for parents to believe that children learn traditional gender distinctions only from Barbies, G.I. Joes, and television. With boys' and girls' toys and television series, we should bear in mind that children are more active, more creative, and more idiosyncratic in their play with toys and television plots than they are usually given credit for by adults.

Television programs and commercials address children of a certain age, but less obviously they address a viewer who is implicitly, or perhaps ideally, middle class, WASP, American, and male. Most children in the United States are poor, ethnic, and female. This means that *most* children will not resemble the heroes on children's television. While cultural studies have provided the insight that the genres of U.S. popular culture have proven to be exceptionally malleable to different interpretations by different groups—and I hope to have demonstrated some of those possibilities with children's commercials and television programs—there is much to criticize about them. Children, especially girls and children of color, may be very creative in the way that they make relevant meanings from and have fun with television, but I wish they didn't have to work so hard at it. I have said that toys and television are the lingua franca of small children, but for most children it is indeed a second language, one that speaks in faint and garbled tones to their own experiences and struggles for identity. The language of consumer culture could stand to incorporate more inflections and learn to speak more dialects.

Commercial television culture should not be singled out, however, as more racist and sexist than the pricier middle-brow alternatives currently offered to parents. Commercial television and mass-market toys are not the sole repositories of stereotypes and prejudices: these are linked to deeply entrenched cultural traditions. Thus, it is necessary to insist that while *Ghostbusters* excludes girls from the action, so does *Sesame Street*; while blue-eyed blonds dominate My Little Pony videos and Barbie commercials, they also dominate most illustrated versions of Alice in Wonderland, Mother Goose, Peter Pan. Racial stereotypes take form in action figures from Robocops to Worldwide Wrestling Federation and populate many animated cereal commercials, but such figures also crop up in Playmobil doll sets and the anthropomorphized animals of such classics as Rudyard Kipling's *Just So Stories*, Beatrix Potter's animals, and Laurent de Brunhoff's Babar.[3] Parents do not buy their way into a prejudice-free world when they ban commercial television, order educational toys from yuppie catalogs, and surround children with European children's classics. We need to combat the false and dangerous belief that racism is a working-class problem. By labeling stereotypes throughout children's literature, we gain a clearer perspective on the scope of racism and sexism throughout the culture—high, low, and middle brow—and can help children identify them more consistently.

Many outstanding picture books featuring ethnic minority characters (many of them female), urban settings, and extended families have been published in the past decade, among them Molly Bang's *The Paper Crane*, Vera B. Williams's *A Chair for My Mother*, Juanita Havrill's *Jamaica Tag-Along*, and Dayal Kaur Khalsa's *How Pizza Came to Queens*.[4] Currently there is a flurry of multicultural titles in children's publishing, including forays by prominent novelists, such as Amy Tan and Alice Walker, into picture books. But such examples still constitute a small fraction of the preschool book market. More common are such popular books and videos (and toy tie-ins) sold to parents for preschoolers as Clifford, The Big Red

Dog, Thomas the Tank Engine, The Berenstain Bears, Wee Sing, and *Barney and the Backyard Gang.* Most often they present a white, middle-class, suburban world with two parents and two children as a norm.[5] Children of color appear rarely, and only as tokens.

These books and videos exemplify a category of children's literature that novelist and critic Alison Lurie defines as books that "hoped to teach manners or morals or both." In these stories small children or animals "learned to depend on authority for help and advice. They also learned to be hardworking, responsible, and practical: to stay on the track and be content with their lot in life."[6] Young children may be satisfied with such stories and characters for a time, especially if the alternatives are kept away from them. But eventually kids are bound to wheel their heads around when they get a chance to see some of commercial television's alternatives—and want to keep watching.

Commercial television and mass-market toys subvert the didactic norm of the approved stories and express a resistance to the middle-class culture of parenting—with its emphasis on achievement, on play as work, and on the incessant teaching of numbers and letters—that may be very healthy indeed. In this respect, television producers and toy designers have capitalized on a tradition of subversion in children's literature and folklore identified by Lurie as stories that "recommended—even celebrated—daydreaming, disobedience, answering back, running away from home, and concealing one's private thoughts and feelings from unsympathetic grown-ups. They overturned adult pretensions and made fun of adult institutions, including school and family."[7] This subversive strand can be seen in many of the materials discussed in this book, from gross or ultrafeminine toys, to commercials in which the children hold a wild dance party behind the teacher's turned back, to the megalomaniac fathers and mothers cast as cartoon villains. Although Lurie herself is no fan of children's commercial culture,[8] and would probably not include any part of it among the texts she approves, I would argue that television and promotional toys have drawn on the subversive tradition in children's literature, and although the efforts of animators, toy designers, and marketers may seem more driven by profit than by creativity, their work is rather similar in its appeal to the subversive classics by Mark Twain and Lewis Carroll that Lurie praises.

One complaint about television is that it has made the subversive themes of childhood culture accessible to children who are too young for it, children who used to be more completely under their parents' control. As a parent, I naturally prefer Mister Rogers, with his kindly pep talks on self-esteem, his gentle suggestions about constructive ways to handle anger, his educational science projects and factory tours, to Teenage Mutant Ninja Turtles. But the fascination of those television worlds beyond the PBS channel, where adults have vanished or figure as despicable villains and where "kids rule," is too great to resist. It is extremely doubtful that any parenting tactics—however clever—will talk young children out of their interest in it. To some, this may sound like merely succumbing because the sides—television culture on one side, the parent on the other—are too unevenly stacked, and that is partly true. But it may be a consolation for parents to be reminded that the subversive appeal of kids' culture, its propensity for inverting adult values, predates television marketing—it has been around in children's rhymes and fairy tales for centuries.

Mothers should not be judged on the basis of their ability to provide "quality" toys and ban commercial TV; and children should not be judged adversely when they know a lot about television. We need to acknowledge how difficult it is to raise young children in a consumer society while easing the workload of mothers where possible and enhancing the chances for all children to feel comfortable and involved in school from the beginning. Instead of recommending censorship as the first recourse, adults need to ponder why certain toys and television shows hold a child's imagination and what this may tell us about the fantasy life of the child—and the child's attempts to grasp the culture of grown-ups.

Children's consumer culture involves rebellion, and that rebellion may convey a resistance to parental culture. For the children of ambitious, middle-class parents, television watching itself may be seen as a rebellion against the ceaseless drive in pedagogy and child-rearing practices to make the child productive every minute of the day—by indefatigably climbing the ladder of cognitive development. As small children spend more of their time in structured day-care environments, their need for the "downtime" of television viewing may be more important. Children's television viewing may be an assertion of privacy. As historian Stephanie Coontz argues, it is difficult to judge whether the twentieth century's decline in parental authoritarianism has led to more or less freedom for children: "While parents have ceased to demand total obedience from their children, offering them the opportunity to make many of their own decisions as well as to inhabit private rooms, they have become more and more insistent that children share their thoughts and feelings. . . . [T]he right to remain silent seems to have become a thing of the past."[9] Children's embrace of toys and television shows that blatantly violate the norms of parental culture, and that their parents do not take an interest in, may be an attempt to reassert some privacy in their play, to resist the attentions of the child-centered parent.

Different children have different things to win or lose when they take pleasure in a peer-oriented mass culture. There are negative consequences of immersion in television culture when it is defined as poor and inadequate in comparison to bourgeois culture. Children may use television in the power struggle with their parents, but television viewing to the exclusion of other activities is debilitating and self-destructive in the long run if it leaves no time for the acquisition of skills that the *public* sphere will require. When dealing with young children, the *disadvantages* of immersion in consumer culture become painfully, abundantly clear, as this is likely to be interpreted as a significant *lack* of mental abilities when the child enters first grade. To be a television fan and only a television fan—not a museum, zoo, or library patron—has negative consequences in poor evaluations of school performance.

I wish to argue that parents and teachers should worry less about the debilitating effects on children—especially affluent children—of toys and television and worry more about ways to improve access to education *and* entertainment for children against whom the odds are already stacked. I believe this needs to include more integration of popular culture into the curriculum at the earliest ages. The best schools and teachers strive for a curriculum of inclusion that takes as its starting point children's knowledge—including knowledge about television and toys—and moves on from there. We need to resist mass culture when it is bad, but we also need to resist the sometimes spurious distinctions put forward by marketers of "quality" educational materials targeting teachers and professionals. Parents and teachers need to be vigilantly self-conscious about the dominance of the middle-class culture of child rearing and be willing to challenge the privileges and unexamined assumptions that this culture masks.

NOTES

INTRODUCTION

1. I am thinking here of some work by scholars Christopher Lasch, Stuart Ewen, Todd Gitlin, and Mark Crispin Miller.

2. Patricia Palmer, *The Lively Audience: A Study of Children around the TV Set* (Sidney: Allen & Unwin, 1986), 142.

ONE. CHILDREN'S DESIRES/MOTHERS' DILEMMAS

1. The line is Judy Holliday's from the film *Born Yesterday*. Charlotte Brunsdon quotes Holliday and discusses the low status of television viewing in her article "Television: Aesthetics and Audiences," in *Logics of Television: Essays in Cultural Criticism*, ed. Patricia Mellencamp (Bloomington: Indiana University Press, 1990), 62.

2. Daniel Miller, *Material Culture and Mass Consumption* (Oxford: Basil Blackwell, 1987), 215.

3. Richard Dyer, "Entertainment and Utopia," in *Movies and Methods*, vol. 2, ed. Bill Nichols (Berkeley and Los Angeles: University of California Press, 1985), 222.

4. Ibid., 224–225.

5. Fredric Jameson, *The Political Unconscious: Narrative as a Socially Symbolic Act* (Ithaca, N.Y.: Cornell University Press, 1981), 69. Dyer's argument is familiar from Hans Magnus Enzensberger and Herbert Marcuse; Dyer, "Entertainment," 229.

6. Some useful reviews of this research can be found in Ellen Carol Dubois et al., *Feminist Scholarship: Kindling in the Groves of Academe* (Urbana and Chicago, University of Illinois Press, 1987), 113–125; Stephanie Coontz, *The Social Origins of Private Life: A History of American Families* (London: Verso, 1988), 349–354; and Dolores Hayden, *Redesigning the American Dream: The Future of Housing, Work, and Family Life* (New York: Norton, 1984), 65–95.

7. Ruth Schwartz Cowan, *More Work for Mother* (New York: Basic Books, 1986).

8. Hayden, *Redesigning*, 55–56.

9. Arlie Hochschild, *The Second Shift* (New York: Avon, 1989), 2.

10. Hayden, *Redesigning,* 64–65.

11. Sarah Fenstermaker Berk, *The Gender Factory: The Apportionment of Work in American Households* (New York: Plenum Press, 1985), 197.

12. Cowan, *More Work,* 213; Arlie Hochschild's book *The Second Shift* paints a vivid picture of the fatigue created by what she calls the "leisure gap."

13. Hochschild, *Second Shift,* 3. The summary of the research is included in Hochschild's appendix, "Research on Who Does the Housework and Childcare," 277–279.

14. Ibid., 9.

15. Cited in ibid., 250.

16. Coontz, *Social Origins,* 337.

17. Phyllis Palmer, *Domesticity and Dirt: Housewives and Domestic Servants in the United States, 1920–1945* (Philadelphia: Temple University Press, 1989), 13.

18. Hochschild, *Second Shift,* 246.

19. Ibid., 232.

20. Cited in Nona Glazer-Malbin, "Housework," *Signs* 1, no. 4 (1976): 913.

21. Bert Leiman, associate director of children's research, Leo Burnett Co., interview with author, Chicago, August 1989.

22. Ann Oakley, *Woman's Work: The Housewife, Past and Present* (New York: Vintage Books, 1974), 210.

23. Christina Hardyment, *Dream Babies: Three Centuries of Good Advice on Child Care* (New York: Harper & Row, 1983), 242.

24. Ibid., 226.

25. Roland Marchand, *Advertising the American Dream: Making Way for Modernity, 1920–1940* (Berkeley and Los Angeles: University of California Press, 1985), 230.

26. Ibid., 228–232.

27. Ibid., 232.

28. Nancy Chodorow, *The Reproduction of Mothering: Psychoanalysis and the Sociology of Gender* (Berkeley and Los Angeles: University of California Press, 1978), 232.

29. Marchand, *Advertising,* 232.

30. See Lynn Spigel, "Television and the Family Circle: The Popular Reception of a New Medium," in Mellencamp, *Logics of Television.*

31. Philip Simpson, ed., *Parents Talking Television* (London: Comedia, 1987), 65.

32. Marie Winn, *The Plug-in Drug* (New York: Viking Press, 1977). Neil Postman, *The Disappearance of Childhood* (New York: Delacorte Press, 1982).

33. For an extensive critique of developmental psychology, see Julian Henriques et al., *Changing the Subject: Psychology, Social Regulation, and Subjectivity* (London: Methuen, 1984).

34. Palmer, *Lively Audience,* 135.

35. Quoted in Julius and Zelda Segal, "The Two Sides of Television," *Parents,* March 1990, 186.

36. Wilbur Schramm, Jack Lyle, and Edwin Parker, *Television in the Lives of Our Children* (Palo Alto, Calif.: Stanford University Press, 1961); I have relied on the summary of this research in Shearon Lowery and Melvin L. De Fleur, *Mile-*

stones in Mass Communication Research (New York and London: Longman, 1983), 267–295.

37. Much of this work is summarized in Jennings Bryant and Daniel R. Anderson, eds., *Children's Understanding of Television: Research on Attention and Comprehension* (New York: Academic Press, 1983).

38. Palmer, *Lively Audience*. Television meanings as inextricable from family interactions and the domestic space has been a focus of attention in research by David Morley, James Lull, Jan-Uwe Rogge, and Hermann Bausinger.

39. Dafna Lemish, "Viewers in Diapers: The Early Development of Television Viewing," in *Natural Audiences: Qualitative Research of Media Uses and Effects,* ed. Thomas Lindlof (Norwood, N.J.: Ablex, 1987), 33–57. See also Paul Messaris, "Mothers' Comments to Their Children about the Relationship between Television and Reality," in Lindlof, *Natural Audiences,* 95–108.

40. *Fangface* was an animated series about the adventures of the werewolf Sherman Fangsworth and his teenage companions Kim, Biff, and Pugsie. Generically, the series was based primarily on a comedy-mystery type of story (sometimes called the "Let's get out of here" adventure formula) found in many examples of cartoons, from *Scooby Doo* (1969–1980) to *Slimer and the Real Ghostbusters* (1986–).

41. Robert Hodge and David Tripp, *Children and Television: A Semiotic Approach* (Stanford, Calif.: Stanford University Press, 1986), 26.

42. Ibid., 71.

43. David Morley makes this point, which has been increasingly taken up by cultural studies, in *Family Television: Cultural Power and Domestic Leisure* (London: Comedia, 1986), 30.

44. Peggy Charren quoted in Margaret B. Carlson, "Babes in Toyland," *American Film,* January–February 1986, 56.

45. T. J. Jackson Lears, "From Salvation to Self-realization: Advertising and the Therapeutic Roots of Consumer Culture, 1880–1930," in *The Culture of Consumption,* ed. Richard Wightman Fox and T. J. Jackson Lears (New York: Pantheon, 1983), 3.

46. Miller, *Material Culture,* 166.

47. Daniel Horowitz, *The Morality of Spending: Attitudes toward the Consumer Society in America, 1875–1940* (Baltimore: Johns Hopkins University Press, 1985), 166.

48. Daniel Miller comments dryly that "the argument that there is a thing called capitalist society which renders its population entirely pathological and dehumanized, with the exception of certain theorists who, although inevitably living their private lives in accordance with the tenets of this delusion, are able in their abstracted social theory to rise above, criticize and provide the only alternative model for society, is somewhat suspicious." (*Material Culture,* 167).

49. For theoretical discussions of Marx's concept of use value that adapt it to contemporary consumer culture see Susan Willis, *A Primer for Daily Life* (London: Routledge, 1991); Wolfgang Haug, *Critique of Commodity Aesthetics* (Minneapolis: University of Minnesota Press, 1986); Jean Baudrillard, *The Mirror of Production* (St. Louis: Telos Press, 1975) and *For a Critique of the Political Economy of the Sign* (St. Louis: Telos Press, 1981).

50. A fascinating pedagogical exercise that demonstrates the inescapability of

the significance of clothing has been developed by Professor Chuck Kleinhans at Northwestern University, Evanston, Illinois, who devotes one day of his class to photographing students' attire, pronouncing that each student will be assumed to be making a fashion statement based on what he or she is wearing that day.

51. The bread-baking phenomenon was sufficiently widespread to be attacked by marketers who now offer a range of gadgetry (flour mills, convection ovens, dough risers) and supplies (whole grains, health foods) to aid in the process.

52. Thorstein Veblen, *The Theory of the Leisure Class: An Economic Study of Institutions* (1899; reprint, New York: Modern Library, 1934), 101.

53. Stuart Ewen, *All Consuming Images: The Politics of Style in Contemporary Culture* (New York: Basic Books, 1988), 62; the concept of "consumption communities" is Daniel Boorstin's.

54. Miller, *Material Culture,* 206.

55. Mary Douglas, "Goods as a System of Communication," in *In the Active Voice* (London: Routledge & Kegan Paul, 1988), 24.

56. Ibid., 24.

57. Sut Jhally, *The Codes of Advertising: Fetishism and the Political Economy of Meaning in the Consumer Society* (New York: St. Martin's Press, 1987), 50.

58. Ibid., 51.

59. Colin Campbell, *The Romantic Ethic and the Spirit of Modern Consumerism* (Oxford: Basil Blackwell, 1987), 203.

60. Daniel Miller points out that Veblen's analysis focused on a newly emerging social group in the late nineteenth century, the nouveaux riches, and the strategies of conspicuous consumption and conspicuous leisure that they adopted in imitation of those with "old money," the aristocratic class.

61. Veblen, *Leisure Class,* 103.

62. Grant McCracken, *Culture and Consumption: New Approaches to the Symbolic Character of Consumer Goods and Activities* (Bloomington: Indiana University Press, 1988), xiv. Georg Simmel, "Fashion," in *On Individuality and Social Forms: Selected Writings,* ed. Donald N. Levine (Chicago: University of Chicago Press, 1971), 302.

63. N. McKendrick, "Commercialization and the Economy," in N. McKendrick, J. Brewer, and J. Plumb, *The Birth of a Consumer Society: The Commercialization of Eighteenth-Century England* (Bloomington: Indiana University Press, 1982), 20.

64. Pierre Bourdieu, *Distinction: A Social Critique of the Judgment of Taste,* trans. Richard Nice (Cambridge: Harvard University Press, 1984), 6.

65. Ibid., 56, 57.

66. Michele Lamont and Annette Lareau, "Cultural Capital: Allusions and Glissandos in Recent Theoretical Developments," *Sociological Theory* 6 (1988): 163.

67. Ibid., 163.

TWO. BUYING HAPPINESS, BUYING SUCCESS

1. Today there are a number of competing publications, such as *Child* and *Working Mother,* that are targeted at professional parents, but all operate primarily as sources of advice and consumer guides. *Parents* is organized according to the same divisions as other magazines for women—fashion, food, home decorating, "crafts"—but has an increased emphasis on how to procure the best medical,

psychological, or educational services for children and the best of consumer goods. The difference between *Parents* and other magazines is a question of degree: an address to women as mothers is a definitive feature of many other women's magazines: *Redbook, Woman's Day, Family Circle, Ladies' Home Journal;* often the same advertisements appear in these and in *Parents* magazine.

2. Viviana Zelizer, *Pricing the Priceless Child* (New York: Basic Books, 1987), 10.

3. Mary Lynn Stevens Heininger, "Children, Childhood, and Change in America, 1820–1920," in Heininger et al., *A Century of Childhood, 1820–1920* (Rochester, New York: Margaret Woodbury Strong Museum, 1984) 30.

4. Zelizer, *Pricing,* 11.

5. Bourdieu, *Distinction,* 78.

6. Elaine Tyler May, *Homeward Bound: American Families in the Cold War Era* (New York: Basic Books, 1988), 166.

7. Ibid., 167.

8. Marchand, *Advertising,* 165.

9. Ibid., 166.

10. The kinds of images of children seen in advertisements for parents borrow only selectively from the scenes and poses of children as seen in general market advertising or decorations. For example, the image of the mischievous boy, which Heininger notes was extremely popular in the late nineteenth century and was used in Norman Rockwell's illustrations, was probably too close to the discipline problems faced by real parents to hold much appeal in toy advertising.

11. This same expression and pose can be found in advertisements for household products, in which the model is an adult woman, marveling at the cleanliness of her sink; it is not a pose used for adult men.

12. In the 1990s there is more emphasis on packaging and brand names, rather than manufacturers' names, as a way to make children remember exactly what they want; small children have the reputation among manufacturers for being fickle once inside the stores, lacking in brand loyalty, and likely to fall for a knockoff of a television-advertised toy.

13. May, *Homeward Bound,* 14. See also Mary Beth Haralovich, "Sitcoms and Suburbs: Positioning the 1950s Homemaker," *Quarterly Review of Film and Video* 11 (1990): 61–83.

14. *Parents,* December 1935, 63.

15. *Parents,* November 1930, 59.

16. Marchand, *Advertising,* 296–297.

17. *Parents,* December 1954, 33.

18. Rachel Dunaway Cox, "What Shall We Give the Children?" *Parents,* December 1928, 32.

19. William Alvadore Buck, "Playthings: Tools for Growth, *Parents,* December 1956, 50.

20. Ibid., 52.

21. Ibid., 52.

22. Brian Sutton-Smith, *Toys as Culture* (New York: Gadner Press, 1986), 25–26.

23. Janet M. Knopf, "Toys That Teach," *Parents,* December 1930, 71.

24. Ibid., 71.

25. "The Right Playthings" *Parents,* December 1953, 92.

26. Helen Thomson, "How Playthings Can Help Your Child Grow," *Parents,* December 1954, 48.

27. Eileen S. Nelson, "Up-to-the-Minute Guide to the Newest in Playthings," *Parents,* December 1953, 62.

28. See McKendrick, in "Commercialization," and Rosalind Williams, *Dream Worlds: Mass Consumption and Late Nineteenth Century France* (Berkeley and Los Angeles: University of California Press, 1982).

29. J. H. Plumb, "Children and Consumption," in McKendrick, Brewer, and Plumb, *Birth of a Consumer Society,* 292.

30. Heininger, "Children," 30.

31. M. Ellen Housman, "Young Ideas in Toys," *Parents,* December 1935, 20.

32. Eventually, in the 1980s, Lego began advertising directly to children on television and became available at discount chain stores.

33. *Parents,* December 1966, 43.

34. The single child in a bare studio set is also a convenient arrangement, eliminating the cost of producing a set, and the style mirrors that of other advertisements.

35. Willis, *Primer,* 94–95.

36. Virginia Wise Marx, "A Guide to the Best in Toys," *Parents,* November 1948, 35.

37. *Parents,* December 1928, 45.

38. Willis notes that the most common plaything of the 1980s was a plastic child-size shopping cart.

39. Marchand discusses the family circle in ads of the 1930s, especially surrounding the radio or newspaper, 248–254.

40. Lionel trains introduced a pink and lavender model in 1957, which was a disastrous failure. Sydney Ladensohn Stern and Ted Schoenhause, *Toyland: The High-Stakes Game of the Toy Industry* (Chicago: Contemporary Books, 1990), 201.

41. Heininger, "Children," 1–33.

42. Richard Dyer, "White," *Screen* 29, no. 4 (1988): 44–65.

43. For discussions of the economics of media advertising, see Felix Gutierrez, "Advertising and the Growth of Minority Markets and Media," *Journal of Communication Inquiry* 14 (1990); for a discussion of the sociopsychological impact of advertising on children, including the effect of ads for adult products on minority children, see Barbara Brown, "Advertising Influences on Majority and Minority Youth: Images of Inclusion and Exclusion," *Journal of Communication Inquiry* 14 (1990): 6–30.

44. I have discussed the various connotations of this type of set as seen in *The Cosby Show* title sequences in Seiter, "Semiotics and Television," in *Channels of Discourse,* ed. Robert C. Allen (Chapel Hill: University of North Carolina Press, 1987), 20–23.

45. Erving Goffman, *Gender Advertisements* (New York: Harper & Row, 1976), 26.

46. This strategy was often used in adult ads in the 1970s and 1980s: for example, there were his and her versions of a Myer's Rum ad, with the individual adult described as a personification of the successful careerist.

47. Terry Lovell, *Consuming Fiction* (London: Verso, 1987), 154.

THREE. THE REAL POWER OF COMMERCIALS

1. *FTC Final Staff Report* quoted in Brian M. Young, *Television Advertising and Children* (Oxford: Oxford University Press (Clarendon Press, 1990), 33.

2. ACT Speaker's Kit (1979), 14.

3. Scott Ward, Tom Robertson, and Ray Brown, eds., *Commercial Television and European Children* (Hants, England: Gower, 1986), 33–53.

4. Lemish, "Viewers in Diapers," 33–57.

5. Richard Adler et al., "Research on the Effects of Advertising on Children: A Review of the Literature and Recommendations for Future Research" (Washington, D.C.: U.S. Government Printing Office), 38.

6. For a review of this research, see Young, *Television Advertising,* 212–214.

7. One exception was a more complex study by Ellen Wartella and James Ettema that examined the various types of commercials, the order in which they were shown, and their use of audiovisual techniques and tried to correlate these factors with children's attention; see Wartella and Ettema, "A Cognitive Developmental Study of Children's Attention to Television Commercials," *Communication Research* 1 (1974): 44–69.

8. Quoted in Young, *Television Advertising,* 30; Dale Kunkel and Bruce Watkins cover the political situation leading to this decision in "Evolution of Children's Television Regulatory Policy," *Journal of Broadcasting and Electronic Media* 31 (1987): 367–389.

9. The Children's Advertising Review Unit (CARU) of the National Advertising Division of the Council of Better Business Bureaus, monitors "audiovisual techniques" that "misrepresent the appearance of children's products or exaggerate product performance." For example, CARU received a complaint against a plush-toy company that "pictured several stuffed animals in groups that appeared to move on their own." CARU advised that the toys be shown in "a realistic play setting" that would provide clues as to the toys' scale (*Advertising Age,* 17 April 1989).

10. ACT Speaker's Kit (1979), 15.

11. "We have no problems with a teacher teaching or a preacher preaching not to watch a particular program but we have problems with a threatened boycott. . . . No matter how you couch it, and no matter how well intentioned it is, that's censorship." Gene Mater, CBS senior vice president, quoted in Kathryn C. Montgomery, *Target: Prime Time* (New York, Oxford University Press, 1989), 160.

12. James U. McNeal, *Children as Consumers* (Lexington, Mass.: Lexington Books, 1987), 250.

13. In one recent example, Reebok introduced Weebok shoes for children up to age five, Reeboks for kids five to ten—backed by a television ad campaign—hoping to capture children for adult Reebok advertising by the age of ten. See Jesus Sanchez, "Children's Advertising Grows Up, but Not Everyone Approves," *Los Angeles Times,* 29 May 1990, D6.

14. Spigel, "Television and the Family Circle," 73–97.

15. The film industry in the 1920s had also designated Saturday morning as the appropriate slot for children's entertainment and offered specialized packages of shorts and feature films at screenings exclusively for children; see Richard deCordova, "Ethnography and Exhibition: The Child Audience, The Hays Office, and Saturday Matinees," *Camera Obscura* 23 (1991): 91–108.

16. Young, *Television Advertising,* 23–24.

17. The 1989 and syndication figures are from "'Turtles' Takes Off," *Elec-*

tronic Media 6 (April 1990): 1; 1990 network estimate from Sanchez, "Children's Advertising Grows Up," D6.

18. Donna Leccese, "Toy Advertising and TV: A Healthy Marriage," *Playthings,* July 1989, 28–31.

19. Beth Bogart, "Word of Mouth Travels Fastest," *Advertising Age,* 6 February 1989.

20. Cedric Cullingford, *Children and Television* (Aldershot, England: Gower, 1984), 121.

21. Ibid., 131.

22. "Toy Makers Get Their Backs Up When Critics Nag at Kid TV Ads," *Variety,* 27 April 1988.

23. Young, *Television Advertising,* 17.

24. Kim Foltz, "TV Ad's Hip Pitch: It's 'Cool' to Be a Boy Scout," *New York Times,* 30 October 1989, C14.

25. Bert Leiman, associate director of children's research, Leo Burnett Co., interview with author, Chicago, 25 July 1989.

26. Quoted in Kate Fitzgerald, "Tapes of Toy Ads Proposed for Kids," *Advertising Age,* 29 May 1989.

27. Young, *Television Advertising,* 201.

28. Anthony Chapman, Jean R. Smith, and Hugh C. Foot, "Humour, Laughter, and Social Interaction," in *Children's Humour,* ed. Paul E. McGhee and Anthony J. Chapman (Chichester: John Wiley and Sons, 1980), 149.

29. Ibid., 148.

30. For a study of the use of cable, VCRs, and network television by the parents of young children in a college town, see Ellen Wartella, Katharine Elizabeth Heintz, Amy Joan Aidman, and Sharon Rose Mazzarella, "Television and Beyond: Children's Video Media in One Community," *Communication Research* 17 (1990), 45–64.

31. Young, *Television Advertising,* 101, notes that Sweden cannot enforce its policy against advertising to children when the Sky channel beams in commercials.

32. Marsha Kinder, *Playing with Power in Movies, Television, and Video Games* (Berkeley and Los Angeles: University of California Press, 1991), 172.

FOUR: UTOPIA OR DISCRIMINATION?

1. Young, *Television Advertising,* 15.

2. Allison James, "Confections, Concoctions, and Conceptions," *Journal of the Anthropological Society of Oxford* 10 (1982): 85.

3. Ibid., 83.

4. Ibid., 92.

5. V. I. Propp discusses this kind of structural scheme for the folktale in his classic study *Morphology of the Folktale* (Austin: University of Texas Press, 1968).

6. See Edward Said, *Orientalism* (London: Routledge & Kegan Paul, 1978).

7. Stern and Schoenhaus, *Toyland,* 201.

8. Susan Willis discusses the anxiety generated by young children's contemplation of adolescence in *A Primer for Daily Life,* 23–40.

9. Dyer, "Entertainment," 222.

10. Robert E. Pitts, Joel Whalen, Robert O'Keefe, and Vernon Murray, "Black and White Response to Culturally Targeted Television Commercials: A Values-based Approach," *Psychology and Marketing* 6 (1989): 324.

11. Personal interviews with Linda Jack, Amelia Lawrence Agency; Jean Gramer, Stewart Talent Agency; Sharon Wottrich, A Plus Agency. The interviews were conducted in August 1990 by my research assistant, Kathleen Rowe.

12. Willis, *Primer,* 119.

13. T. E. Perkins, "Rethinking Stereotypes," in *Ideology and Mass Communication,* ed. Michèle Barrett et al. (New York: St. Martin's Press, 1979), 150.

14. Burroughs quoted in Sheila Gadsden, "Seeking the Right Tack in Talking to Blacks," *Advertising Age,* 12 December 1985.

15. Gloria Joseph, "Black Mothers and Daughters: Their Roles and Functions in American Society," in Gloria Joseph and Jill Lewis, *Common Differences* (Boston: South End Press, 1981), 95.

16. Kim Foltz, "Mattel's Shift on Barbie Ads," *New York Times,* 19 July 1990, C18.

FIVE. TOY-BASED VIDEOS FOR GIRLS

1. Elizabeth Segel, " 'As the Twig Is Bent . . .': Gender and Childhood Reading," in *Gender and Reading: Essays on Readers, Texts, and Contexts,* ed. Elizabeth A. Flynn and Patrocinio P. Schweickart (Baltimore: Johns Hopkins University Press, 1986), 171.

2. Increasing sales through segmentation is tricky, but with children's goods it works on a per family basis when brothers and sisters can no longer share the same clothes, books, and toys.

3. Segel, " 'As the Twig Is Bent . . . ,' " 175.

4. Sybil DelGaudio, "Seduced and Reduced: Female Animal Characters in Some Warner's Cartoons," in *The American Animated Cartoon,* ed. Danny Peary and Gerald Peary (New York: E. P. Dutton, 1980), 212.

5. My sources for this survey of female characters on children's television are Stuart Fischer, *Kid's TV: The First Twenty-Five Years* (New York: Facts On File Publications, 1983), George Woolery, *Children's Television: The First Thirty-five Years, 1946–1981* (Metuchen, N.J.: Scarecrow, 1983), and Hal Erickson, *Syndicated Television: The First Forty Years, 1947–1987* (Jefferson, N.C.: McFarland, 1989).

6. It is interesting to note that when Fred Rogers first appeared in 1955 on a show called *Children's Corner,* he worked behind the scenes as a puppeteer and a woman named Josie Carey hosted the show; see Fischer, *Kids' TV,* 68–70.

7. *Eureeka's Castle,* a program for preschoolers on Nickelodeon, which was introduced in 1990 with the deliberate intention of snagging the *Sesame Street* audience, clearly redresses this situation. The presence of a female lead both offers the possibility of some segmentation—getting the girls' and mothers' attention—and lends an air of nonsexism to the show. Eureeka, however, remains more of a figurehead than a developed personality.

As of the 1991 schedule, Nickelodeon seemed to be orienting itself to girls in its daytime programming with some animated series, *The Little Bits,* and *The Koalas,* and the situation comedy *Clarissa Explains It All.* This mimics the way the cable network *Lifetime* specializes in adult women viewers.

8. Miss Piggy has been read more positively by feminists Judith Williamson and Kathleen Rowe; I agree with these interpretations but do not find them pertinent to the experience of young girls.

9. The Care Bears were reintroduced in 1991 with a new, explicitly ecological

bent to their characters: now they were interested in such things as kindness to animals and keeping the environment clean.

10. The girls' toys that were part of this phase outnumber the boys' toys: He-Man and the Masters of the Universe, the Transformers, the Thundercats. He-Man was merely a "swords and sorcery" version of superheroes who were long familiar to the boys' toy and media market such as Superman, Batman, and Spiderman. There was certainly nothing new about producing an animated series for boys' whose licensed characters were "tied in" with toy merchandising.

11. Tom Engelhardt. "Children's Television: The Strawberry Shortcake Strategy," in *Watching Television: A Pantheon Guide to Popular Culture,* ed. Todd Gitlin (New York: Pantheon, 1987), 84.

12. Ibid., 97.

13. See Robert C. Allen, *Speaking of Soap Operas* (Chapel Hill: University of North Carolina Press, 1985), and Ellen Seiter, " 'To Teach and to Sell': Irna Phillips and Her Sponsors, 1930–1954," *Journal of Film and Video* 41 (1989): 150–163.

14. Engelhardt, "Children's Television," 97.

15. For a comprehensive discussion of the critical reception of Disney's work and the elaborate care that went into the drawing of the characters' movement, see Richard Schickel, *The Disney Version* (New York: Simon & Schuster, 1968). Ariel Dorfman attacks the content of Disney on ideological grounds in "Of Elephants and Ducks," *The Empire's Old Clothes* (New York: Pantheon, 1983), 17–63, and *How to Read Donald Duck: Imperialist Ideology in the Disney Comic* (London: International General, 1975).

16. Stephen Kline, "Limits to the Imagination: Marketing and Children's Culture," in *Cultural Politics in Contemporary America,* ed. Ian Angus and Sut Jhally (New York: Routledge, 1989), 299–316.

17. My informal survey ranges from the children of university faculty to the children of low-income, unemployed families served by a free day-care program I worked at in 1988–1989.

18. Stern and Schoenhaus, *Toyland,* 117.

19. Roland Marchand has noted that introducing a choice of colors became a standard advertising technique in the 1920s. Marketers began to suggest changes in color scheme for bathroom fixtures, towels, sheets, fountain pens, and kitchen cabinets and appliances once the market had become saturated. Colors going in and out of fashion helps to drive the market for many consumer goods bought by adult women; see Marchand, *Advertising,* 120–127.

20. Hasbro, United Kingdom, 1988.

21. Mattel, 1989.

22. For an animated series to be considered for a network series, at least sixty-five episodes must be made.

23. Bourdieu, *Distinction,* 7.

24. "Translated into ritual terms, the quest-romance is the victory of fertility over the waste land." Northrop Frye, *Anatomy of Criticism* (Princeton, N.J.: Princeton University Press, 1957), 193.

25. The frozen blight is reminiscent of the winter Demeter causes while she grieves over the separation from her daughter Persephone; in cartoons the blight appears, but the mother is always already absent.

26. Frye, *Anatomy*, 93.

27. Valerie Walkerdine, "On the Regulation of Speaking and Silence: Subjectivity, Class, and Gender in Contemporary Schooling," in *Language, Gender, and Childhood*, ed. Carolyn Steedman, Cathy Urwin, and Valerie Walkerdine (London: Routledge & Kegan Paul, 1985), 224–225.

28. Allison M. Jaggar, *Feminist Politics and Human Nature* (Totowa, N.J.: Rowan & Allanheld, 1983), 45.

29. In this respect it is very similar to a lot of somewhat older girls' play with Barbie dolls. Part of the success of the pony line may have been the way that it extended this possibility to younger girls, who may not have had the rather formidable hand-eye coordination required to style a Barbie doll's hair—and to dress her. It also places the hair care issue at some remove from its meaning in heterosexual romance.

30. See Tania Modleski's description of the "ideal mother" as the soap opera viewer's position in "The Search for Tomorrow on Today's Soap Opera," *Film Quarterly* 33, no. 1 (Fall 1979): 3–18. Modleski discusses both romance and soap opera in *Loving with a Vengeance: Mass-produced Fantasies for Women* (New York: Methuen, 1982).

31. See Janice Radway, *Reading the Romance: Women, Patriarchy and Popular Literature* (Chapel Hill: University of North Carolina Press, 1984).

SIX. ACTION TV FOR BOYS

1. Quoted in Jim Black, "Licenses Spell Success for Toy Companies," *Playthings*, June 1990, 96.

2. Marsha Kinder discusses the Ninja Turtle phenomenon, its relationship to video games, its postmodern elements, and its gendered appeal in *Playing with Power*.

3. The producers have defended the change in Janine's part from the film version, saying that they originally had a feistier Janine but when they tested the character, girls didn't like her.

4. Vivian Sobchack, "The Virginity of Astronauts: Sex and the Science Fiction Film," in *Alien Zone: Cultural Theory and the Contemporary Science Fiction Cinema*, ed. Annette Kuhn (London: Verso, 1990), 106.

5. Brad Leithauser, "Dead Forms: The Ghost Story Today," *New Criterion* (December 1987): 30.

6. In Northrop Frye's terms, the boys' cartoons are low mimetic and the girls' cartoons are high mimetic. *Anatomy of Criticism: Four Essays* (Princeton, N.J.: Princeton University Press, 1957), 366.

7. The most influential essays associated with psychoanalytic feminist film criticism have been collected in the volume *Feminism and Film Theory*, ed. Constance Penley (New York: Routledge, 1988).

8. Laura Mulvey, "Afterthoughts on 'Visual Pleasure and Narrative Cinema' Inspired by *Duel in the Sun*," in Penley, *Feminism and Film Theory*, 72.

9. For a full discussion of these issues, see the *Camera Obscura* special issue entitled "The Spectatrix," vols. 20–21 (1989), edited by Janet Bergstrom and Mary Ann Doane; Marsha Kinder has adapted the psychoanalytic model to the special problems of television and child viewers in the first chapter of *Playing with Power*.

10. Christine Gledhill, "Pleasurable Negotiations," in *Female Spectators,* ed. Deidre Pribram (London: Verso, 1990), 64–89.

11. Bruno Bettelheim, *The Uses of Enchantment: The Meaning and Importance of Fairy Tales* (New York: Knopf, 1976), 7.

12. Erikson's book *Childhood and Society* (New York: Norton, 1950) incorporated some of the methods and ideas about play as material for psychoanalysis developed by Melanie Klein nearly two decades earlier. Erikson's work achieved much greater influence in the United States than Klein's did, in part because of his emphasis on "normal" personality development rather than Klein's emphasis on innate drives and the primacy of aggressive urges and fantasies—ideas that were difficult to reconcile with the popular image of childhood innocence and joy. It is therefore usually a version of Erikson's ideas, not Klein's, that is found most commonly in parental advice literature about play.

13. Ibid., 115.

14. Ibid., 98.

15. Erikson preferred to use abstract toys, such as blocks, in this work. The use of abstract toys in clinical experiments, and their praise by child educators such as Montessori and Froeber, constitute one legacy of the cultural mapping of types of toys. Usually representational toys made of plastics and synthetics are denigrated by comparison with "natural" materials for the manufacture of toys and abstract, nonrepresentational items. Psychologists use blocks for child observations because psychologists must concern themselves with replicating experiments and situations, and wooden blocks are readily available and do not vary a great deal. Rudolf Steiner and the Waldorf school also used blocks as preferred playthings The philosophy of the Waldorf school emphasizes the cultivation of individualism, creativity, uniqueness, abstraction, and originality in children rather than social play, shared codes and meanings, narrative genres and conventions, and ritual.

16. Erikson, *Childhood and Society,* 100.

17. Kinder, *Playing with Power,* 58.

18. Vivian Gussin Paley, *Boys and Girls: Superheroes in the Doll Corner* (Chicago: University of Chicago Press, 1984), 92.

19. Patricia Marks Greenfield, Emily Yut, Mabel Chung, Deborah Land, Holly Kreider, Maurice Panroja, and Kris Horsley, "The Program-Length Commercial: A Study of the Effects of Television/Toy Tie-ins on Imaginative Play," *Psychology and Marketing* 7, no. 4 (1990): 252.

20. N. C. James and T. A. McCain, "Television Games Preschool Children Play: Patterns, Themes, and Uses," *Journal of Broadcasting* 26 (1982): 783–798.

21. Willis, *Primer,* 31.

SEVEN. TOYS "R" US

1. See, for example, Kline, "Limits to the Imagination," 299–316, and Engelhardt, "Children's Television," 74–108.

2. Ellen Wartella and Sharon Mazzarella, "A Historical Comparison of Children's Use of Leisure Time," in *For Fun and Profit,* ed. Richard Butsch (Philadelphia: Temple University Press, 1989), 173–194.

3. Letter from the publisher, "Industry Must Support China's 'Status,'" *Playthings,* June 1990, 4.

4. President Bush moved to restore China's most-favored-nation trade status in June 1991.

5. Quoted in "Licensing Opportunities Abound for Everyone," *Playthings,* October 1989, 52–54.

6. Ibid.

7. Film critic Charles Eckert was an astute commentator on this phenomenon; see "The Carole Lombard in Macy's Window," *Quarterly Review of Film Studies* 3 (1978): 1–21, and "Shirley Temple and the House of Rockefeller," *Jump Cut* 2 (1974): 1, 17–20.

8. Schickel, *Disney Version.*

9. Quoted in Marisa Cohen, "All Work and All Play," *Toy and Hobby World,* July 1990, 28.

10. Marisa Cohen, "The Package Deal," *Toy and Hobby World,* June 1991, 49–51.

11. Ibid., 51.

12. Grant McCracken, *Culture and Consumption,* 119.

13. Russell Mitchell, "Waldenbooks Tries Hooking Young Bookworms," *Business Week,* 11 May 1987, 48.

14. Quoted in Nina Flournoy, "Teach Your Children Well," *Toy and Hobby World,* July 1990, 25.

15. Quoted in Karen Paxton, "A Woman's Touch," *Toy and Hobby World,* February 1990, 44.

16. "Imaginarium Promotion Offers French Flavor," *Playthings,* February 1991, 46.

17. Bourdieu, *Distinction,* 223.

18. Ibid., 224.

19. Henry Scott, director of children's merchandise, quoted in Flournoy, "Teach Your Children," 25.

20. Playmobil 90, "The Good Old Days," 1989 catalog, 2.

21. Ibid., 8.

22. Music for Little People, Fall 1992 catalog, 16.

23. Ibid., 23.

24. HearthSong, Autumn 1992 catalog, 36.

25. Early Learning Centre, 1990 catalog, 1.

26. Ibid., 24.

27. Horowitz, *Morality of Spending,* 167.

28. An excellent selection of comments on this subject from British intellectuals is included in Simpson, *Parents Talking Television.*

29. Simmel, "Fashion," 299.

30. See Hodge and Tripp, *Children and Television,* and Paley, *Boys and Girls.*

31. Paley, *Boys and Girls,* 113.

CONCLUSION

1. Eleanor Berman, *Working Mother,* November 1988, 126.

2. Louis Menand, "Savonarola Comes to the Multiplex," *The New Yorker,* 5 October 1992, 169.

3. Ariel Dorfman has brilliantly demonstrated this in *The Empire's Old Clothes,* 17–66.

4. *The Paper Crane* (New York: C. N. Potter, 1985); *How Pizza Came to Queens* (New York: Greenwillow Books, 1989); *A Chair For My Mother* (New York: Greenwillow Books, 1982); *Jamaica Tag-Along* (Boston: Houghton, 1985).

5. Although the characters are animals, the Berenstain Bears are steeped in white middle-class culture, while their neighbors, the rabbits and beavers, seem to refer to Latino and Chinese families.

6. Alison Lurie, *Don't Tell the Grown-ups: Subversive Children's Literature* (Boston: Little, Brown & Company), 1990, x.

7. Ibid.

8. Although her work does not deal with television, she has been quoted in the *New York Times* saying that the link between media and toys leads to an impoverishment of the imagination; see Janet Maslin, "Like the Toy? See the Movie," *New York Times,* 17 December 1989, 24.

9. Coontz, *Social Origins,* 355.

INDEX

ACT, *see* Action for Children's Television

Action for Children's Television, 5, 30, 37, 96–102, 112, 150, 191

activity, 71, 166; as parental goal, 54; purported importance to children, 33; in toy claims, 62; toys, 73

Adventures of Johnny Quest, The, 148, 173

advertising: age-appropriateness, 99, 111; animation techniques, 103, 115; anti-toy, 64; childhood health in, 55; for children, 5; children's "three-in-one" appeal, 103; Christmas, 55–62; claims for educational value in, 46, 47*ill*; class representation in, 55; deceptive, 98, 101, 241*n9*; for educational materials, 63–74; as entertainment, 105, 106, 108; expenditures, 104; in form of parental advice, 27*ill*; gender representation in, 5, 11, 55, 74–87, 116, 126, 134; for girls' toys, 74–87, 128*ill*, 128–130, 129*ill*; and hedonism, 38, 39, 45; industry self-regulation, 101; language in, 1–2; to parents, 5, 51–95; racial representation in, 5, 55, 57, 87–95, 132, 134–136, 137*ill*, 138–143; "reason why," 105; regulation of, 97–102; revenues, 104; as social tableaux, 54–55; television, 5, 59–60; of toys, 51–95; view of children, 96, 102–110

Advertising Age (magazine), 103

All-Star Basketball toys, 90, 91*ill*

Alphabet Soup, 213

American Baby (magazine), 22

American Baby (television series), 22

Anderson, Daniel, 34

Anderson, James, 34

animation techniques, 103, 108, 115, 122, 152

anti-authoritarianism, 117–118

Appalachian Artworks, 195

Apple Jacks, 139

Auerbach, Paul, 96, 108

authority: freedom from, 50; mother's, 21, 23; punitive assertion of, 24

Babar, 110, 214, 216

Bang, Molly, 231

Barbie, 7, 38, 49, 131, 142, 150, 156, 193, 201, 202, 203, 219, 224; African American, 88; Animal-Lovin', 203; Holiday, 203; Style Magic, 136; Wet-n-Wild, 203

Barney and the Backyard Gang, 232

Barnyard Commandoes, 173

Batman, 7, 199

Beauty and the Beast, 146, 198

Beetlejuice, 199

behavior: aggressive, 229; television-watching, 34

Bell, Daniel, 38, 39

Berenstain Bears, 232

Bert and Ernie, 149

Bettelheim, Bruno, 189

Big Bird, 149

Bloch, Ernst, 11

About the Author

Ellen Seiter took her M.F.A. and Ph.D. degrees at Northwestern University's Radio-TV-Film Department. She taught for twelve years at the University of Oregon before joining the Indiana University faculty in 1993 as Professor of Telecommunications and Graduate Coordinator. A Fulbright Scholar, Seiter specializes in feminist criticism and audience research. She is co-editor of *Remote Control: Television, Audiences, and Cultural Power* (Routledge, 1989), and author of articles in *Cultural Studies, Screen, Feminist Review, Journal of Communication,* and many other scholarly journals.